ACADEMIA AND PEACE

THOUGHTS AND STRUGGLES

BY

AVIVI I. YAVIN

BOOKS

Cover and book design by Zeev Bar-Gil

Note for libraries: A catalogue record for this book is available from Library and Archives Canada at
www.collectionscanada.gc.ca

ISBN: 978-0-9812476-7-0

MW Books
Garden Bay, BC
Canada
http://mwbookpublishing.com
info@mwbookpublishing.com

10 9 8 7 6 5 4 3 2 1

Opinions of Readers on the Book

Avivi Yavin's book reflects the work of a professor in academia with a burning aspiration for peace and a deep conviction that it can be achieved in the Middle East. As described in the book, Professor Yavin's efforts to promote peace serve as a living example that the strength of Academia is not in theory alone, and that the academic communities in Israel and in the Arab World can make an effective contribution to the advancement of the peace in the Middle East.

Haim Ben-Shahar is a professor emeritus of economics and was president of Tel-Aviv University in Israel in the years 1975-1983.

Avivi Yavin has spent all of his adult years in thinking and acting on matters pertaining to peace between Israel and its neighbors. He fought in the war which created the state of Israel but he already empathized with the people on the other side of this conflict. Throughout his long and brilliant career in physics, carried out across the globe, he simultaneously engaged in the struggle for peace. He courageously made many trips to Egypt for this purpose. He fostered many ideas which could bring Arabs and Israelis closer together. As long as there are persons, like him, who are strongly committed to a peaceful and friendly elationship between Israel and its neighbors we can have great hope for the development of the Middle East. May his work prosper!

Professor Erich Vogt is a professor emeritus of physics. He was vice president of the University of British Columbia and the director of the Canadian national laboratory TRIUMF.

For several decades Professor Yavin has pursued a goal of establishing professional ties between academics in Israel and in the Arab world. This volume presents an interesting chronicle of his efforts in this pursuit. While results to date may seem disappointing, his contacts have provided useful insights and perspectives on the problems involved in developing more productive relations between Israel and its neighbors, certainly a worthwhile outcome.

Professor Parker Alford is a professor emeritus of physics from the University of Western Ontario, Canada.

There is a special breed of people, people who are not afraid to dream, who do not hesitate to tackle the toughest of challenges, who are not discouraged by setbacks and by failure. My colleague, my friend, Avivi, is one of them. I was fortunate to witness the birth of his dream of promoting peace in the Middle East through academic initiatives, I was deeply impressed by his imagination and perseverance in pursuing his project almost single handedly, and I was saddened with him when reality did not live up to his vision. Yet, the lessons I learned from him throughout this period had a deep and significant impact on my own personal life. For this I shall be indebted to him for as long as I live.

Itzhak Kelson is a professor emeritus of physics from Tel-Aviv University in Israel.

A university is not an ivory tower, it has a unique role in society.

A university is the only institution whose main task is thinking. All consensuses in all fields are investigated. Frozen thinking is identified and alternatives are suggested. Creative thinking is done by individuals, by groups, and sometimes with public participation.

Thinking, and not only teaching and research (and the specific thinking which goes along with them) is the essence of university existence.

In summary: In every healthy democratic society there are traditionally three independent authorities: legislative, executive, and judicial. A fourth authority has recently been added, namely mass media, the watchdog of democracy. Academia should be the fifth authority, whose duty is to investigate all the consensuses and to suggest and grope forward in all fields.

Scientific collaborations of Arab and Israeli scientists could help advance, acquire, and maintain Arab-Israeli peace.

Peace should enable Arab - Israeli scientific collaborations; thus advance science.

Dedicated to the memory of Professor Mohamed El-Nadi
A great scientist and a talented scientific leader
A teacher of many generations of Egyptian physicists
An Arab patriot and a man of peace
A warm human being and a close friend

Contents

PREFACE
by Harry Lustig

Contrary to the impressions fostered by popular culture, physicists in many parts of the world, not least in the United States, have been eager participants in world affairs. In particular, they have fostered international collaboration, not only because they think, rightly, that it would advance their science, but also, in many cases, because they wanted to contribute to the attainment of peace in the world. Of all the involved physicists I have known, none has worked harder and more tenaciously at this goal than the prominent Israeli physicist Avivi Yavin.

Yavin was born and reared in Israel as an ardent Zionist. He bravely fought in that country's war of independence in 1948, and he had his schooling there, culminating in an M. Sc. in Physics, Mathematics, and Philosophy from the Hebrew University. He received his Ph.D. in physics from the University of Washington in 1958 and for several years thereafter he was a leading researcher at the cyclotron of the University of Illinois, Urbana-Champaign, rising to the rank of full professor in 1968. In 1970 he was called back to Israel to establish the Department of Nuclear Physics at Tel-Aviv University and he served as the Dean of the Faculty of Exact Sciences at the University from 1971 to 1976. Beginning in 1982 , he spent most summers and three sabbatical years at TRIUMF, Canada's national laboratory for nuclear and particle physics in Vancouver. He is a fellow of the American Physical Society.

Yavin's book is an account of his unflinching endeavors to advance the cause of peace between Israel and the Arab world. His primary motivation has been, I believe, an extraordinarily developed sense of moral responsibility and an unquenchable conviction that all of us and, in particular, intellectuals, have an inescapable obligation and an usual opportunity to lead in creating a moral universe and to advance amity between nations and peoples. The most effective agency for getting there was, he believed, perhaps too optimistically, academia.

Avivi Yavin's untiring efforts took many forms. One of them was the creation and leadership of an unprecedented interdisciplinary Research Project on Peace, at the University of Tel Aviv, spinning off several "think tanks". It involved nine faculties and the top leadership of the University and its aim was to produce well-researched studies on every aspect of peace and collaboration between nations. Undoubtedly Yavin hoped that these studies would lead to actual cooperative projects between Israel and the Arab countries. But this was not to be. In fact, most of the proposed cooperative studies were not carried out. Several factors contributed to that failure. One was the traditional isolation and lack of common ground between the different disciplines, another the jealousy of other Israeli universities who felt that they had been excluded, and a third the hard line position of some of the participants at Tel Aviv, including some members of the administration, that peace with the Arabs was not attainable and perhaps not even desirable.

The most persistent efforts of Avivi Yavin were his many attempts to bring about collaboration among Israeli and Arab scientists, not only in physics (although this was clearly a leading candidate), but in other fields as well. For this he had a promising model: the holding of joint conferences and the collaborative research of American and Soviet scientists, mainly physicists, long before there was a governmental rapprochement between the two countries. This cooperation arguably made an important contribution to the eventual political détente between the two superpowers. Not so incidentally the clear-headed insistence by the American scientists to advance the human rights of their Soviet colleagues was an important and positive contribution of the collaborations.

Yavin's fertile brain came up with a plethora of ideas and proposals for bilateral, trilateral and multilateral proposals for conferences and research collaborations. They were to be carried out in Israel, in Arab countries and in the several European countries where Avivi Yavin himself was an active and respected participant in research. He was sensitive to the fact that the Arab scientists were weaker in some of the fields to be encompassed than the Israelis and the Europeans and aware of the dearth of resources that the Arab countries and institutions could or would provide and he promoted arrangements that would minimize the reality and the perception of these disadvantages. Perhaps his most ambitious proposal and one which would have had the greatest impact, had it been carried out, was the creation of a Middle-East University.

Arguably the greatest opportunity for bilateral cooperation came with the unexpected visit of the Egyptian president, Anwar Sadat, to Israel and the conclusion of a peace treaty between the two countries in 1979. Yavin immediately seized the opportunity by traveling to Egypt and meeting with dozens of Egyptian scientists and academic leaders and even some high government officials, including the foreign minister, Boutros Boutros Ghali, who later was to become secretary-general of the United Nations. He ascertained their needs and with them entertained and energetically worked on a number of proposals for cooperative projects. He received enthusiastic moral (if, wisely, not publicized) encouragement from the US science attaché at the embassy in Cairo and the promise of financial support from American foundations. Over the next years, Yavin made three more visits to Egypt to see if any of the projects could be salvaged or new ones substituted for them. In the end all of this came to practically nothing. Against the wishes of much, but not all of the Israeli establishment and people, as well as a number the Egyptian scientists, there was no warming of relations between Egypt and Israel: the peace remained "cold". Sadat was simply afraid of the continuing enormous antagonism against Israel by the Egyptian people and even more so of the intractable hatreds of the other Muslim nations whom he had alienated by concluding a peace treaty in the first place. Not that Israel was entirely blameless: attitudes and politics in that country swung to the right and the invasion of Lebanon was the straw that broke the *gamal's* back. As it turned out Sadat had ample reason to be afraid: in 1981 he was assassinated by Egyptian Muslim fanatics.

Although chastened, Avivi Yavin never gave up. He launched many more initiatives for cooperation with Arab scientists and their leaders. The one I am personally familiar with as a result of my participation in the planning was to be a week-long conference of young Arab and Israeli physicists on aspects of nuclear and particle physics (quarks and gluons) to be held under the auspices of the American Physical Society. This effort is accurately described in *Academia and Peace*. The meeting was to be held on neutral ground, possibly on the Greek Island of Crete. Lectures were to be given by leading American and European physicists, but not by Israelis, in order to minimize any feelings of second class status by the Arabs. Among the several movers on the American side, Avivi perhaps does not pay enough tribute to the 1985 president of the APS, the extraordinary Robert Wilson. (As a young scientist at Los Alamos in the Manhattan project, Wilson did what he could to persuade J. Robert Oppenheimer that the two atomic bombs should not be dropped on Japan without warning. Later he became the designer and sterling director of Fermi Lab. When testifying before Congress to obtain the funds to build Fermi Lab, he was asked – harangued would be a better word – what the Lab would contribute to the military defense of the United States. Wilson replied, in paraphrase, "nothing at all Senator, but it will make the country worth defending".) No wonder that this sensitive, intelligent, and courageous man would at once grasp and support Yavin's proposal. Because the conference was to be held in Europe, we decided that it would need the endorsement of the European Physical Society. After leading us on for a number of months, the European Physical Society passively sabotaged the proposal. Yavin uses more diplomatic language to describe this debacle.

Although Avivi Yavin's lifelong efforts to bring about peace and collaboration between Israel and the Arab world in the end came to naught, no one should think that he was an impractical dreamer who promulgated beautiful theories but washed his hands of the "dirty" details of their implementation. Nothing could be further from the truth. As his book makes clear, he tirelessly led *and* did yeoman's work at every level. Particularly because of the failed effort to hold the quarks and gluons conference on Crete, it would be tempting to describe his political life as a Greek tragedy. It wasn't and it isn't, because the fatal flaw lay not in his character, but in the small-mindedness, ignorance, and selfishness of other men and their cultures. But perhaps his work has not been in vain. Some have suggested that, like those of many thinkers and reformers, Avivi Yavin's ideas and initiatives were merely premature and that they will yet be implemented. We can only hope so and make our small contributions to make this happen.

Harry Lustig, initially a nuclear physicist, is Provost Emeritus and Professor of Physics Emeritus of the City College of the City University of New York, and Treasurer Emeritus of The American Physical Society.

ACADEMIA AND PEACE

THOUGHTS AND STRUGGLES

INTRODUCTION

The skeptic might ask, "What has academia got to do with peace?" The expert in political science will then undoubtedly give the following answer, "Peace as well as the ways to achieve and maintain it are legitimate topics for academic research, similarly to disciplines such as agriculture and physics or even topics such as military strategy or human relations." Such an answer is correct, but in my opinion not complete. Academia certainly has the right to investigate the many aspects of peace just as it investigates all the above-mentioned topics, but in my opinion it also has a moral and social obligation to do so. It is unfortunate that Israeli academia as a whole failed to recognize and appreciate this obligation in time before the 1973 Yom-Kippur War, before President Sadat's peace initiative, and again before the Palestinian intifadas. Due to these failures, I, as a member of Israeli academia, feel somewhat ashamed. I reached this conclusion later in my academic life, and then decided to devote time and effort to contribute to peace.

This autobiographic book is not a treatise dealing in depth with the many aspects of either academia or peace; rather it deals mainly with the interrelations, which exist or should exist between these two concepts. The book describes in some detail the many thoughts that crossed my mind and all the time and efforts that I devoted, over almost fifty years, to the promotion of academic cooperation among all the peoples of the Middle East. My strong belief has always been that cooperation between scientists of enemy nations could and should help advance peace between these nations; and on the flip side peace will make it easier to cooperate, and so will advance science. Unfortunately, some of the collaborators in these endeavors are not with us any more, but their names and valuable contributions will be extensively described in the book.

The first thirty years, which are covered in the first chapter, describe how my views were formed. These views put the human being - be he an American or a Vietnamese, an Indian or a Pakistani, a Jew or an Arab – at the center of all moral considerations. I also initiated in these years some actions to promote peace in the region. The bloody war in Vietnam took place during that period, and I was emotionally and intellectually involved in that war, both in the US and in Vietnam, which I visited in 1967. Millions of people, mostly Vietnamese but also Americans, died in that war; and I observed with pain the enormous damage caused to the good American people by politicians, people from the military, and businessmen, who sought power and financial profit and shamelessly led their young people to kill and be killed under the guise of national security. I describe this tormented period in three yet unpublished books: "On Love and War", "The Rape of a Country", "Doves and Hawks".

The second chapter deals with the fascinating period following President Sadat's unexpected declaration, "No more wars!" and his visit to Jerusalem in 1978. The third chapter describes in detail a unique project which I founded at Tel-Aviv University called The Research Project on Peace. This Project combined two values in which I always believed: academia and peace. One of the first major activities of the Project was the establishment of a national authority for economic planning.

The entire fourth chapter is devoted to my first visit to Egypt along with my wife, Rivka. We describe our meetings and our talks with Egyptians in the streets of Cairo and in several academic and research institutions.

The following two chapters (fifth and sixth) describe various activities of the Research Project on Peace, and present in full the work and conclusions of a think-tank which was formed by the Project.

My efforts to establish scientific collaborations between professors from Tel-Aviv University and Egyptian professors are described in the seventh and eighth chapters, which also include the description of some dramatic meetings with the Egyptian Minister of State for Foreign Affairs and with the Head of the Egyptian National Academy of Science. Chapter nine is devoted to my correspondence with the Egyptian Minister of State for Foreign Affairs.

The tenth chapter describes my efforts to use the prestige and power of the American Physical Society to organize, under its auspices, a meeting of scientists from East-Mediterranean countries to deal with scientific matters.

Chapter eleven describes my attempt to recruit first-rate writers or film producers to present a picture of a possible optimistic future in the Middle East, with the hope that such a picture would have at present a positive and motivating effect on the peoples and politicians of the region.

My last major efforts to achieve cooperation among academics in the Middle East region are described in the twelfth chapter, which presents the proposal put forth by a Palestinian physicist and me to establish a Middle-East university in the Taba-Eilat-Aqaba region, in close proximity to Egypt, Israel, and Jordan. Such a university could be supervised by UNESCO, which gave the idea its blessing. Efforts to have me nominated for a UNESCO chair are also described in chapter 12.

I believe that at a certain stage the reader will wonder why an established physics professor decided one day to leave the quiet life of teaching and research, and to spend years in somewhat Sisyphean efforts related to peace. The answers are presented twice in the book, at the end of the third chapter and also in the last (thirteenth) chapter.

This book is a translated and slightly shortened version of a book with the same name of the original Hebrew manuscript. In writing the book I made use of the many written documents, as well as some written material which the late Major-General Aharon Yariv left. Except for trivial changes and the deletion of unessential parts, I have not changed anything in the presented documents, which will appear either in the text or in the appendices. The reader will therefore have the opportunity to read about extensive thoughts and efforts, a generation ago, in both Israel and Egypt, to achieve scientific collaborations where none had existed before. I believe that our successes and failures will help guide future efforts in the Middle East and elsewhere to achieve peace through scientific collaboration, and to advance science via such collaborations.

Finally, I was somewhat surprised to realize the degree of cynicism in the academic world concerning my activities. Few who were aware of my work believed that my motives were solely unselfish, and that I was not seeking power, money, or fame. Most people involved doubted that my actions stemmed only from the belief that they would help science and peace through scientific regional cooperation. On the other hand, I tried to avoid entirely the assumption or insinuation that selfish motives drove those who objected to my methods.

The Establishment of the State of Israel. A war between the Arabs and the Jews broke out on November 30, 1947, right after the United Nations General Assembly had voted to establish two states west of the Jordan River, a Jewish state and an Arab state. The Palestinian Arabs, who did not accept the decision, launched attacks on the Jewish communities throughout Palestine (or Eretz Israel as the Jews call it). After the British left the country on May 15, 1948, the Palestinian Arab gangs were joined by the regular Arab armies of Egypt, Jordan, Syria, Lebanon, and Iraq. The Jews then declared the formation of the State of Israel, and called the fighting their War of Independence, while the Arabs subsequently called it, or rather its result the Nakba (the disaster).

In the nineteen thirties and forties, many young Israelis received their ideological education in youth movements, such as the Scout Movement. That education, mostly socialist, was aimed at convincing them to form new kibbutzim (communal villages). After World War II, another goal was added to the education program: convincing and preparing young Israelis to fight the British mandatory regime, which blocked the immigration of most of the remnants of the Holocaust from entering the country. These young Israelis were hardly interested then in what was happening elsewhere in the world, with the exception of the military struggles (actually civil wars) in Vienna and Spain before World War II, or the ones in Greece and Korea after the War. At that time they did not think much about Arab-Jewish relations, and saw the local Arabs as ungrateful people who did not appreciate the economic and cultural progress that Zionism was bringing them.

The young Israelis were told that the Arabs hated us. There was no talk in the Arab community about Palestinian nationalism. We were told that the Arab society was feudalistic, controlled by five families, whose spiritual leader was Haj Amin El Husseini, the Mufti of Jerusalem, who had collaborated with the Nazis in the extermination of the European Jews. Our idols were fighting people such as the one-armed Joseph Trumpeldor, who was killed in 1920 in the defense of the small village of Tel Hai from the attacks of Arab gangs, and people from Hashomer (the watchman) organization. We also admired the British major, Charles Ord Wingate, who trained the members of the first Israeli paramilitary organization. In schools and youth movements we learned extensively about the pogroms that the Arabs had carried out in Hebron in 1929. We also learned about Arab attacks on Jewish towns and villages throughout the whole country in the Arab uprising of the years 1936-1939. One of the great local ideologues was Berl Katzenelson, who called for Avodah Ivrit (Jewish labor); i.e. that Jews should hire Jewish rather than Arab workers. This is the atmosphere that characterized the Arab-Jewish relations in which I grew up.

Just before 1948, there were several ideas in the Jewish community about the desired (or possible) political solution of the Arab-Israeli conflict.

(a) The Revisionist group, the predecessor of today's right-wing Likud party, called for the establishment of a Jewish state on the two banks of the Jordan River (i.e. in area that today contains Israel, the West Bank, the Gaza Strip, and Jordan).

(b) Some groups left of center would settle for a Jewish state only west of the Jordan River (i.e. Israel, the West Bank, and Gaza).

(c) The socialist party, Hashomer Hatzair, called for the establishment of a bi-national state west of the Jordan River.

(d) Small groups had other solutions: Brit Shalom (peace union), whose members were Jewish intellectuals such as Martin Buber, called for a state of 60% Arabs and 40% Jews, while the communists demanded the establishment of a democratic state, which would effectively be governed by the Arabs who were two thirds of the population. There was also a small group of the so-called Canaanites, who advocated the severing of the special relations with the West and with the Jews in the Diaspora

(e) Mapai, the United Labor Party, headed by David Ben-Gurion, was in control of the community. It espoused the so-called Biltmore Plan, which called for the partition of the country into two states, Jewish and Arab.

Because of the ideological education that we received, which today I might call indoctrination, I considered the Arabs to be an uncivilized enemy, not realizing that I hardly knew them. This attitude was strengthened further when the

War of Independence (or Nakba) broke out on November 30, 1947. Guarding the mutilated bodies of the 16 Israeli soldiers who were killed in Atarot near Jerusalem (I knew some of them), affected me very much. Gush Etzion, south of Jerusalem, was under considerable Arab attacks. A platoon of soldiers was dispatched on foot to help, and I was among them. In the last moment it was decided to replace our squad with another one. All these dispatched 35 Israeli fighters were killed on their way to Gush Etzion and their bodies were badly mutilated. This event increased my anti-Arab feelings. I also lost close friends in the war, in which thousands of young Israelis as well as remnants of the Holocaust were killed. The number of Arab killed in the war was much bigger. When my conscience bothered me for my participation in killing Arab fighters, it was only because I thought then about their mothers, not about them as human beings or young people who had lost their lives. At times, I had philosophical doubts about my own actions as a soldier, but there was one thing I never thought about, during the war and right after our victory: the terrible disaster, which we inflicted then on one million Arabs, one million human beings like me. There were several reasons for that indifference: The Arab hatred of the Jews before and after the war, the fact that they initiated the war and were later assisted by five regular Arab armies, the thoughts about the Holocaust, and my Zionist upbringing. All these left no room for pity or sympathetic feelings for the tragedy we inflicted on the Arabs.

I was in Jerusalem during the pogrom that Jewish soldiers carried out in Dir Yassin; I heard about many Arab villages that were completely destroyed, and about hundreds of thousands of Arabs that left the country voluntarily or were forced to leave and become refugees, but at that time I did not share their agony. Like most of my friends I believed that they received what they deserved. Today it is hard for me to believe that I was then so indifferent to the misery of so many human beings - men, women and children – who lost everything they had, partly because of me and the Zionist movement to which I belonged.

In the following years, after reading extensively about the misery of the expelled Arabs, my conscience started to bother me, but I still believed that we were absolutely right and that justice was entirely on our side. A long time later, I started to understand that the Palestinian Arabs did not suffer only personal tragedies, but also a national one. One of the reasons for this delay in my understanding is that they too did not see themselves as a nation. Only in the mid-sixties did they elect governing bodies in Israel, in the west Bank and Gaza Strip, and in the neighboring Arab countries. Their main expression of Arab nationalism up till then was their hatred of Jewish nationalism, namely, of the Zionist movement and the State of Israel. Only in the late sixties, after the formation of the Palestine Liberation Organization (PLO) and of the El-Fatah movement, did I and some of my friends start to realize that the struggle between us and them was national, and that both sides had some measure of rightness. We also reached the conclusion that the question of who was guilty of the disaster and of the mutual bloodshed was less important than the question of how to solve the problem politically and prevent further bloodshed.

My Political Activity in the United States (1954-1969). My Zionist education, and that of most of my friends, was briefly described above, and could be called nationalistic, even chauvinistic. During my studies in the Hebrew University (1949-1954) I was not involved in political activity. After my arrival in Seattle in 1954 for my doctoral studies in physics, I found myself involves in such an activity, often against my will. On one occasion I was invited by an NBC reporter, along with another Israeli student, to argue the Israel case with two Arab students. We called for a discussion of possible and desired peace settlements, while the Arab students wanted only to discuss the right of the Palestinian Arabs for a national home. We agreed that they had such a right, but the Arab students still did not agree to discuss solutions.

After moving to a faculty position at the University of Illinois in 1958 I tried several times to meet Arab faculty members and students, but they always refused. For this reason I was surprised and encouraged by the following event. A representative of the Arab League gave a public lecture in the Department of Physics. In an answer to a question from the audience, he elaborated on the reasons why Arab students were forbidden to talk with Israeli students. I stood up and reminded the speaker that he was talking in a University, which was a temple of free thinking. I said that students from all over the world came to the university in order to think freely, and not to get orders from politicians with whom or on what they had the right to talk. The majority of the audience applauded me; among them I noticed many Arab students and Arab faculty members.

The desire for a discourse between the Arab and Israeli academic communities changed slowly in the following years. In particular, I remember a case in which it was the Arab students who suggested meeting in public with their

Israeli counterparts, and even insisted that all issues would be debated. To my surprise, most of the Israeli students rejected this suggested, and one student explained this attitude, "I am afraid that in such an open meeting, they might convince me and the public that we Israelis do not have a right to live in our state, Israel".

I then made one attempt to get mediation from the outside on one tough issue. I wrote a letter to the French philosopher Jean Paul Sartre, who had bitterly attacked Israel for her unwillingness to tackle the problem of the Palestinian refugees. In my letter I offered him my help in finding a constructive and human solution to the problem, but Sartre did not respond.

Soon after the Six-Day War in June 1967, I wrote a letter to Professor Yuval Ne'eman, an outstanding physicist and an advisor to the Israeli Prime Minister Levi Eshkol and Defense Minister Moshe Dayan, offering there that the Israeli Government should settle the residents of the Arab refugee camps in the West Bank and Gaza in those occupied regions. I argued that financial help could be expected from the United States, which was losing the war in Vietnam, and which saw our victory in the June war as their victory. (In this victory, an ally of the United States had just beaten several allies of the Soviet Union). I argued further that the whole Western World might assist us in such an endeavor, which could put an end to a human tragedy, which served as a cause of political instability in the Middle East. Later on I realized that I had addressed the wrong person, since Professor Ne'eman had completely different plans (i.e. annexation) for the occupied territories.

The various scattered incidents described above do not show any complete political agenda on my part; rather they describe the political atmosphere at that time in relation to the Arab-Israeli conflict as well as my own slow emancipation from the dogmatic education I had received in my teen-years. The following section will describe some dramatic events, which became the first chapter in the interesting saga, which will be described later in the book.

My Egyptian Student. One day I was approached by a student named Tabark Noweir, who was taking my theoretical-mechanics course, and asked for a job in the cyclotron of the University of Illinois. I took her as my assistant, and she turned out to be a very devoted worker. There was only one problem in her work; each time James Allen, the director of the laboratory, came in, I noticed that she positioned herself behind my back, as if she was hiding. I asked him if he too noticed it, and he surprised me by saying that she apparently knew that he did not especially like foreigners and women in his laboratory. I told him that she was a good assistant, and added that I too was a foreigner. "For me, Israelis are not considered foreigners", was his surprising answer.[1] One day, while several of us were working as a group, a student asked me, "You are always criticizing us, Americans, on the issue of Vietnam; let's see how you are solving your problems with your Egyptian student." Clearly, I did not answer him, since we never talked politics in the lab, except for during lunch or coffee breaks. She asked him afterwards for the reason for his question, and he said, "Don't you know that Dr. Yavin is an Israeli?" She turned pale and left the laboratory. Two days later she came back, and we continued to work together as before until the next crisis.

Several days before the June (or Six-Day) War in 1967, the university TV station called me and Ali El-Saidi, Tabark's husband, who was the president of the Egyptian organization of nuclear students in the USA, with a request to appear together on a TV program and discuss the tension in the Middle East. I agreed, but Ali refused to appear with me on the same program. Several days later the War broke out, and Tabark did not come to work for several days. One day I saw her coming into the laboratory with a pale face. I understood that she was worried about meeting me. I therefore walked to her, stretched my hand forward for a hand shake, and said, "Our countries are at war, but we are scientists and human beings, and therefore we will continue to work together. She shook my hand, and with tears appearing in her eyes she quietly went to her desk. The other students told me later that my words moved her, and added that she was also worried about her two brothers who served in the Sinai. We learned later that they were safe and healthy,

After two months, a day before I was leaving for a conference in Japan, on my way to join Tel-Aviv University, I received a phone call from Ali, and this is what he said, "The war between our two countries has ended, but we are still enemies. I don't know if we will ever see each other again; so I am calling to thank you and to tell you that I will never forget what you have done for my wife." In the next decade, while in Israel, I received from Tabark two requests, sent to me via the University of Illinois: In the first one she asked me to tell

---

1 James Allen was a great physicist and a warm human being, but with strange opinions about running a scientific laboratory. He was not Jewish, and was not particularly interested in politics, but he once told me the following amusing anecdote: His grandmother applied for membership in the Daughters of the American Revolution, because one of her ancestors had fought in the Revolution. Her application was denied, because they checked and found out that he had indeed fought in the Revolution, but for the wrong (English) side.

her Ph.D. committee in Egypt that the research which she had done with me in Illinois had never been used in the thesis of another student. The second request was a question, asking whether I would agree to serve on her Ph. D. committee in Egypt. I gladly responded positively to both requests. I often wondered afterwards if I would ever see Tabark and Ali again.

American Leaders Facing Dilemmas of Internal and Foreign Affairs. I first arrived at the United States during the McCarthy period. It was painful to see how the great American people behaved in that period, but I admired people such as Edward R. Murrow, who stood up courageously to Senator McCarthy and his infamous accusations in Senate hearings. I painfully followed the Bay of Pigs fiasco, when President Kennedy attempted to invade Cuba and failed. A couple of years later, the Soviets introduced missiles to Cuba. President Kennedy could have attempted to restore his honor by invading Cuba, but this great leader decided to use peaceful means and the Soviets peacefully pulled their missiles back. In the summer of 1963 the whole country was awaiting a speech by President Kennedy, wondering whether he would speak up in favor of human rights for the African-Americans (or Blacks as they were then called), and he did.

Two American leaders intrigued me in the sixties; President Lyndon B. Johnson and Martin Luther King. They both faced dilemmas of internal versus foreign affairs, but their decisions were so different. President Johnson helped the civil-rights movement, already when he was a senator. As a president he sent young Americans to the killing fields of Vietnam, where close to sixty thousand Americans and more than a million Vietnamese died. It is strange that many Americans, even today, keep saying that Johnson was good on internal affairs, as if - unlike jobs, schools, and houses - lives of young Americans are not considered *internal affairs*.

Martin Luther King, the leader of the civil-rights movement, was a student of Mahatma Gandhi, and advocated getting equality of the races only via non violence. He was asked for his stand on the war in Vietnam. Most of his advisors warned him not to speak against the war, since such a speech would hurt the still weak movement. The country was tense, awaiting his decision. In his speech, he acknowledged the possibility that speaking against the war could hurt the struggle he was leading, but said that as a religious leader he had to speak against all evils, and the war was evil. How impressive was this man of God, a giant in comparison with religious leaders such as Billy Graham, who encouraged his followers to go on a crusade against a miserable people in Southeast Asia. From Martin Luther King I learned that you could not be ethical only in matters that don't affect you. Later I disagreed with many of my Jewish friends in the US that like me had held dovish views on the war in Vietnam, but turned hawkish after the Six-Day War.

The Conference in Dixon, Illinois (1969). Although I was deeply involved, emotionally and intellectually, with the senseless, bloody war in Vietnam, and with what it was doing to the American people, my main concerns and thoughts were with my people in Israel and with the Arab-Israeli conflict. I was reasonably pleased with the activity of the academic people and of the intellectuals in general in Israel, where the politicians started to enjoy the possession of the new territories gained by the Six-Day War (the Golan Heights, the West Bank, the Gaza Strip, and in particular- the Old City of Jerusalem), while many intellectuals came up with ideas of how to exchange the newly gained territories with peace with Arab world.

The Arabs, mainly the Palestinian Arabs, were still in a state of shock. Their intellectuals then invented a relaxing political idea for their people. Rather than calling them to search for ways to solve their problems in a peaceful way, they came up with a comparison between Zionism and the Crusades, and predicted that the fate of Zionism would be the same as that of the Crusades; namely, it would evaporate in thin air by itself. I felt that such an attitude was very unfortunate, first of all for the Palestinians. I wished I could tell them my opinion that Israel would not evaporate, and that there was another way – peace - which would gain them national as well as personal progress. However, I knew that it was almost hopeless to advise one's adversary what to do, but I felt very strongly that it was worth a try. So I looked for an opportunity to speak to Palestinian intellectuals and urge them to do their duty to their society rather than dream about Crusades and Israel's disintegration. That opportunity came from an unexpected direction.

I was invited by the External Studies of the University of Illinois to speak at a world-affairs conference in Dixon, Illinois. The subject of the conference, held on April 18-19, 1969, was The Middle-East Crisis – Prospects for Peace. The Israeli Ambassador Yitzhak Rabin was also invited, as was Fred Gottheil, a Jewish professor from the University of Illinois; the three of us representing the Israeli side. The Saudi politician of Palestinian decent, Fayez Sayeg, along with two Arab professors in American universities, represented the Arab side.

In his speech, Ambassador Rabin impressed the audience by his special deep voice and by his sincerity, this in spite of some difficulty the American audience had in understanding his *Israeli English*. For instance, he said that the Arabs were interested in a *deluxe war*, and that we will not give it to them. The audience did not understand the words and meaning of the term, which sounded to them as *delooks war*. The Israelis in the audience knew that a deluxe war was a war in which the Arabs attacked us and we only retaliated at that time and place. The local hostess of the Arab delegation told me that she had been pro-Arab, but the minute Rabin started to talk she fell in love with him and changed sides.

Ambassador Sayeg started by saying "I have a dream", imitating Martin Luther King. His dream was about Palestine as a secular democratic state, in which Jews, Christians, and Muslims would live in peace. In order to achieve this goal, Israel would have to dissolve, and allow democratic elections in Palestine. In the discussion that followed I told him that his dream sounded beautiful. However, if he was serious about a real peace, there was no need to dissolve the State of Israel. There was another option that should be considered, the establishment of a Palestinian state side-by-side with Israel, and then the two states could form a federation or fuse through mutual agreement. He obviously was not interested in discussing my idea, and the audience understood that his so-called *dream* was nothing but a call for the dissolution of the State of Israel.

One of the Arab professors, whose field was political science, presented quotes from a few founders of Zionism on the extreme right (Zabotinski and other Revisionists) as well as from Israeli extreme right-wing leaders such as Israel Eldad. Then he read a carefully selected letters to the editor of right-wing Israelis, which he found in Israeli papers, and claimed that this proved that Israel wanted to conquer the whole Middle East, and expel the Palestinian Arabs. I asked him if he taught his students how to select only quotes that fitted a theory that they were presenting, because by doing so they could "prove" every theory, even the most extreme and idiotic. The three Arab lecturers mentioned the Crusaders extensively, and predicted that the "Zionist state" would end up like the Crusaders state.

In my talk, entitled the Political Role of Arab and Israeli Intellectuals – Hopes And disappointments (Appendix I), I criticized the disservice that the Arab intellectuals are doing to their people by letting them dream about the Cru-saders rather than leading them to look for peaceful solutions for their bad situation. I criticized them in strong words, perhaps too strong, for their relin-quishing their duties as intellectuals by just echoing their politicians. I ended my talk by calling on Arab intellectuals to get together with Israeli intellectu-als and search together for peaceful solutions.

The audience listened attentively to my talk, and to this day I do not know the reason for that; was it the text of my talk or the introduction the Chair had given me which did it?[2]

The Shock of the Yom-Kippur War. Upon returning to Israel and joining Tel-Aviv University, I almost stopped completely to deal with peace issues. The exceptions were lectures which I gave at homes of friends on topics such as The Arms Race in the Middle East or The Dangers of Being Too Depen-dent on a Super Power.

The stubbornness of Prime-Minister Golda Meir and her chief advisor Israel Galili bothered me, as did the statement by the Defense Minister General Moshe Dayan, who said that if he had to choose between peace with Egypt or keeping Sharem El Sheikh with no peace, he would choose the latter[3]. I could feel the approaching danger from the neighboring Arab countries, which had lost some of their lands in the 1967 war. The Israeli government rejected all reasonable suggestions for compromises offered by important world lead-ers, such as Gunnar Jarring of the UN and the American Secretary of State William Rogers. The two mediators-to-be basically suggested that the goals of Israeli-Arab negotiations should be total peace and complete withdrawal of Israel from the occupied territories. Anwar Sadat, the president of Egypt, responded with "Yes, but…" Golda Meir, the prime minister of Israel, said plainly "No". Several Israeli intellectuals also suggested ways to advance peace, but Golda kept saying "No."

My fear materialized on Yom Kippur (the Day of Atonement) on October 6, 1973, when the Egyptian and Syrian armies launched a surprise attack on the complacent, unprepared Israeli army, and dealt us a terrible blow. At a certain point, some Israeli leaders were afraid that the Syrian and the Egyptian armies would overrun the country, but the war ended roughly where it started, while

2 *The Chair read in my CV that I had written a paper on Super High Energy Accelerators, and so the Chair introduced me as a super high energy physicist, a strange and untrue title, but an audience-capturing one.*

3 *Years later Dayan said that he changed his mind on that.*

16

thousands of soldiers died on both sides. Most people in the government, the armed forces, and the general public blamed the military for the failures and them being surprised by the Egyptian and Syrian attacks. Almost everybody believed that the failure was mainly caused by the wrong military concepts and preparedness, and this failure was given the Hebrew name Hamechdal (the oversight or foul-out). I believed that the *political* concepts and not the *military* ones were mainly responsible for the disaster, and that they should be called Hamechdal.

Following the Yom-Kippur War, and having gone through the days in which we thought that Zionism was facing its end, a group of Israeli professors volunteered to go on tours to universities of the United States, to tell what had happened and to ask for support. The tours were organized by APPME (American Professors for Peace in the Middle East). I took part in one of the tours, and gave lectures in several universities, mainly in the Midwest.

About a month after the war ended I invited to my home professors, writers, and journalists, as well as mayors, members of Knesset, and other politicians, in order to discuss the situation and what to do about it. Close to one hundred people gathered in my home, and the meeting lasted for more than six hours, an indication of the level of anxiety in the country. The following is the text of my opening talk in the meeting[4]:

THE PEACE – WHAT ARE ITS CHANCES, WHICH WILL BE ITS COMPONENTS, AND WHO SHOULD BRING IT ABOUT

Like many in the audience, I have now had the feeling for quite some time that the leaders of the country do not understand some of the important processes that are taking place in our region. For instance, very few leaders realized the depth of the Arab pain at losing the Six-Day War and some of their national territories. These leaders mistakenly related the Arab reactions only to their historical hatred of Zionism. Our leaders did not fully understand that in that war the Arabs were also terribly humiliated. Their reaction to their loss of territories resembles that of the human organism when a thorn penetrates the body; all its antibodies are called upon to repel the invader. Also, our leaders consciously or uncon-

---

4 *The text of my talk is presented here in full, because it describes the Israeli society and the political situation as it was right after the war, and differs in many respects from what is described in official accounts or in most books on this era.*

sciously ignored the existence of a national Palestinian problem, using pseudo-historical and pseudo-political arguments, and insisted that there was no such a thing as a Palestinian nation. Most of all, I have been saddened by the realization that we actually had all the necessary means to solve these dangerous problems, but stubbornly refused to consider possible peaceful solutions.

You may ask, and rightly so, "If you knew all that, what did you do? Why were you quiet? Don't you and your friends, who share your thinking, feel guilty for not being involved? Such an involvement could perhaps have prevented the war that did not have to take place." Since the accusing finger is not pointing only at the political and military leaders, but at me too, and because I believe that most of you have similar feelings of guilt, I have decided to invite you all here.

In this evening we will talk about the many aspects of an Arab-Israeli peace; we will ask ourselves if there is a new chance now for peace; we will point out all the necessary components of any possible peace; we will look at existing political bodies, which can help bring about peace; and we will suggest how we will be able to contribute to the endeavor. Clearly, none of us has the right to use the names of our dead soldiers in order to justify a political theory. But we have the duty to see to it that young people will not be killed any more.

We have with us here people from the whole political spectrum. I believe that following the shattering of illusions and beliefs, many in the country are looking for new political solutions, and we could look for changes of opinions and for new political alliances. I hope that our discussion tonight will verify my expectations. The politicians among us will clearly have the right to speak tonight, but I hope that they will mainly use the opportunity to listen to a cross section of a large public, that will no longer be passive and quiet. This meeting will hopefully be the beginning of a balanced and healthy interaction between the intellectual community and the politicians. No more will we allow a situation in which they speak and we blindly do as we are told. A new partnership should now emerge, in which we think together and act together on questions of war and peace.

18

Three basic facts

I will start by pointing out three basic facts that were and still are true facts, but very few pay the necessary attention to them:

Basic Fact No. 1. We and the Arabs indeed have opposing national interests in the region. Apart from some small fringe groups, most of the Israeli and Arab leaders recognize this true fact when they emphasize the need for the strengthening of their armed forces. However, the recognition that the other side has national rights which should be fulfilled, even for one's own interests, is unfortunately not one of the building blocks of the political thinking in any of the sides of the conflict.

Basic Fact No. 2. There is a national Palestinian problem, which will not disappear by itself, and a solution for it should, therefore, be found. We recall that there were many people in the world who claimed that the Jews were not a nation, since before 1897 they did not have a desire to be a nation, and they lacked some of the characteristics of a "normal" nation. Similar superficial analyses with regards to the Palestinians, like the ones made by Israel Galili, will not cure the misconception. Let us also remember that a constructive solution of this problem is not only in the interest of the Palestinians and the Arab countries, but of our state as well.

Basic Fact No. 3. It is possible to find a compromise between the basic national needs of the Arabs and the Jews, but it is clearly impossible to find a compromise between the extreme demands of the two sides of the conflict. A realistic definition of the *basic* interests of the two sides will show that the difference between them is not insurmountable. One of the main political roles of the intellectuals in the region is to define these true and basic interests, and to suggest ways to a compromise. They also have a duty to bring this information to the Arab and Israeli public and to their political leaders.

Six Wrong Assumptions

Several wrong assumptions and half-truths were popular in Israel before the war. It is up to us to analyze these assumptions and half-truths, and to bring it to the attention of the public, so that they will stop being used as "natural truths" that justify futile policies. The following are some examples:

Wrong Assumption No. 1. All the Arabs, always wanted, still want, and will always want to destroy the State of Israel. This extreme, but popular assumption was based on some loose ideas, such as: such is the character of the Arabs; or we are outsiders, and they will never get used to us; and the declarations of the Arab leaders prove this assumption. There are undoubtedly many Arabs who wanted, and will always want to see Israel destroyed, and perhaps also to see us physically exterminated, just as there are Israelis who would like the Arabs to disappear from the country, but this does not justify the assumption that *all* the Arabs *always* want us and the state to be destroyed.

Wrong Assumption No. 2. There is no fundamental difference between Jaffa that was conquered by us in 1948 and Nablus that was conquered by us in 1967. The one who says so ignores the fact that the 1948 borders, accidental as they might be, were used for the establishment of the state, which was our basic goal; while the addition of territory is beyond our basic needs, and deprives the Palestinian of one of their basic needs.

Wrong Assumption No. 3. The Arabs did not accept the border before the Six-Day War (the Green-Line) as the border of Israel; therefore, they will not agree to it now. This view that "there is nothing new under the sun" assumes that a nation never sobers up, and never changes its mind. In order to refute this view, I will point out that the Herut Party of Zabotinski wanted and still wants us to have Eretz Israel on the two banks of the Jordan River, but will be satisfied today with only the Eretz Israel west of the Jordan River. Does only Herut have the right to sober up?

Wrong Assumption No. 4. The withdrawal of the Israel Defense Forces (Zahal) from the Sinai Peninsula, and the return of the Egyptian Army to it are one and the same thing. The basic national interest of the Egyptians is to have Zahal withdraw from all the occupied territories and to get political sovereignty over the evacuated territories. They undoubtedly also want the return of the Egyptian army to Sinai, as part of their complete national sovereignty, and also for the possibility that a new Israeli-Egyptian war will break out. However, any objective observer should realize that moving the Egyptian army to the Sinai is only a *secondary* interest of Egypt, while preventing it from doing so is a *basic* interest of ours. The Egyptians, apparently, understand the difference, and this could be the reason for their request that Zahal will withdraw from the Sinai, leaving open and unclear the question of what will happen in the evacuated territory.

Wrong Assumption No. 5. *Planning wars takes a long time, is expensive, and requires the best brains; on the other hand, making peace is easy, does not require planning and steps, and can be carried out by fools. Moreover, a Peace Treaty is essentially a piece of paper, which relies on trusting the Arabs.* Just as we have a big defense ministry with some of the best brains and a huge budget, preparation for peace requires imaginative brains and adequate budget.

Wrong Assumption No. 6. *Our insistence on negotiations without preconditions is sincere, reasonable, and natural; it is not by itself a precondition, and therefore does not present an obstacle to peace; on the contrary, it clearly shows our desire for peace.* In order to see the hypocrisy of this claim, let us look at the following hypothetical situation. Let us, for a moment, make the frightful assumption that in June 1967 Egypt conquered the southern part of the country, all the way to a line from Sodom through Beer-Sheba to Ashdod. Let us further assume that the Egyptians then called for negotiations without preconditions, but refused to declare that they would be willing, eventually, to withdraw after the negotiations. Would we have agreed to negotiate, or would we have tried first to get American arms and expel the Egyptians from the occupied territory?

The Pre-war Main Political Groups

1. The Whole-Land-of-Israel. These people wanted to keep all the occupied territories. Their motives are historical, mystical, religious, geopolitical, or strategic. For most of them, the use of the term "security borders" is only for argumentation, because these people would want Nablus to be Israeli even if there would be no chance that an Arab Nablus will ever pose a danger to the security of Israel.

2. Peace-and-Security. These people, believed in a step-by-step solution; in each step, Israel would withdraw a little, security would be kept, and additional normalization would follow.

3. The Pragmatic Center. The Labor party was the main factor in the pragmatic center. They believed in keeping the occupied territories as a bargaining chip. They slowly annexed the territories, always proclaiming their wish for a compromise.

In practice, the country was led by the Pragmatic Center, which was strongly supported by the Whole-Land-of-Israel people (the right). For different reasons, both groups believed that we should not withdraw at present from the occupied territories. The Pragmatic Center believed, and still does, that we should not draw maps of a possible final compromise solution, because this would split the public, and there was no chance for peace at present; the right agreed, as they did not want a compromise either now or in the future. The Center believed that there was no harm if peace was delayed, because we were using the time to build new settlements and increase our strength, and this would apply pressure on the Arabs to negotiate; the right agreed. In fact, both groups were in agreement that time was on our side. They based their view on the assumption that the strategic depth, which we had gained in 1967, would save us from a surprise attack, and at any rate, Zahal was strong enough to discourage any potential enemy from launching a surprise attack. The war has clearly shown that this assumption was wrong. I imagine that there is little disagreement on that in this room

Why Was Our Political Establishment Wrong?

Our political establishment was wrong in its assessment of the intentions of both Egypt and Syria, and not mainly because of military considerations. It is popular to discuss the mistakes of our military intelligence, but this is not what I wish to do now; rather, I would like to elaborate on the connection between the erroneous policy of our government, which was briefly mentioned above, and the fact that it fell into the trap, prepared for us by the Arabs. The main mistakes were three: the government did not fully appreciate the humiliation, which we inflicted on the Arabs in 1967; it counted too much on the military gap between the Arabs and us; and it relied completely on the so-called "strategic depth" of the Sinai and the Golan Heights, and on the deterrence and retaliation capability of the Zahal. With this attitude, the government made it easy for the Arabs to surprise us. Our government thought that since the Egyptians knew that we were so much stronger, they would not dare attack us. Instead, they would only pretend that they were going to attack in order to scare the West that an Israeli-Arab war was imminent, and could escalate into a world war. "If this were their trick," so thought our political leaders, "we would not play their game and would not mobilize our reserves whenever the Arab countries moved their armies during maneuvers." But there was also a political reason for not mobilizing the reserves, which had been mobilized a few months earlier at a time of tension. Their thoughts were the following: "If every time the Egyptians and the Syrians decide to cause an artificial tension we mobilize our reserves and send them to the borders, the Israeli public will start asking what kind of security these borders provide." For these reasons the government decided not to fall for the trick, and not mobilize the reserves; but it was no trick, as we all know quite well.

Is The Situation Hopeless?

Is there any chance for peace? Before I try to answer this important question, I wish to read to you some quotes from an article in Saut el Arab on November 11 of this year, just a few weeks after the end of the war: "Now, after the balance that was created by the October 6 war, there is an opportunity to achieve a political balance, and separate the issues of territories from those of security, i.e. to achieve simultaneously full withdrawal of Israel, security, and peace. The opportunity to achieve a just peace in the region seems more than good if the intentions are sincere, and it is possible that this is the last opportunity. As to the responsibility of the Arabs, we have taken the first steps in the movement towards just peace in the region. Our intentions are sincere that this time will be different from previous times when wars erupted between our enemies and us." Let us also recall the warm words about peace, which Mrs. Sadat wrote in a recent article.

Why do so many people here and abroad think that the situation now is more conducive for peace than before the war? I see several reasons for that: 1. the Arabs have gained security and self-respect, but they have also realized that they cannot win and destroy Israel even in a surprise war; 2. the position of President Sadat, the rational and moderate president of Egypt, has been strengthened, along with his ability to make peace; 3. the stubborn policies of the government of Israel have proven to lead nowhere; 4. the superpowers have now recognized the danger to them from the tension in the Middle East, and have started to act more decisively to ease the tension; and 5. the main Palestinian underground groups have recently indicated that they wish to be included in negotiations, which would lead to a state for them.

The Main Elements of Any Realistic Solution

Let me end my presentation by listing the main elements of any realistic solution of the Arab-Israeli conflict. This is important for practical as well as strategic reasons. Negotiations usually succeed when each side is realistic. Before coming to the negotiating table each side should recognize the basic interests of the other side, as well as its red lines. Let me therefore list some of the important facts that we have to accept before we start negotiations, if we sincerely want them to be successful:

1. Peace will necessarily be based on a compromise between the basic interests, after they are defined, of both sides to the conflict.
2. An occupation by force will not be accepted either by the Arabs or by the international community. We are not a superpower like the Soviet Union, and even for them, we may not have heard the end of the story.
3. The withdrawal of the I.D.F. from the occupied territories will eventually be carried out as part of a peace treaty. We will obviously be able to negotiate the pace of the withdrawal or the compensation that we will get in return, but not on the withdrawal itself.
4. Our right to an independent and viable state is legitimate. The state must be recognized, and will have recognized borders.
5. The Arab armies will not return to most of the evacuated ter-

ritories.

6. The Palestinian problem, human as well as national, will have to find its solution in the West Bank and the Gaza Strip.

7. A complex formula will be needed for Jerusalem, which will ensure that it will be united and be the capital of Israel, and at the same time it will have in its midst some political Arab presence (Palestinian, Jordanian, or that of the Arab League).

I will not discuss in detail the various new political unions in our country that will hopefully be formed now in order to promote peace, and leave it to the discussion that might follow. But I will end my presentation by turning to a woman in this room, who is the champion of human rights in the country. Member of Knesset, Shulamit Aloni! You have founded the civil-liberties party in Israel. You should be credited for the growing attention being paid now everywhere to the rights of the individual. Since the right to live is the most important right a person has, we do hope that you will decide to include the work for peace in the agenda of your popular new party.

****

In spite of the late hour almost nobody left the room during the coffee break that followed, except for one person. Before leaving, he turned to me and said, "I think that you are an enemy of the country. I am leaving because I can't listen to such heresy anymore." A young man with a patch on his eye then said to me, "I am so pleased to hear you say clearly and openly what I was feeling in my post on the Golan Heights during the war." Some participants argued against the views presented in my talk, but most people who spoke had encouraging words, and added some thoughts of their own. A large number of young people expressed agreement with me, and inquired what they could do to help. The meeting ended at daybreak.

The Rabat Resolutions. The hopes for peace suffered a big setback about a year after the Yom-Kippur War. Yasser Arafat, the head of the Palestinian Liberation Organization, delivered a speech at the UN General Assembly full of hate for the State of Israel. At a meeting of the Arab League in Rabat, Morocco, extreme anti-Israeli resolutions were adopted. One of them stated that any evacuated piece of land in Palestine will be given to the control of the PLO. The Israeli establishment had hoped to come to an agreement with the moderate Jordan. It therefore believed that the Rabat resolutions all but brought an end the chance for peace.

Contrary to the pessimistic atmosphere, I saw a possible ray of light in the new situation, because it could enable us to achieve two important goals: to convince the political establishment in Israel to start the evacuation of the occupied territories and to drive a wedge between the extreme anti-peace PLO and the Palestinians in the occupied territories. I therefore wrote a letter on the new aspects of the situation, and mailed it on January 2, 1975 to Foreign Minister Yigal Alon, Defense Minister Shimon Peres, and the Chairman of the Foreign Relations and Security Committee in the Knesset, Yitzhak Navon. The following is a complete text of my letter.

HOW TO TURN THE RABAT RESOLUTIONS
FROM A GAIN FOR THE PLO
TO A POLITICAL ADVANTAGE FOR US

Introduction. The Rabat resolution of the Arab League and the appearance of Arafat in The UN General Assembly have shocked many statesmen and countries. Many think that this is the end of any chance for peace, and that Israel has suffered a decisive defeat. The purpose of this manuscript is to show that not only is there no place for frustration and panic, but that we have now the possibility to change the turn of events from a gain for the PLO to a meaningful success for us.

Previous years are characterized by lost opportunities. We keep saying, "We wish we could turn the clock back. If we could only turn the clock back to before October 1973, we could have negotiated with the Arab states in a different way, full of initiatives and from a position of strength. If we could only turn the clock back a few years, we could have helped rather than hinder the selection by the Palestinians of a moderate local leadership. If we could only turn the clock back a few months, we could have made some gestures to Jordan, and perhaps prevent the Rabat Resolutions."

There are a few problems, for which the clock has not yet moved irreversibly forward, and in which we can still initiate action from a relatively comfortable position. We have to note that our comfortable position will weaken with the progress of time, and that the problems will not be solved by themselves. Therefore, the time to act on them is now, not later. One of these problems is the nuclear potential, in which – at least in the eyes of the Arabs – we have a temporary advantage over them, and an Arab-Israeli negotiation on this issue will be from a position of strength for us. The second one is the Palestinian problem, and in particular, the control over the West Bank (and the Gaza Strip). This manuscript deals with the second problem. I will first point out a couple of basic facts, and will then suggest some actions that should be taken.

1. The Arab world should certainly be blamed for the fact that the Palestinian problem has not yet found a solution. The Arab countries kept the Palestinian refugees in camps hoping that this would apply pressure on Israel, and did not care if the refugees suffered greatly from this.

2. Since June 1967 we had under our exclusive control about 50% of the Palestinians in the Middle East, as well as a large area (the occupied territories) in which the Palestinian problem could have been solved. Because of the relative weakness of the Arab World, we also had six years in which we could unilaterally have started to find a constructive solution to the problem. Every one knows *now* that our inaction damaged our own interests. Rather than act, we were proud of our policy of "open bridges" (to Jordan), which was nothing but a temporary substitute for a long-range policy. One of the main reasons for our inaction with regards to this problem was the lack of national consensus about what to do with the West Bank, since a sizable percentage of the Israelis dreamed (and is still dreaming) about keeping the West Bank for ever, with a large percentage of Jews settled in it. Like in many other issues, this internal situation led the governments of Levi Eshkol and Golda Meir not to act.

An Opportune Situation. Our external situation vis-à-vis the whole world is not favorable for us when we deal with most issues except for one, the problem of the West Bank (and the Gaza Strip). Here most of the trump cards are *still* in our hands. We control the area and the population, and Zahal is positioned along its entire perimeter. We also control the development and economics of the West Bank. Any Arab attempt to find a solution to the problem of this region and its residents has to take these facts into consideration. It is today impossible to solve this problem without our good will, and without collaborating with us. King Hussein was aware of this fact, as was George Habash. But Yasser Arafat, being drunk by his imaginary military victories, as well as by favorable statements by world leaders, "succeeded" in gaining another "victory" in Rabat, against the advice of Hussein and Habash. In view of the whole world, and in particular those of the residents of the West Bank, he received in Rabat the exclusive responsibility for the future of the West Bank, or of any part of it, which would be evacuated by Israel.

Let us ask some simple questions: Supposing that we immediately evacuate the West Bank, will the PLO even try to move in? And how will it get there? I do not believe that there is anybody who will seriously suggest that they will parachute into it. And how will it manage its economics, its security, and its foreign trade? Will the PLO be able to manage the electricity and water supply, etc? Is there any chance that they will be able to do any of these things without the good will and full Israeli collaboration? They cannot even rely on King Hussein, their closest Arab neighbor, but who is the PLO's enemy. In simple words, on this issue we are holding the trump cards, and should act quickly, lest we again lose valued time and say afterwards, "If we could only turn the clock back." The time to actively face the PLO and the Palestinian problem is now, when the PLO released Jordan from its responsibility, made promises to the residents of the West Bank, which it cannot fulfill.

A Proposal for Action. As a consequence of what I said above, our policy should have two goals: It has to show the political weakness of the PLO, and at the same time to start solving the Palestinian political problem for the residents of the territories.

As a first step, we have to stop our automatic refusal to let the local Palestinians participate in international political conferences. Furthermore, we should state that we are starting to evacuate the territories, which we have never intended to annex, and we will hand them to any Arab entity, which is willing to govern them.

What we could have done unilaterally in the Sinai before the Yom-Kippur War in October 1973 and did not do, we will and should do now in the West Bank. We should unilaterally decide on the order and pace of the evacuation, according to our interests. We will announce that our goal is to evacuate all (or most of) the occupied territories, and in the first step we are going to tell the residents of Nablus, Jenin, and Tul-Karem, or those of Hebron, Bethlehem, and Jericho that we are giving them the control of their region, and we are not interested in who they select as their leaders. Our only condition will be that our security will be maintained. If their leaders will be interested to collaborate with us economically or in any other field, they will have to ask us, and we will make the decision as dictated by our interests.

Will the PLO be able to govern the evacuated territories as it declared in Rabat? If we act quickly, the PLO will have to decide quickly whether it is ready to come to us with a request for collaboration, or to announce to the world and the residents of the territories that it is unable to fulfill its promises. We will undoubtedly be accused of intrigues and evil intents, but in fact the residents of the territories will be able to run their lives freely because of an Israeli unilateral decision, and in collaboration with Israel. It is expected that a political conflict between the residents and the PLO will take place. It is possible that the residents will also turn to Jordan asking for economic aid, and it will again be up to us to agree or disagree. We note that before the "PLO's victory" in Rabat, the PLO could have asked the UN to take control over the evacuated territories. After the Rabat resolutions, and with our proposed "help", it is safe to say that the PLO will not be able to go this way.

We will remind those who worry about the introduction of military units and weapons to the evacuated territories, that as long as we control all the borders, we will be able to inhibit it and to go into the territories in case of terrorist attacks. It is hard to believe that the PLO will endanger losing big units and heavy weapons in an enclave surrounded by Zahal. As for the danger of the Soviets moving into the West Bank, we will count on the Americans to prevent them from doing so.

The Responses. Itzhak Navon acknowledged the receipt of my letter, but added no comment. Shimon Peres said in his short letter, "I enjoyed reading your letter, although I do not agree with your conclusions". In his letter to me, Yigal Alon said, among other things, "There is no doubt that your analysis is deep, and that the policy, which you are proposing is daring and imaginative. The question is whether it is not too daring and too imaginative." At the end of his letter, which is brought in full as Appendix II, he wrote, "And again – thank you for sending me the manuscript, which although I disagree with its conclusion and its recommendation, I found it to be very interesting and thought provoking." Although I was sorry that the three political leaders did not accept my suggestion, I was somewhat pleased with the last part of Alon's letter, since I always believed that a logical analysis and the encouragement of the political leaders to think and act are among the main duties of the scientists and intellectuals in their society.[5] Those who read my letter today, which was written thirty three years ago, when the conditions were so much more convenient to us, cannot but be sorry that the three high-ranking recipients of my letter did not have the necessary far-looking view and political courage, which were needed to execute the program outlined in my letter.

A letter to the Egyptian Dean. My experience in the United States taught me that contacts between scientists from different countries, even enemy ones, could contribute not only to science, but to the reduction of tension between their countries. For instance, the scientific collaboration between high-energy physicists from the United States and the Soviet Union started a long time before the era of the famous political detente, and most likely contributed to that detente. In the Middle East, there had been no contact between Israeli scientists and scientists from the Arab countries, except for those who found themselves in the same research group abroad. Such was the case of my relations between me and my Egyptian student at the University of Illinois, as described above. Israel and the Arab countries in the Middle East were, to a large extent, isolated from the scientific world, and they all could have ben-

5 *I elaborated on this point in my talk in the Dixon conference presented earlier "The Political Role of Arab and Israeli Intellectuals – Hopes and Disappointments."*

efited from scientific collaboration among them. I saw an added advantage of such collaborations, since then Arab and Israeli scientists would get to know one another, and would learn that we all were human with similar feelings. The probability of collaboration in the natural sciences, small as it seemed at that time, was greater than that in any other field, because of the apolitical nature of the natural sciences.

Being the dean of the Faculty of Exact Sciences, I decided to try to establish scientific collaborations is the same disciplines as those in my Faculty (mathematics, physics, chemistry, and environmental sciences) with scientists of our largest neighboring state – Egypt, with which we were still officially at a state of war. I therefore wrote a letter to the dean of the same faculty in Egypt, in which I summarized my considerations, and made a few practical suggestions as to how we can start some scientific collaboration. I emphasized that I would be happy to hear from him alternative suggestions. Since I did not know the name of the dean, I did not put down a name. The Following is the text of that letter:

Dean, Faculty of Exact Sciences
Cairo University
Cairo, Egypt

September 21, 1975

Dear Sir,

The purpose of this letter is to explore the advisability and feasibility of some scientific contacts between the faculties of exact sciences of Cairo University and Tel-Aviv University.

I hope that you, sir, will agree with me that science is one of the most universal and nonpolitical of all human endeavors. Scientists and intellectuals from the U.S.A. and the U.S.S.R. had been exchanging ideas long before the present era of political détente started. In fact, it can even be argued that these exchanges contributed to the political détente, at least in creating an appropriate psychological atmosphere.

We in this geographical area have not yet reached political détente. I hope that you will share my belief that the time might be right to consider taking the first steps in exchange of ideas, at least in the field of science.

Many ideas for such contacts may come to mind. Egyptian and Israeli scientists can, for instance, meet on neutral ground and discuss scientific subjects previously agreed upon; or I can suggest a program of correspondence as a good start. We might even agree on a simpler, more direct and personal approach of an exchange of visits. I would welcome the opportunity to host you (or another member of your academic staff) at Tel-Aviv University, as my guest; and I will be honored if you find it possible to reciprocate and extend an invitation to me.

Clearly, I am open to any suggestion from you, and have brought up only a few examples, which occurred to me. Certainly, I will welcome alternative ideas, which you may choose to suggest. The most important question now seems to be whether or not we can agree on the advisability of scientific exchanges. If I get an encouraging response from you, I will look into the practical possibilities of implementation. Here too I am open to suggestions from you.

Please accept this communication as a personal letter. I have not requested, and have therefore not accepted, official permission or blessing from the University or the Government. I intend to keep the letter and subsequent correspondence confidential until we decide otherwise.

This letter is being sent to an American who has recently visited both your country and mine. I will ask him to forward it to you, with the hope that he will agree to do so. I sincerely hope that you will accept the letter in the same spirit in which it is written, and that together we will find a satisfactory way to build up some scientific collaboration between our two neighboring universities. Being familiar with science here, and having had scientific contacts with Egyptian scientists in the USA and Europe, I have no doubt that we both could and would benefit from such collaboration.

With best wishes to you and to your Faculty,

Sincerely yours

Avivi I. Yavin
Dean of Faculty of Exact Sciences
And Professor of Physics

Since Egypt was an enemy country, I thought it was my duty to let the government know about my intention to send the letter, in order not to damage the security of my country. I was in the active reserves of Zahal, so I reported to the office of military security. They told me that the law forbade the sending of such a letter. When I asked what could happen to me if I went ahead and sent it, I got a surprising answer, "My personal opinion," so started the short answer, "is that nothing will happen to you." I told him that my conscience required that I should send the letter, but I was going to leave him a copy, and I would also send a copy to the foreign ministry; I would then wait a week to enable both offices to keep me from sending the letter, if they thought that it would damage the security of the country. I did not hear from them; after eight days I mailed the letter to my friend in the United States, Rabbi Henry Cohen; and he, in turn, mailed it to Egypt. I did not receive an answer from the Egyptian dean, and years later I heard from Professor Mohamed El-Nadi that his government did not allow him to answer my letter. Is it true that nothing happened to me for mailing the letter? In Appendix III, I will answer this question, and discuss the issue of "Big Brother" in Israel.

CHAPTER 2.
PRESIDENT SADAT ARRIVES IN ISRAEL

A Surprising Announcement. Following the disaster of the Yom-Kippur War, and in spite of public protests, the Labor Party did not allow the changing of any of the pre-war arrangements for the upcoming national election. No new alliances were possible, no new parties were allowed to run in the post-war election, and no new candidates could run in their own party. When Foreign Minister Yigal Alon was asked whom one should vote for, his answer was that he intended to swallow a pill against throwing-up, and then to vote for the Labor Party. So Labor won the election.

This shrewd political move of the Government that failed so abysmally in the War was not its only one. The most serious one was the appointment of an investigating committee, the Agranat Committee, whose charge was to investigate what the *military* did wrong before the war and through its first several days, excluding the possibility that this national committee would find the *Government* responsible for the Yom-Kippur foul-up. The top brass was indeed found guilty by the committee, while Prime-Minister Golda Meir received, soon afterwards, the Israel Award for her lifetime achievements. All these maneuvers did not help much Prime-Minister Meir and Defense-Minister Dayan, and the public uproar forced Golda Meir's Government to resign. Yitzhak Rabin, who during the Yom-Kippur War was the Israeli ambassador to the United States, was called by his party, Labor, to come home and replace Golda as prime minister. His Government lasted about two years, and ran into trouble with the religious partner in his coalition. Then an Israeli reporter in Washington discovered that Yitzhak Rabin and his wife Lea were still holding an open bank account in the US, which was then against the Israeli law. Prime-Minister Rabin then decided to resign. In the special elections that were then held, in mid-May 1977, the Likud Party, headed by Menachem Begin, won a smashing victory. So ended a period of nineteen years, in which the Labor Party had run the country. In order to strengthen his Government and broaden its political base, Prime-Minister Begin invited former Defense-Minister Dayan to be the foreign minister in his Likud-led government

****

A conference organized by the monthly journal New-Outlook was organized in Tel Aviv, in November 1977, to deal with the many aspects of the quest for peace between Israel and the Arab World. The title of the conference looked very theoretical, since no Arab leader of stature had ever even mentioned the possibility of such a peace, and at a meeting in Khartoum the Arab League had agreed on three taboos: no recognition of Israel, no negotiations with Israel, and no peace with her. Moreover, an academic guest from the United States spoke at the New-Outlook conference and "proved" with the help of documentary evidence, that even if there had been a positive expression about peace from any Arab intellectual, it had always been by a junior one.

At a certain moment in the conference, it was announced that the Chair had just gotten a surprising piece of news from Cairo saying that the president of Egypt, the biggest of the Arab countries, was willing to negotiate peace with Israel. Later President Anwar Sadat added the historic and electrifying statement "No more Wars!" The news was received by the participants of the conference with pleasure mixed with doubts. The people who had experienced so many wars and disappointments were not entirely ready to believe that an end to wars was just beyond the horizon. The skepticism was reinforced by the Israeli Chief of Staff Mota Gur, who warned the public against an Egyptian deception. However, the organizers of the conference welcomed the news, saying that it proved that the path New Outlook was pursuing was correct. Although the invited speakers had not prepared talks on the announcement, most of them devoted some time to it. The most eloquent speaker was Professor Shaul Friedlander, the liberal historian and political scientist. He warned the audience not to believe that a separate peace with one Arab country was possible, important and big as this country might be, and that if such a peace would take place, it would not induce other Arab countries to follow suit. As expected, the majority of the audience was convinced by his arguments. I was not. I stood up and argued that the change of direction was of utmost importance, and that Egypt's action could induce other Arab countries to do the same. One thing, however, became clear; namely, that the taboos of Khartoum were broken.

The whole country was in a state shock. Having talked about peace, for decades, nobody really expected it, and it came as a real surprise to an unprepared public. The pace of political events was fast and accelerating. It appeared that prior to Sadat's announcement in Cairo, secret talks between Foreign-Minister Moshe Dayan and Hassan Tuhami, the special envoy of President Sadat, had been held. The main elements of a future peace treaty had apparently been agreed upon in these talks. President Sadat announced in the Egyptian parliament that he would visit Jerusalem and would speak in the Knesset; and indeed, the visit took place as planned. Defense-Minister Ezra[1] Weizmann, who had just broken his leg, traveled from Tel Aviv to Jerusalem to meet and talk with Sadat. The Egyptian President indeed spoke in the Knesset, and all went well until Prime-Minister Begin made a diplomatic error, and called the relatively young Egyptian foreign minister "young man". The latter was insulted by this paternalistic act.

As for me, I hoped that Menachem Begin, who appeared to be a great leader willing to withdraw from the whole Sinai, would go one step further, and invite the Palestinian leader Yasser Arafat to also speak in the Knesset, but Begin did not do that.

Why did Sadat decide to come to Jerusalem and sign a peace treaty with Israel? Many observers claim, and rightly so, that Sadat was a great national leader, who correctly analyzed the new situation in which, for the first time, both Israel and Egypt were under the same umbrella – the American one. I do not doubt that Secretary of State Henry Kissinger, the man holding that umbrella, indeed knew how to use it. In my imagination I saw what might have taken place in the Egyptian Government, and I published what I "saw" in an article in New Outlook on June 1985. The title of the article was: Can Israel Achieve Economic Independence? The relevant paragraph follows:

Why did Sadat come to Jerusalem? There is a modern legend that runs as follows: The economic situation in Egypt had deteriorated abysmally. When the war failed to halt the rapid decline, Sadat asked his aides: "Is there a way, any way, to avert an imminent economic disaster?" When all standard solutions, such as more irrigation, increasing tourism, cutting services or a new appeal to the USSR, were considered and proven ineffective, an unknown adviser suggested the idea of peace with Israel. Only with peace, he argued, will Egypt's tremendous military investment come to a halt, and the way will

1 His name is actually Ezer, but the Egyptians, who liked him, nicknamed him Ezra.

be opened to massive American aid, an increase in tourism, the reopening of the Suez Canal, and a renewed search for oil. Most advisers and members of the cabinet greeted the bizarre proposal with scorn, as it ran counter to all accepted ideas in Egypt and the Arab world. Sadat then silenced them all and asked: "Can you suggest an alternative way to avert the approaching catastrophe?" When nobody spoke up, the great Egyptian leader stood up and said: "If peace is a solution, and if it is the only solution, I am going to Jerusalem".

A New Challenge for Academia. I saw many opportunities in the new political situation, but many dangers as well. Peace between us and the Arab countries had always been a dream for me, and peace might now take place with one of them. It soon became clear that there was almost no person or institution which was ready for the new situation. The Begin Government, in fact any Israeli government, had always dealt with current problems, and had never spent any time on hypothetical questions, such as how to bring about peace and how to maintain it. All it had always done was to say that we wanted peace, without really doing anything about it or even thinking or planning peace activities. The situation should have been different in the Israeli academia. I was disappointed that although academia had no responsibility for pressing national problems, it had not done its duty in preparing itself and the nation for peace,

Since I was a member of academia, I wondered whether I had done *my* duty. To quiet my conscience I could have been satisfied by my efforts at the University a few years earlier to have the new institute for strategic studies deal also with peace studies. And this is what had happened: The rector of the University proposed at a meeting of the Central Committee (made up of the rector, the vice- rector, and the nine deans) to open a new institute for strategic studies, headed by Retired General Aharon Yariv. Everybody at the meeting agreed, but I suggested that the institute should deal with peace studies as well as war studies, claiming that "peace and war are two sides of the same coin." My suggestion was rejected. I raised it again in the next meeting of the Central Committee, and it was rejected again. I raised it for the third time, this time in the following Senate meeting. My efforts failed there too, because the proposed institute's head, Aharon Yariv, objected to adding peace studies to the institute's areas of activity. The University Senate then voted to establish an institute only for strategic studies. In spite of these efforts my conscience still bothered me. Although my expertise was physics and not political science, I felt that I too had failed by not trying even harder to convince the University to think about all the aspects of peace, and to convince the Government and the public to make the necessary preparations.

In talks with my friend, the late Professor Judah M. Eisenberg, about the new situation following Sadat's visit to Jerusalem, we reached the conclusion that one of the likely possibilities or dangers was that Prime-Minister Begin would change his mind in view of what he would have to sacrifice for peace. We did not know Menachem Begin personally, but we knew his personal history, and believed that we understood his frame of mind. We thought that he might be afraid that he would get into history as the one who drastically diminished Theodor Herzl's and Zeev Zabotinski's dream of greater Israel. I argued that theoretically there was another alternative for a leader like Begin; namely, that he might see himself as the one who started a new great stage for Zionism, in which Israel would help the whole Middle East move forward. I also argued that some of us in academia stood a chance of convincing Begin to accept the new challenge. Judah disagreed, and said that members of the University would not want to undertake such an action, since it was political in nature. Alternatively, he suggested getting together several senior members of the faculty to discuss the possible contribution that the University could make to the promotion and maintenance of the budding peace. As a result of this conversation I invited to my home for a meeting a few senior members of various faculties: The rector - Shalom Abarbanel (mathematics), Judah Eisenberg (physics), the president - Haim Ben-Shahar (economics), Eitan Berglas (economics), Yoram Dinstein (law), Zeev Hirsch (management), Shimon Shamir (history), and Amos Shapira (law).

In my invitation letter I did not follow Judah's advice and suggested two topics for discussion:
- Are we facing today the reduction of a vision or a beginning of a new great era?
- What can the University do to help the peace process?

The following is the text of my opening talk:

(1) As to the first suggested topic, let me start with a short personal comment. In various conversations with friends and other people, I often paint the following ideal picture of a future in twenty or thirty years. *There is then cooperation among all the countries of the Middle East. Roads, railroads, aviation lines and trade routes go through all the countries in the region, including*

countries such as Israel and Palestine, and the borders between states lose their relevance. The whole Middle-East region then operates as a superpower, competing with the other superpowers. All present difficulties look small in view of this rosy picture. Therefore, it is important that present difficulties will be solved in light of this possible picture of the future. As for security, each step will be small and slow to make sure that the security balance is maintained. When I present these ideas, the audience is usually surprised, and I get comments such as, "What you are saying is interesting; I have never heard or thought about such an idea." I therefore reached the conclusion that the country lacks a vision of a desired and possible future, in the light of which present problems should be addressed and solved.

My conclusion is that we therefore need a new vision, sort of a new Altneuland, like Herzl's book, that will give an optimistic view of what a future could be like, so that then we would be able to say, "If you will it, it is no fairy tale". Let me bring another example of a book with a vision, like that of Altneuland, which had a great influence on society, I mean "1984" by George Orwell. This book too talked about a future, though its future was grim, but it too had a great influence on the future, as a warning. My suggestion is that we will create a kind of anti-1984 picture; a picture of a possible optimistic future, with a hope that such a picture will help solve the current difficulties. All political sacrifices will not be seen then as surrender to pressure, rather as cleaning up the surface, to enable progress toward a better future. More specifically, a future with economic and political cooperation could almost automatically solve, by itself, the following problems: security, borders, Jewish immigration, Palestinian refugees, etc. Why is that so? Suppose that big industries and agricultural plants are built in the region in which there is full Israeli-Palestinian-Jordanian-Egyptian collaboration; this is done with the help of big investments from the Arab countries and other countries in the world, which are interested in a peaceful Middle East. Will there be great importance where exactly the national borders are?

In order to promote such a vision, which I have just outlined to you, we will have to do three things: 1. Draw out to the public and the leaders of our country the possibilities embodied in the new era, and explain to them that we are not facing the diminution of the old vision, rather the beginning of a new vision, which is in fact the extension of the old one. 2. Prepare clear and extensive economic, political, and educational plans. 3. Get the international community interested, so that it will become involved in the new economic enterprises, and this involvement will be used as a positive feedback in the dynamics of achieving peace.

(2) As to the second topic in the agenda of what the University can do, I wish to start by comparing what might politically be happening to a natural phenomenon. I believe that in many respects, our situation resembles that of a water-dam that has been keeping the water of a lake from flowing out, and once the dam breaks down, the water rushes out in all possible directions. Our challenge is to direct the flow.

Some people might wonder what a university has got to do with peace. My answer is that we have recently been discussing what the faculty could do to help our society, and not stay only in the "ivory tower". We discussed possible contributions in traditional fields such as: security, ties with Jewish communities abroad, education in disadvantaged communities, etc. If we had to invent a test for the relevance of our University to our society, apart from our teaching and research, we could not have found a better example than the one before us. Our country is marching in a fast pace into a big and unknown future, when almost no thinking has been done to prepare it for this future. My question is: Will the University be willing to do the thinking, and will each professor want to help in his or her field of expertise? This is a terrific challenge and a great opportunity to prove to our society that we are not secluding ourselves in an ivory tower.

Although there is no limit to the imagination concerning the vacuum that will soon be filled, I will use the opportunity and present a few examples of what academic actions faculty members could take: We can look for scientific collaborations with individual Egyptian faculty member or groups (or departments) working in the same field, or plan regional projects, such as power plants, roads, and railroads, as well as hospitals and clinics or schools and universities.

Let me be more specific and suggest some actions that our University could take: 1. Hold an open workshop for the faculty members in order to discuss the following question: Should the university be involved with peace matters, in what fields, and how should it be done? 2. Announce that the University assigns this activity top priority. 3. Set up immediately a coordinating body, perhaps a new center for strategic studies, which will deal with all aspects of both war and peace. 4. Have this center establish ties with other universities in the country to coordinate activities on the developing peace; it can also try to establish ties with a similar center in Egypt, if and when such a center will be formed. 5. Establish a place, in and around Tel Aviv, for public thinking and planning. 6. Supply the Government, the Knesset, and the whole public with ideas, suggestions and plans.

As had been predicted by my friend Judah, the discussion that followed my opening presentation concentrated exclusively on the second topic, on what the University could and should do for the approaching peace; in general, the participants liked the idea, and made a few suggestions. The reaction to the first topic was sympathetic, but much less enthusiastic than mine. The rector, Shalom Abarbanel, said that there are limits to the ability of the University to deal with social and political matters, and added that there might be different opinions in the faculty on these topics.

The Yariv Committee. Professor Ben-Shahar, the University president, could not come to the meeting at my home, so I gave him a full report afterwards. As a result of this report, and perhaps also of reports of discussions of other groups, Vice-President Mori Sokolovski appointed a "Committee for Strengthening the Peace", headed by Retired General Aharon Yariv, whose members were the following senior professors: Asher Arian, Gideon Gera, Zeev Hirsch, Baruch Raz, Jonathan Shapira, Shimon Shamir, and Avivi Yavin. Dr. Reuven Choresh coordinated the Committee's work, and Ms. Nina Wolf acted as its secretary. The Committee was charged with the following task: "To prepare a working document that will deal with the definition and the mapping of the subjects and the national goals in the future relations between Israel and Egypt, and perhaps the rest of the Arab World." The Committee was also asked to consider the new internal challenges in Israel, which could be created by these relations, and to consider the contribution of Tel-Aviv University in finding solutions to the subjects and national goals that it will define.

The Committee or think-tank, under the experienced hands of General Yariv, started right away to work intensively. Shimon Shamir, the University expert on Egypt, supplied the Committee with information and assessments as to the possible Egyptian attitudes. Several members of the Committee then submitted working papers; among them were: "Israel after peace" by Jonathan Shapira, "Egypt – Objective Needs" by Gideon Gera, and "Areas in Which Cooperation between Israel and Egypt Can Be Foreseen When peace Takes

Place" by Baruch Raz and Reuven Choresh. I submitted the following working paper, entitled "Fundamental Considerations in Dealing with the Israeli-Egyptian Cooperation."

In our discussions we assume that peace is desired and that maximum cooperation will strengthen it. I will now present a set of fundamental considerations or criteria needed for the investigation of the opportunities and dangers in the general subject of cooperation, as well as in individual areas.

A basic consideration. The simple and immediate consideration for the selection of an area for collaboration is time; namely, that it will be possible to agree on, and start collaboration in a short time.

Real needs. A collaboration has to take place where there are real needs (at present or in the near future) of each side; it should not be undertaken only as a tool for strengthening peace.

Interface with outside interests. Even in bilateral relations, the interaction with outside interests (the superpowers, the oil countries, the Jewish people, etc) has to be evaluated. It is possible that sometimes the inclusion of a third party will enable a desired collaboration; on the other hand, it is possible that in certain cases, Israeli-Egyptian collaboration might spoil important relations of one of them with a third party (such as Egypt with the rest of the Arab World).

Interaction among various areas or considerations. There are cases in which the set of considerations should include more than one area. I will now present three examples: 1. A successful collaboration in the academic area could help collaborations in business, industry or agriculture. 2. In certain cases, the real-need criterion (No. 2 above) can be met only if two areas are involved; for instance, water and energy. 3. Success in one area could hurt another area; for instance, if industrial plants are built in which the know-how and management are Jewish but the blue-collar workers are Egyptians, the plants could be successful economically, but could hurt the relations between the two peoples.

Timing, order, and speed. A separate consideration should be given to the following question: When to start with a specific collaboration, where should be its place in the set of collaborations, and what should be the rate of its progress? For instance, in the beginning it is advised to have only small-scale collaborations, which stand a better chance of being successful, and will serve mainly to create a positive atmosphere. Tourism is one such example.

New areas. There are areas, which each party could not handle by itself because of the lack of critical mass (for production and/or consumption) or because of barriers (for instance, construction of ground transportation lines between Europe and Africa). These areas should have priorities.

Internal dangers. Every Egyptian-Israeli enterprise could, in principle, create internal dangers in Israel or in Egypt, in the same area or in other areas. Also, the whole topic of cooperation might affect the Israeli or Egyptian society, their national goals, and their relations with outside parties, such as the Jewish Diaspora for Israel and the Arab World for Egypt.

Overall balance. When the plan for collaboration in various areas is presented, it should be verified that there is a balance in the advantages and contributions of each side in the whole program as well as in each area. An example for an unbalanced program is one in which Israel will have only political advantages and Egypt will have only economic ones, or visa versa.

Collaboration and not aid. Because of possible sensitivity of Egypt to collaborations with a more developed country, it is important that real collaborations and not aid programs will be undertaken. In those cases in which there will also be some level of aid in one part, attempts should be made to progress toward a balanced collaboration as soon as possible. It is therefore recommended to start with areas and programs, which will be suggested by the Egyptians.

Non-identification with a specific social power in Egypt. In order to prevent the collapse of the whole program in case of a major political or social change in Egypt, it is crucial that the cooperation program will not depend only on the ruling layer, and that it will not appear as if the program is especially intended to strengthen this layer.

Positive feedback to the peace process. If it will be possible to start collaborating in some areas even before the formal peace process ends, these collaborations should be encouraged, because they will contribute to the process.

A Proposal. It is suggested to investigate the possibility of forming soon "An Egyptian-Israeli Committee for Strengthening the Peace". This Committee will be charged with the following tasks:

To suggest basic considerations in the subject of Egyptian-Israeli collaborations.

To prepare a list of possible areas for collaboration.

To overlook the process of cooperation.

During his Committee's work, Chairman Yariv sent a letter to all the University faculty members. In this letter he informed the faculty about the appointment of his committee and about the proposals for research topics that the Committee had already received. He also asked the faculty members to go over the list of proposed topics for collaboration, and to add new ones.

On March 13, 1978 the Yariv Committee submitted its final report to Vice-President Sokolovski. The report included a list of 27 research topics to be suggested to the faculty (See Appendix IV). It also included an estimate of the necessary budget for the various proposed activities such as: research, bi-party or tri-party conferences, and administration, for a total of $500,000, to be gotten from outside contributions. The University itself was asked to allocate $100,000 from its own sources.

The Committee recommended that the University would charge a central body with the coordination, encouragement, and support of all the activities in the University related to peace, by forming a body for handling peace activities. This body's tasks will be: 1. To overlook all peace activities in the University. 2. To handle all the existing ties between individual faculty members and scientists in Arab countries. 3. To take care of academic people from Arab countries visiting the University. 4. To organize common activities such as: research, conferences, and publications. 5. To supply University assistance to such common activities. 6. To form ties with other public bodies in Israel (other universities, the Government, Tel-Aviv Municipality, etc) on peace issues. 7. To form ties with similar units in Arab countries if and when such units are formed.

CHAPTER 3.
THE RESEARCH PROJECT ON PEACE

Forming the Peace Project. The Yariv Committee recommended forming a central body for the coordination of all the activities in the University related to peace, and the initiation of new activities. My own feelings were that we had been negligent with our duties to our society in the past many years, and had not prepared ourselves to the challenges of peace; however, we had at least made big steps forward in the previous several months, and had succeeded in moving along with the actual events, and not only in explaining them a posteriori. Lots of things had to be done, and from my failing efforts in the Senate a few years earlier I knew that Aharon Yariv would not agree to add a new responsibility to the ones he already had in the Institute for Strategic Studies. I knew that the one faculty member, who would undertake to coordinate the existing peace activities and initiate new ones, would knowingly freeze his own scientific career for at least several years. My hesitations did not last long. I asked the University president to form the new body, and he in turn asked me if I was willing to take the responsibility of forming the new coordinating body. I agreed not only because of the importance of that responsibility, but also because of the President's enthusiastic support of the idea, and our similar views as to the University's responsibility to society.

How do you form such a unique body with such unique tasks? I could not learn from the experience of others because of the uniqueness of our situation. I soon realized that my three first major tasks would be: 1. To select an advisory board or a management for the new body, which would advise me, and would help in selling the new ideas to the faculty. 2. To estimate the necessary budget for at least the first year, and find sources for that. (Here the estimate of Yariv's committee would be of great help). 3. To understand in full the dimensions of the new challenge. My first steps were consultations with my friend Judah Eisenberg and with Yoram Dinstein from the Law Faculty; both of them had been present at the meeting in my home several months before. We all agreed that we needed a balanced advisory board made of the best people in the University in the relevant disciplines. In addition to the three of us and Vice President Mori Sokolovski, the following people were selected: Aharon Yariv, the head of the Institute for Strategic Studies, Shimon Shamir, who had formed the Shiloah Institute[1], Asher Arian, a political scientist and the dean of the Faculty for Social Sciences, Zeev Hirsch, an economist and the dean of the Faculty of Administration, and Baruch Raz, a chemist and head of the Institute of Technological Forecasting. Later three more professors were added to this group: Eli Reches from the Shiloah institute, David Horn from the Physics Department, and Eitan Berglas, an economist. I selected the lawyer Drora Beit-or to be my secretary and later the Project's administrative director, leaving the job of secretary to Ophira Reffen. The team of the three of us acted in a friendly concert.

As promised in our first meeting, President Ben-Shahar approved a small sum from the president's budget for my first steps, and later got from the Knesset the sum of 1.0 million Israeli Lira (about $50,000) by the recommendation of the Finance Minister Simcha Erlich. In the course of my thinking about directions to go and the actions I should take, and even before the first meeting of the newly appointed Management, I decided to get new ideas and perspectives away from home - in the United States, so I took a trip there.

A Study Trip to the United States (April 1978). Before I describe my visit to the US, I will describe a very unusual event, a visit of an Arab professor to the University, several weeks earlier. Professor George Assousa, an American astrophysicist of Palestinian origin, visited Israel and the University in February as a guest of the Israeli National Council for Research and Development. We were told that he was a nephew of a former Jordanian defense minister, and that he was interested in Arab-Israeli cooperation in research projects. In his visit he met many top University staff members, who described the University activities to him. Aharon Yariv described the work of his committee, and I told Assousa that we would be interested in academic collaborations even before a peace treaty was signed. I told him that we would like to find a Jordanian university that would be willing to organize conferences on agreed subjects together with us. We mentioned the Jordan valley, in which both sides were interested, as one such example.

---

1 *It later became the Dayan Center*

Since we knew very little about the Arab states, we asked him to talk about one of them, and he selected Jordan with which he was mostly familiar; and this is what he told us: The number of Jordanian students studying abroad was larger than the number studying in Jordan. He recommended collaborations in higher-education and said that the following areas were candidates for Israeli-Jordanian collaboration in research: agriculture, water, solar energy, public health, transportation, and the Jordan valley. At this point President Ben-Shahar said that the University would be willing to accept Jordanian students and to exchange faculty members. Assousa suggested that the West Bank would be the best location for Jordanian-Israeli meetings, with no need for governmental commitments, and added that such meetings would have positive political effects (an idea that resonated well with me). At the end of the meetings, all the participants commended the good spirit of the meetings and praised Assousa for his constructive approach.

Before leaving for the US I called Shlomo Aaronson, a political science professor at the Hebrew University, who was staying then in UCLA, and who was apparently selected by the Hebrew University in Jerusalem to head their peace activities. He invited me to visit him in Los Angeles, and asked if we were interested in collaboration with the Hebrew University. President Ben-Shahar encouraged me to stay in touch with George Assousa and with Shlomo Aaronson, and added that there were some unfriendly voices at the University about our peace activity. He did not elaborate. This was for me the first time that I heard that the peace activity was causing some tension in the University. In the first meeting of the Management, a few weeks after I returned from the US, I understood part of what the President had said.

I flew to Los Angeles to meet Shlomo Aaronson. I still assumed that we would work together, and planned to suggest that we would set up a national academic committee for peace activities. I also intended to suggest that we would have an international steering board made up of people such as: Henry Kissinger, George Bull, Stanley Hoffman, Mendes France, Bernard Lewis, Bruno Kreisky, Nikolai Chauchesko, the King of Morocco, Willy Brandt, and the Persian Shah. Aaronson[2] was very cooperative, and stressed that he was very interested in working with us. He described what was happening

2   In my talks with Professor Aaronson he repeated the following phrases, "This subject has been investigated, and there is no need to deal with it further", or "this subject will be investigated", and other such comments on various political questions, as if we were dealing with a mathematical problem that had only one solution. I thought that this had to do with his personal style, but I learned later that it might have to do with the difference in cultures between someone from the exact sciences, and one from the social sciences.

in UCLA, where there was support, but also opposition to peace activities on their campus, probably because of the Saudi money that they were getting. I then met with Steve Spiegel, one of the authors of the famous Brooking Report on the Middle East, and with Ray Orbach, the provost of UCLA, who was an expert on arms control. They were very interested in our ideas, gave advice about sources of financial support, and offered to help my activity in the future.

From LA I flew to Washington DC, mainly to talk to George Assousa. In our meetings he gave me his political assessment as follows: If there was going to be separation between Israel and the West Bank, the Palestinians would agree to the demilitarization of the West Bank. There should be an intermediate period of 5-7 years in which the Palestinians there would get autonomy, and Israel would get security; all under the supervision of the United States, Japan, and Romania (the Tripartite Commission). An Egyptian geophysicist, who came with him to this meeting, said that the situation in Egypt was desperate, because there was actually no effective government. Assousa added that he was afraid that we would be swallowed by the "Egyptian sponge", and therefore he recommended starting collaborations with Jordan and not with Egypt. I wondered whether he realized that Israel was facing peace with Egypt and not with Jordan. Assousa then described the situation in the three colleges in the West Bank, Bir-Zeit, Bethlehem, and Nablus, and repeated his request that Israel would help higher education in the West Bank. He suggested that the Americans, mostly of Palestinian origin, should build industrial plants in the West Bank in collaboration with Israeli industries, and the products would be sold in the Arab World and in the Third World. In his opinion, 20% of the professional Palestinians living in the United States would then be willing to return to their country. In summary, Assousa was interested in academic collaboration that would help develop the West bank, but my main concern then was mainly academic collaboration with Egyptians.

I reported my meetings to Hannan Bar-On from the Israeli Embassy. Upon returning home I was informed by President Ben-Shahar that I already had been allocated $15,000 from the University and $50,000 from the Knesset, all for the first-year operations.

The Project Management. One of my first actions upon returning to Israel was to have a meeting with my advisory board, which had already received the official appointment from the vice-president and was called the Management. I thanked the members for agreeing to help me. We decided to call our body The Tel Aviv University Research Project on Peace, or in short, the Peace Project. Shimon Shamir said that the task was pioneering and very difficult, and then added, "Let us remember that usually success has many parents, but failure has only one (meaning me)." We identified several subjects for our first efforts: We should start by identifying all existing research projects at the University related to peace and then start new ones. These projects should get some financial support from us. We should then encourage collaborative research with Arabs, especially Egyptians as well as research on the effects of peace on the country. I insisted that research projects that point out the various political and social dangers to the country from peace should also be included. I was asked to report to the University faculty on the formation of the Peace Project and to ask for research proposals. These would be judged by a research committee as to their academic levels and their relevance to the peace issue. If approved, financial support would be granted.

These deliberations were in a good, constructive, and friendly spirit, as expected. However, I failed to expect what happened next. I reported to the Management on what I had learned in the US, and about our approved budget, and proposed to expand our activities, and form an Israeli academic body, in line with my talks with Shlomo Aaronson from the Hebrew University. Most members of the Management objected, some of them violently. There were some members who objected because they said that some people in political science in the Hebrew University were more senior than our people. Others claimed that we were ahead in the peace endeavor, and we alone should harvest the fruits, as we had already done with the support from the Knesset. Judah Eisenberg and I fought hard, saying that the effort was hard and important, and that collaboration with the Hebrew University would improve its chances for success. But we were in the minority. It meant that the collaboration and exchange of information with Shlomo Aaronson would have to stop. This was the first time, but not the last one, that I discovered strong sectarian attitudes, mainly in the disciplines of the west-side of the Campus (liberal arts, political science, law, art, and management).

We worked very hard to set in motion all that had to be done. I wrote some letters to the faculty, we set up a research committee to evaluate research proposals, we chose public persons to be on a newly formed supervising committee which we called the Steering Board, and drew up plans for the future. All these activities will be described in more detail in the following sections

In one of the first Management meetings we decided to prepare a document, which would describe our goals and activities to date. We called it the Project Document. We kept expanding the Document to follow our expanding activities. Rather than presenting the changing Document repeatedly, following every new major activity, the expanded Document, as it looked after about a year of activity of the Peace Project, is presented in Appendix V, but the reader should bear in mind that it describes some activities, which would actually take place later.

The Board of Governors of the University was scheduled to meet in the beginning of June. Since the "peace-buds" had started to blossom, and since the University had worked hard on the peace issue in the previous months, it was decided to have one session of the Board meeting devoted to the University plans in regards to peace. Three talks were planned for this session (6.6.1978): 1. Aharon Yariv would talk about his institute and about the committee he headed. 2. Zeev Hirsch would talk about the various plans to build a channel from the Mediterranean to the River Jordan (or the Dead Sea)). 3. I would talk about the Research Project on Peace. Vice President Sokolovski felt that there was not enough material for a full talk of half an hour, but he was wrong. Since our activities and plans are described at length in other sections of the book, I will present here only the introductory part of my talk:

A Talk in a Plenary Session of the Board of Governors
In English they call it peace, in Arabic it is called Salam, but it is known universally as shalom. What a word! It contains a world of ideas, human experience, suffering, expectations, disappointments, and still hopes. In his first speech in Arabic, the new president of Israel, Itzhak Navon, called peace "the most beautiful adjective of God". The spontaneous joy in Israel from the visit of President Sadat to Jerusalem, and in Egypt from that of Prime Minister Begin to Ismailia, were a vivid proof that the people of the Middle East, by and large, want peace; in fact, desire peace in all their hearts and souls. And still, peace is hard to achieve and keep.

But you may ask, and understandably so: What has all this got to do with a university? Shouldn't a university concentrate on teaching and research, and leave politics to the politicians? The answer is simple: We are not talking about politics, which should be outside the university domain of activity. We are talking about something entirely different, something big, and something that has unfortunately been little tended to. And by this I mean research in, and planning for the many aspects of peace in the Middle East.

The Egyptian attack on Yom Kippur of 1973 caught us all by surprise, and one of the major factors responsible for the surprise was the notorious concept or *conceptsia (Hamechdal)*, as it is colloquially known here. In simple English, the word describes the freezing of the mind into one rigid concept. No more considerations of all aspects and alternatives, no more doubts; instead – the dangerous state of being led by pre-conceived ideas, by wishful thinking, and by one-track minds, characteristic of a complacent society. The recent exchange of visits between President Sadat and Prime-minister Begin caught us again by surprise. We had talked so much about our desire for peace that when peace appeared to be within reach, we realized that the country had not planned for it at all. In their hearts, the people had always wanted peace, but their minds were not ready for it. There were few, if any, plans for achieving peace, let alone plans for the time after peace would be achieved. Various economic possibilities for regional cooperation, with all their enormous challenges, had not been considered. Legal problems of peace and beyond had not been fully dealt with. The mutual advantages of collaboration in science, medicine, agriculture and the arts had not been fully realized. In short, not only did we not have, as a nation, the answers to the challenges of peace, we did not even have the questions, the right questions, and all the relevant ones. So here too we see a case of insufficient, if not total absence of free, responsible and imaginative thinking. Both in the challenge of war in October 1973 and in the challenge of peace in November 1977, the state of the People of the Book, which is known for its contribution to free and imaginative human thinking, failed precisely where it was supposed to excel. And Israeli academia, which is charged with the responsibility of teaching and leading the people in thinking, has - I am afraid - failed, and badly so.

Perhaps a little late, but still quite a while back, Tel Aviv University decided to take up the challenge of planning for the approaching peace. We knew that in the area of peace, as in all areas, a university should ask the right questions, and all the relevant ones. A university should also prepare plans, and Professor Hirsch has just given you an example of thinking and planning, which have been done at the University on one specific question. General Yariv has just described to you how Tel Aviv University decided to meet in full the new challenge for academia. One of the recommendations of his committee was to undertake an all-University effort in research on peace, and give it a high priority. As a result of this recommendation, the University has created the Tel Aviv University Research Project on Peace. As its name suggests, the Peace Project will deal with all the many aspects of the peace-making process, and we will deal with them not as politicians but as scholars. As a University project, we cannot do more, but as I have just explained, we cannot and should not do less…

The audience seemed very interested in the talk. Some of them said that they were proud that their University was a pioneer in this important subject.[3]

Steering Board. One of the main goals of the Peace Project was the interaction with the public. Therefore, the Management decided to ask the president to appoint a public Steering Board, and to appoint Aharon Yariv as its head. The Board would overlook the actions of the Peace Project, would pass to us the requests of the public, and would pass to the public the results of our research and actions. President Ben-Shahar, Aharon Yariv, and I talked to many people who, we thought, would represent a broad cross section of the Israeli society, and asked them to agree to serve on the board. The response was usually positive, and at times even emotionally so. In very few cases were we turned down for personal or political reasons. Some people with right-wing ideology thought that dealing with aspects of peace, even if it was done inside a university, had left-wing connotations. It is possible that Aharon Yariv, who was respected by most Israelis, repelled others because to the famous Yariv-Shemtov formula, which said that Israel should talk with any organization that recognized it.

3   *The Public Relations Department of the University, out of too much enthusiasm (and little thinking), almost caused us a lot of embarrassment. In preparation for the session on the University's contributions to peace, this Department laid a folder on the desk of each participant with material about the talks of Yariv, Hirsch, and Yavin, along with material from another session. I was astounded to see that the material from the other session was a proposal by Professor Edward Teller, a member of the Board, that the University should put itself in the frontline of the international struggle against the Soviet Bloc. Luckily I had sufficient time to see to it the Teller's proposal would be taken out of the folders describing the University's contributions to peace.*

We ended up with an impressive Steering Board[4], which included high ranking representatives of the treasury, industry, courts, the press, the foreign ministry, the health system, the local government, and the University. On of the first question to be discussed by the Board was the inclusion of Israeli Arabs in the Peace Project's activities. It was pointed out that it was still difficult to include an Israeli Arab in the Board or Management, but not in all the other activities. Members of the Board kept bringing subjects for research to be suggested to the faculty and supported by the Peace Project.

Since the main goal of the Peace Project was research, the Management and I spent most of our time and efforts dealing with this question. I wrote several letters to the faculty, in which I described our goals and plans. I pointed out that we had a budget aimed at supporting our researchers, including students, in subjects related to peace, and added that we were ready to support researchers from other institutions as well as public experts. A special emphasis was put on research projects, which would be carried out in collaboration with Arabs. One such letter is shown in Appendix VI.

In addition to sending the letters I asked the nine deans to let me speak in their faculty councils, and my request was granted by all of them. Most of the discussions were interesting and taught me a great deal; there were questions and answers, and I was given several pieces of advice. Although the attitude of most people was positive, some participants had criticism and even objections to the Peace Project's activities. One question surprised me, "Why should we collaborate with Egyptians? The poor people of your city should have a preference." The professor who asked this question was apparently against peace with Egypt and against the Peace Project, and decided that our only goal was to help Egypt. Strange! Following my two letters to the faculty and my meetings with the nine councils, we were flooded by suggestions from senior as well as junior staff members. Several graduate students volunteered to help us, and we received dozens of research proposals. My work load grew quickly, so I asked Professor

4　The members of the Steering Board were: Ms. N. Arad, Mr. I. Ben-Aharon, Justice H. Ben-Ito, Mr. M. Bar-on, Mr. D. Brodet, Mr. B. Gitter, Mr. M. De-Shalit, Prof. D. Vital, Ms. H. Zemmer, Mr. B. Yekutieli, Mayor S. Lahat, Mr. A. Levin, Ms. A.M. Lambert, Prof. B. Modan, Mr. A. Sivan, Mr. T. Peleg, Mr. M. Fraenkel, Mr. G. Rafael, Prof. A. Shapiro, Prof Y. Shapira, Prof. H. Shaked, Mr. A Sheffer, and Mr. P. Tamir.

David Horn to help me by becoming the Chair of the research commit-tee, and he agreed. The whole list of the supported research proposals will be presented later; here I will bring just the three, which were completed in the first several months:

Egypt's international trade policies, by Zeev Hirsch and Alfred Tobias.
The Palestinian problem – electoral behavior, coalition aspects, and ex-pected trends in its operational vicinity, by Shaul Mishal.
Mediators and the Israeli-Arab relations, by Saadia Tuval.

Consultations with Outside Personalities. With the appointment of the Management, the Steering Board, and the Research Committee I finished building the infrastructure of the Peace Project. I could therefore turn to the formation of contacts with relevant people in Israel and the rest of the world, hopefully in Egypt too. Up until the Camp David Accords between President Anwar Sadat and Prime-Minister Menachem Begin on September 17, 1978, I held dozens of such meetings. I will present here only some of them, those that had historical significance or that had suggestions and assessments as to the Peace Project's future activities, and these too only briefly. I will not include in this section accounts of the meetings with the many faculty members who came to discuss their ideas for research. I will start by presenting brief accounts of talks with people from outside the University.

Ann Marie Lambert. She fought with the Maquis in France, and the Nazis tortured her. She was then the Israeli representative in UNESCO, where I met her in 1972 and 1974 when I represented Israel on the UNESCO Science Committee. She offered to volunteer working one day a week for us with no pay.

*Professor Stanley Hoffman*n. He was a distinguished professor at Harvard visiting the University. After an exchange of only a few sentences, and to my surprise, he uttered a sigh of relief, saying that finally he could speak in Israel with somebody with an open mind. He said that he had a stom-ach full of the frozen minds he found in Israel, and that included Shimon Peres and the Shiloah Institute. He said that our thoughts and plans in the Peace Project were sound, and added that he was doubtful about the participation of Arabs in our activities, but he would pass the informa-tion to the Arabs at Harvard, and would help us deliver invitations to our future conferences to those Arabs. He warned us about involving, in our activities, controversial figures such as Henry Kissinger, The Persian Shah, and the King of Morocco.

Nahum Goldmann. I went to meet with this old Zionist leader. We had a long talk in which he said that he had excellent relations with the Egyptian Ambassador to the United States, Ashraf Ghorbal. We then discussed collaborations through his representative Kolodnick in organizing international meetings and conferences.

Yochai Bin-nun. He had been the legendary commander of the Israeli navy, and at that time he was the head of a civilian institute for seas and lakes in Haifa. He told me that George Assousa was trying to get the US Congress to allocate 2.5-4.0 million dollars to be used by an Egyptian-Israeli-Jordanian collaboration to develop seas, lakes, and rivers in the region.

Professor Shlomo Avinery. He was the senior professor of political science in the Hebrew University. Following his phone request I traveled to Jerusalem in order to tell him about our Peace Project and to invite him to join our Steering Board. He welcomed me with questions such as: What is a physicist doing in such a project, and why are you the director and not Aharon Yariv? He then stated that the structure of our Management and Steering Board was not good, and that as a professor of one institution he did not want to be on a Steering Board of another institution. His last "friendly" comment was that one does not research peace; one makes peace. I wondered why he had invited me to travel up to Jerusalem, since he had known what my request would be, and that his answer to that would be negative. I also started thinking that the Management might have been right in refusing to collaborate with the Hebrew University.

Gideon Rafael. This charming retired diplomat too invited me to come up to Jerusalem, and thanked me for coming. He said that he was enthusiastic about the Peace Project, and would gladly accept our invitation to be on the Steering Board. He added that he would love to help us get contributions. After he had attended several meetings of the Steering Board, he advised me that the "civilians" on the Board were not very happy that we dealt almost exclusively with research projects.

Peleg Tamir. He was the general manager of the Manufacturers Association of Israel and a close friend of Ezer Weizmann, the defense minister. After I had told him about the Peace Project, he agreed to serve on the Steering Board. When I told him that someone (it was actually President Ben-Shahar) had proposed that the University undertook to coordinate all the economic activities in the country concerning peace, he said that this man was a genius. We then agreed that there should be two bodies: one body, the Peace Project would deal with research, and his Association would deal with the actual economic bodies.

Consultations with University Professors. My talks with some of the University professors were interesting and very educational to me. Some were helpful, others gave me the first signs of undercurrents of different and opposing personal views; I detected discipline differences concerning the goals of the Peace Project as a University body. I should have been alert to that from the beginning, but at that time I was perhaps still naïve because of my total belief in the cause and my belief that all my colleagues felt likewise. The following are some of the ideas presented at a meeting in the President's office attended by senior faculty members.

Professor Shimon Shamir suggested that we, in the Peace Project, should stay away from all political aspects as much as possible, and that we should, in the beginning, concentrate on two tasks: 1. Mapping: what was done in the Arab countries; ties that our professors had already with Arab professors; third parties who were involved with the subject and could be used as sponsors; and sources of funds. 2. Bi- and tri-lateral symposia.

Vice President Mori Sokolovski, who is the one who appointed the Yariv Committee and was a member of the Project's Management, said (to my surprise) that he was disappointed with the results of the Yariv Committee. He said that in the research that would be done with the Peace Project's support, it was essential that we determined not only what we wanted to publish, but also what information we would like to keep to ourselves.

President Haim Ben-Shahar said that he was afraid that we might lose the opportunity to be first in doing important things. Therefore, he suggested that we should establish quickly a large institute for economic planning using mainly outside experts, since we did not have a sufficient number of our own. He then added (to my surprise) that we should consider changing the Peace Project's direction to become an institute for economic collaboration in the Middle East in subjects such as transportation, industry, and energy.[5] Ben-Shahar then made a different or alternative suggestion that the University should establish a national authority for economic planning.

Professor Eitan Berglas, who was at that time in the Ministry of the Fi-

5 *In a later conversation between the two of us I said to him that some people in the University cautioned me by saying, "Don't be naïve, Avivi; from the outset, the aim of President Ben-Shahar in the Peace Project is to form a big economic institute for himself." He did not react to that, and I added that I myself did not object to putting emphasis in the Peace Project on economics in the first stage, but without neglecting the other areas. I then added, "Do not forget that you are the president of the entire university."*

nance (the Treasury) as a director of the budget, spoke on the question of the establishment of a national authority for economic planning, and said that it should be established in the Government and not in the University. *Professor Ben-Shahar* interrupted him and said that for the country there were, in principle, two kinds of decisions to make, those which would usually have immediate consequences and those which would have only medium or long-term consequences. The decision of whether and when to withdraw from the Sinai was an example of the first kind, because it would have immediate economic consequences and the Government should therefore consider the consequences of such an action. On the other hand, the Government could not deal with the medium and long-term consequences of its decision on the withdrawal, and this would be up to a body like the University to do so. He summarized his opinion by saying that the University (via the new economic authority that he proposed to establish) should be the thinking arm of the Treasury on such issues.

Professor Zvi Hadar contributed the following example where only the University and not the Government could fully investigate. There was a dilemma concerning the Sinai, actually there were two concepts; namely, should the Sinai be turned into a fertile region by Egyptian-Israeli collaboration, or should it stay as a desert separating militarily between Israel and Egypt. By its nature the Treasury could not deal with such a question.

Following these and other discussions with various faculty members I started wondering whether there was a genuine conflict of interest between the establishment of a national authority within the University, which required intensive involvement in economic matters, and the goals and future activities of the Research Project on Peace. My conclusion was that, in principle, there should not be such a conflict, because the Peace Project was an umbrella for all activities on Campus dealing with aspects of peace. If there was a lot of activity in economics, we should help it, and never compete with it. (A body could not, and should not be in conflict with one of its parts). Later we would encounter the same problem of a possible conflict of interests between the Peace Project and University bodies such as the Shiloah Institute and the Strategic Institute, in dealing with relations with Egypt. My answer there would be the same. Furthermore, if a conflict developed, it would be the fault of the Peace Project, indicating that it was not doing what it should do; namely, be only a co-ordinating and helping body, with no interest of its own. As we will later see, not everybody on Campus agreed with me, and what was worse, not everybody believed that such were my intentions. One professor even said to me: If not for power, why did you take this job in the Peace Project.

A National Authority for the Repercussions of peace and for Planning Regional Cooperation. The title of this section may sound a bit complicated, and it represents the complications of the situation and of my position. In order to help the reader to avoid confusion, I will start with pointing out a few basic historical and political facts, before I describe, in this section and the following one, what actually transpired next in the Peace Project.

The time was September 1978. The country was in an excited and optimistic state, but nobody really knew clearly what was going to happen and what the Government and the universities should do. Apart from the natural loyalty to the country, I had 4 loyalties or 4 hats to wear, some of them overlapping with one another, and some even in conflict as I soon discovered. I had a loyalty to academia, to peace, to the Peace Project, and to the University President as his advisor and aid on peace matters.

Following the discussions and uncertainties, which were described in the previous section, President Ben-Shahar asked me to prepare a proposal for him to be presented to the University leadership, so that we could start acting without losing time. The following is the proposal which I prepared, in the week that the Camp David Accords were signed.

A PROPOSAL FOR THE ESTABLISHMENT OF A NATIONAL AUTHORITY FOR PLANNING COLLABORATION IN THE MIDDLE EAST CONNECTED TO TEL-AVIV UNIVERSITY

Four years ago the University Senate approved a series of recommendations aimed at the encouragement of the faculty members to be involved in national projects. The Research Project on Peace was founded on this basis. Today it is accepted by almost everybody that planning peace has a high national priority, and that there is a need for a central national body that will deal with regional cooperation and with coordination of all the planning activities related to peace in the country. Along with the recognition of the importance of the subject and with the need that the University will coordinate such activities, we have to be careful not to change the character and classical duties of the university to the society, should the University or a major part of it decide to become a central body for planning. Furthermore, it is doubtful that the University could perform such a task without additional staff with the needed planning expertise. We therefore propose:

- A central national Authority for planning cooperation in the Middle East should be established in connection with Tel-Aviv University.
- In the first years of its activity the Authority will use the University's academic and physical infrastructure.
- Interested faculty members will join the Authority in the areas of their expertise.
- The Authority will be open to additional faculty members from the country, including Arabs.
- The Authority will also hire planning experts from the country and from the rest of the world.
- The Authority will gather and coordinate the existing research projects and plans concerning regional cooperation.
- After several years, the Authority will become independent of Tel-Aviv University.

It is necessary to prepare a comprehensive proposal dealing with all the aspects of the proposed Authority in order to get approval from the main bodies (the Government, industry, the University, etc.) The proposal should be prepared within a week, and both the Government and the Central Committee of the University Senate would be notified right away of our intention. It is proposed that the President and the Rector shall appoint a group made of faculty members and outside experts, which will prepare the proposal. The tasks of the group will be: 1. to define the tasks and modus operandi of the Authority. 2. To suggest the structure of the Authority. 3. To propose the connection between the Authority, the Government, and other public bodies. 4. To suggest topics for the work of the Authority. 5. To suggest a time table. It is proposed that this group shall meet for one day in the beginning of a week, shall then split to subgroups, which shall work for the whole week, and the full group shall meet again the following week to summarize its decisions. The Research Project on Peace shall take the responsibility of submitting the final report to the relevant bodies.

This proposal was submitted to the next meeting of the Management of the Peace Project, which was also attended by President Ben-Shahar, and was approved there. The University Directorate then decided to hold a workshop on the subject. The impressive list of the University people and outside experts who were invited and attended the workshop is presented in Appendix VII.

Four introductory lectures were presented at the workshop, followed by a general discussion. A brief account of these lectures, emphasizing their main points, and deleting the reports of activities which were presented in previous sections of this book, is presented here. The whole discussion is presented here because it shows the reader the situation, ideas, hopes and fears that existed in the first year after President Sadat's historic visit to Jerusalem.

1. Prof. Haim Ben-Shahar, the University President. The situation in the country is full of uncertainties, requiring thinking, hard decisions, and actions. There could also be pitfalls in the integration of our plans into the region. The Government handles the immediate dilemmas, while we have to think about the future. The initiative is ours, and the Government knows about it. We started several months ago, and established the Peace Project, managed by Professor Avivi Yavin, but the pace of events is catching up with us. The main question is: What should we do next?

2. Retired General Aharon Yariv, Chair of the Steering Board of the Peace Project. The goals of the Peace Project, which my committee recommended to establish, are the following: To coordinate the University actions concerning peace; to encourage the faculty, the public, and the Government to deal with peace issues; to examine the existing concepts and consensuses; to look at the existing economic and medical plans; to examine the dangers; to collaborate with Arab groups and individuals; to exchange professors and students with Arab universities; and to look for funds that will help us in our activities.

3. Mr. A. Tieberg (representing Mr. P. Tamir). I will be a bit of a spoiler. I will look at industry, because what is good for industry is good for the country. I will emphasize the dangers, which are usually in the short range (2-4 years) rather than the advantages, which are usually in the long range. For instance, I don't see what products we will be able to sell Egypt for 80 million dollars, as suggested by the Treasury, or how to transfer the Nile's water to Israel. The following are the economic dangers that I foresee: 1. Slowing down of needed growth in certain areas, and at the same time, acceleration of growth in unnecessary directions. 2. Renewed worsening of the balance of payments. 3. Escalation of inflation, due to the increase in Government spending on defense, on building airports, etc. 4. Directing our limited manpower not to where there are problems that need to be solved. 5. A real and continuous decrease in the investments in our industry. On the other hand, there are some prospects for positive developments because of the expected opening of new markets and the improvement of psychological tendency in the world to invest in the region. As for bi-lateral relations, Egypt with its 40 million people is poor, but there are subjects, such as the development of Sinai or of energy sources, which are worth examining. Bringing cheap labor from Egypt to work here might have serious social consequences; therefore, it is preferred to use it in Egypt.

4. *Professor Shimon Shamir.* I am supposed to talk about a view into our future economic relations with Egypt. I will concentrate on 4 points:

1. the normalization of relations with Israel is hard for Sadat and for Egypt for political reasons, and we have to take that into consideration. Egypt is now being attacked because it has agreed to start the normalization along with our withdrawal from the Sinai, and not after the withdrawal is completed. 2. In the question of cooperation there has lately been a reversal of position in Egypt. For years the Egyptians have been afraid of us economically, and now they have economic expectations from the peace. We should beware of tying ourselves to these expectations, because of a possible eventual disappointment. 3. The Egyptians are not going to be highly impressed by our new technologies, because they are already used to it in the West. Our contribution should not be in initiating and planning, rather in concrete work in the field. 4. The political structure in Egypt is different than that in the West. A fast action without the knowledge of the political and social structure there might be harmful. For example, Alexandria is a center of opposition to Sadat; if we rush there because there is a good university in Alexandria, we may be disappointed. In conclusion, we need to make a great effort to study the background; not to rush things; and to do the planning with considerations of how it is done in Egypt, and not only as it is done in Israel.

A vivid discussion followed the introductory talks, and a brief protocol of the new ideas is now presented.

Professor Zeev Hirsch. I wish to present some of the problems we have in dealing with future economic relations in the Middle East. We have to examine the following questions: What do we want? What is realistically possible? And what is the price we are ready to pay? Up till now economics (the boycott) was part of the war against us, and our first goal was to stop this war; but the war was being led by Saudi Arabia and Kuwait, and not by Egypt. We should apply pressure in this respect on the West and not on Egypt. A common market is usually mentioned, and this requires deep examination. Bi-lateral dependence might change our economy. For instance, we might go from chemical and electronic industry to civil engineering, and we have to check and see if this is desirable over a long run. Let me first bring two examples where peace could help our economy. 1. The automobile industry. We can expect investments in industry in which the motors will be built in Israel and the bodies in Egypt. 2. The Jordan-Valley project. This can be done only when there is peace.

Let me now bring an example of a hidden pitfall. Irrigation of the Negev with the Nile water. Every year, 550 billion cubic meters of water are extracted from the Nile for irrigation in Egypt. Let us assume that our experts will be able to raise it, say, by 10%, and we will be able to benefit from this increase. After some time the needs in the growing population of Egypt will increase, and the Egyptian public will ask why their Government is selling water to a foreign country, while it is needed locally. The conclusion from these examples is that each collaborative project should have a net positive gain for each side; and the more equal the gain, the better. Also, we should always bear in mind that conditions change (like in the Nile-water example above).

Professor J. Gross. It is possible that because of the large percentage of people in our country who speak foreign languages and because of our capital market, Israel could become a financial center like Switzerland or Great Britain.

Mr. B. Rabinovitz. The main task of the proposed Authority should be to protect the country, mostly its social structure, and to defend the peace by regional cooperation. Moving the army back from the Sinai to the Negev will accelerate greatly the development of the Negev. There are still several open questions concerning the West Bank: What will happen at the bridges with Jordan and how to form ties with Jordan? What about the Israeli money in the West Bank and what about the taxes, once a Palestinian autonomy is established there? As to the discussion concerning the nature of the new body that we may recommend to form, I would like it to be both influential and independent.

Vice President Av. Shloosh. We should learn from Israel's experience in collaboration in Africa, which is being praised, and remember that with the Arab countries we should be more careful. Our experience with Romania is also worth learning from, because there we have made several doubtful deals.

Mr. A. Reches. I am concerned mostly with the Israeli Arabs. Even without the Israeli-Egyptian negotiations there were problems with them, which have been aggravated by these negotiations. Once there is a decrease in the security and political tension, the social-economic tension between Jews and Arabs in the country will increase.

Professor H. Ben-Shahar. Let me summarize the discussion and add my preferences. I would like to form a group outside the existing bodies, which will complement them and not compete with them. Although I suggested calling it "an Authority", I do not insist on this name. I am not worried by competition from other universities, and I will not consider it a disaster if the Government will decide to turn to another university and not to us. I suggest that the proposal that we will prepare will stand by itself, and our willingness to undertake the task will be mentioned only in the cover letter; in other words, the question as to the academic institute that will be responsible is only secondary.

Following President Ben-Shahar's summary talk we organized five committees that started to work immediately. These were the charges of the five committees (the chairmen are in parenthesis): 1. to define the tasks of the Authority and its areas of activity (Professor J. Eisenberg). 2. To propose the organizational structure (Mr. A. Jacobson). 3. To suggest the ties between the Authority and the University, the Government, and other public institutions (Professor J. Gross). 4. To identify and analyze projects (Professor Z. Hirsch). 5. To prepare the proposal for the establishment of the Authority (Professor A. Yavin).

The workshop ended. We did what I always believed that a university should do for society; namely, we spent time thinking and using our expertise to suggest plans for our society in a critical moment. Moreover, in this workshop, the University was a center of thinking, where experts from the Government and the public sectors got together with us to think and plan. This was very satisfactory to me, because I had felt very bad about the negligence in academia to do the thinking and preparations before a major event such as peace with an enemy country was happening; but at least we did it now. I also wished, or even believed that the tremendous amount of work done by so many good people, who took a week off from their busy agendas, would bear important fruits. But should I have been that satisfied? After all, I was a director of a brand new big project, the Peace Project, which had barely started to work. Was the proposed National Authority part of the Peace Project? Should it be?

*****

As it had always been my custom, I turned to some wise friends to ask for their opinion and advice. Professor Eitan Berglas had been a dean and a vice rector; he was a well known economist, and a very influential figure in the Treasury; and more importantly, Eitan was very intelligent, to whom many people turned for advice. He was also a good friend of President Ben-Shahar and of mine.

Eitan suggested that we first send a letter of intent to the Government, then continue with the work of the workshop-committees' work, and when we were ready, submit the full proposal. He thought that we should concentrate on two major tasks: planning the cooperation with Egypt, and investigating the possible consequences to our country from the forthcoming peace with Egypt. He said that nobody in the Government was thinking seriously about the autonomy for the Palestinians. He agreed with Ben-Shahar's idea that our University should offer itself as a home for the new Authority, and that it should accept experts from other universities and the public. He also gave me a new and surprising piece of information; namely, that for the previous two years Ben-Shahar had been planning to establish a new economic center headed by David Rockefeller and former US Secretary of the Treasury Paul Simon, and said that he objected to merge this proposed center with the proposed Authority or Peace Project. I wondered: Why had Ben-Shahar not told me about his proposed Rockefeller-Simon Institute? Did I have to worry about three new bodies: the Peace Project, the National Authority, and the Rockefeller-Simon institute? Eitan then said that adding the adjective national to the proposed Authority would not help much, and might even hurt it. Finally, he suggested to call the new body a Center and not an Authority and to weaken the ties to the Government, because too strong ties were not good for either the Government or the University, which should stay independent or the Government. The new body should serve all the people, while also accepting work requested by the Government. His last suggestion was to leave open the possibility that together with the Government we might, in the future, turn the Center into a national body.

My qualms had not been quieted. Helping the Government was important, but what did this have to do with the Peace Project? Our main task in the Project was to plan the collaborations with Egyptians in order to strengthen the peace, and not to do other things even if they were important to the Government. And for the country, could the establishment of the Center or the Authority be the right step at this stage towards the goal of strengthening the forthcoming peace?

*****

My discussion with Eitan Berglas and my qualms should be classified as constructive attempts to find the right direction for the University and the Peace Project. What transpired afterwards could not be called constructive, and was again an indication of undercurrents, which I tried to understand in vain.

I first talked with Professor Yoram Dinstein, who had been with me from the first discussion at home, and was a member of the Project's Management. (Professor Dinstein later became the rector and then the president of the university). He had objected to my early attempt to work together with Shlomo Aronson from the Hebrew University, and now he repeated his objection by emphasizing that the importance of the Peace Project to the University was as a tool to get money for the University as a whole. *What a strange idea,* I thought. He then surprised me further by criticizing me for undertaking on myself to push our President's idea of a National Authority. When I said that this had been decided in the Project's Management, he said that people had voted for it because the President was present. He finally threatened to resign from the Management of the Peace Project, but after some more talking he agreed to stay "in order to help you", so he said.

Aharon Yariv expressed fears that campaigns for the new Authority (or Center) would hurt his campaign to get money and new staff for his Center for Strategic Studies. Rector Shalom Abarbanel said that turning the Peace Project into a Center or an Institute would require putting it in a specific

Faculty, so the Center would not stay any more as a whole-University body.

It was President Ben-Shahar who encouraged me at this point. He urged me to continue with the Peace Project, and added that if the Peace Project became a Center, where other universities and private experts could become members, then we should add a third governing body (to the Management and Steering Board chaired by Aharon Yariv) – an International Advisory Board. He asked me to talk to M.K. Abba Eban and ask him to co-chair this Board together with David Rockefeller.

In his talk to me, Mr. Eban accepted the offer. I was then asked by the President to re-write a new document about establishing a new proposed body, somewhat along the ideas of Eitan Berglas. It was presented to the Central Committee of the University Senate, which decided to name the document: "The Establishment of a Center for the Study of Peace". It was very similar to my original document, which had been presented to the Peace Project's Management and to the workshop.

On 12.10.1978, following the intensive work of the workshop-committees, I submitted this new document to the Central Committee of the Senate and to Simcha Erlich, the Minister of Finance (Treasury). He welcomed the proposal, and promised it 10 Million Israeli Lira (about $500,000), but the Central Committee did not push the idea further, most likely for reasons of internal politics at the University. This is how the intensive work of so many professors, Government officials, and public experts was wasted. Needless to say, I was very disappointed! (To my dismay, this was not the last time that such a thing happened.) I thought that this was the end of my efforts to help the President on this issue, so I went back to my main job of running the Research Project on Peace.

A Second Trip to the United States (Mid-December 1978). With mixed feelings I returned to my main job. On the one hand I felt satisfied that I finally got my university, my academia, to think and work together with public experts on a very important national and even regional issue. But since the proof of the pudding is in the eating, my academia, or its Senate and ruling bodies, all but killed the result of this important work (or at best, put it on a deep freeze).

Professor George Assousa visited us again, after spending a few weeks in

Israel, Jordan, and the West Bank, with some sobering information. His talks with Israeli Jews and West-Bank Arabs gave him the impression that the Israelis are more interested in peace than the Palestinian Arabs, who saw peace as surrender to the Israeli policy. Therefore, any Israeli initiative would be met with suspicion, suggesting that progress here should be very slow. The Jordanians were not ready for peace talks with Israel; perhaps the Palestinians could help us on that. As for the Egyptians, they see the expected normalization different than the Israelis do. The Egyptians were looking mainly or even exclusively for assistance and financial help. His advice to the Peace Project was that we should not be only academic vis-à-vis the Egyptians, because their needs were immediate and very tangible. Professor Joseph Loya, a marine biologist, and I then took Assousa for a two-day visit to Eilat and the Sinai, after which Assousa said that there was room for collaborative Egyptian-Israeli research on the Sinai. Later I realized that he was no expert on Egypt.

In his meeting with the Project's Management Assousa was asked a variety of questions, and the first one was about the way he viewed the Israeli universities with regards to peace; and this in short is what he said: The Peace Project should not be only passive. You should not despair if in the beginning you will not find partners on the other side; they will come, but slowly. Tel Aviv University is more dynamic than the other Israeli universities, and it has a president who is pushing in this direction. Your advantage over the Weizmann Institute is the existence here of a strong faculty of social sciences. On the other hand, The Hebrew University has an advantage because of the relative large number of Arabs students there.

Talking about the West, Assousa said that both Europe and the United States were interested in collaboration with the Middle East, and might soon come up with something like a Marshall plan; the idea had already been raised in the US Congress, and the Peace Project should prepare itself to answer the questions that might be raised in this respect.

Baruch Raz asked Assousa where he thought we might fail. His answer was that too much enthusiasm was dangerous. Even when good ideas are presented, it should be done with moderation. He added that it was important to bring many Arabs to Israel to see, as he had done, that freedom of debate existed in Israel.

President Ben-Shahar asked me to take another trip to the US in order to help him in creating public relations for the University in the right circles in the United States. This was needed for the establishment of the center for Peace, an idea that he still believed in and was pushing for. He then added that I would be going as his personal representative, as if he himself was going. The President then elaborated on his reasons for his request: The Peace Project, which might turn into a center, is gaining momentum; In the US there was a large new group of potential contributors, beyond the usual group of rich Jews, who might be interested in helping our peace efforts; a peace treaty with Egypt could be signed in the near future, and we should be ready for that; and other universities might enter the field where we seem to have an advantage. He then enumerated the specific goals for my trip: 1. Assist the Friends of Tel Aviv University in their campaigns; 2. Coordinate with them the organization of academic symposia that we would want to hold in the US; 3. Establish ties with the US regime (White House, Congress, various agencies, etc); 4. Meet Arab academicians, and pass information to them about our peace efforts. Finally he stressed that the main goal of my trip was to investigate the various options for holding symposia by the Peace Project in a small number of US cities, including New York and Washington.

Just as I had felt earlier when asked by the University President to activate the study for the Center, I felt now that the President's ideas were in line with my own thinking. However, judging from our recent experience with the proposed National Center, the President and I were a little more cautious this time, and expected that some members of the Management would claim that they wanted to help us, but in fact would do everything they could to put obstacles in my (and the President's) efforts. The President therefore advised me to take preemptive measures and talk with Vice-President Sokolovski and Professor Dinstein and agree with them on the goals of my trip. The following were my thoughts then: *Our Project was pioneering and all our steps were original. I needed people, who agree with the Project's goals to help me in my hard task and not only put obstacles on my way. At the same time, I would welcome people who would warn me of pitfalls, but I definitely did not need people who would only put obstacles in my path from within. The tasks were hard enough without those obstacles.*

The meeting with the two professors was tense, and as expected, they only put limits on what I should do in my trip. After a long debate they gave their own okay to my trip in writing (strange as it was), with the request that I would only deal with the administrative aspects of the proposed symposia and not with their subjects or speakers. In other words, as far as they – the two Management members - were concerned, I could go, but handcuffed behind my back. Indeed a great help!

Upon arrival in the US, and on the request of President Ben-Shahar, I called Robert Aboud in Chicago, a banker of Lebanese descent, who was supposed to be open to the idea of Arab-Israeli collaborations. I left him a message, but he never called back.

In Washington I met a large number of people, and I will describe briefly only the talks that either taught me something new, or were interesting for our future activities in the US. George Assousa organized my meetings in the first day, and actually joined me in those meetings. Officials from the A.I.D and from the American Enterprise Institute (sort of the Republican parallel of the Brookings Institution) were interested in the Project's activities and plans, and promised to help organize a conference in Tel Aviv and a symposium in Washington. I got a similar reaction from Dean Brown of the Middle East Institute, which was largely pro-Arab, as many of its members were former ambassadors to Middle-East countries or doing business with Middle East countries.

My meetings at the American National Academy of Science were very encouraging. Three of their top officials suggested that the Academy would host the proposed symposium in Washington. They would provide us rooms of various sizes for simultaneous discussions, as well as a hall, which could seat 750 people. At one point, Thomas F. Malone, the Foreign Secretary of the Academy, joined us. He was very enthusiastic when I told him about our Peace Project and about our intention to hold a symposium in Washington. He said that the Academy would be interested in hosting the symposium, and would bring to it all the important people, including senators and congressmen. In his opinion, the problem would be to limit the list to 750 people. He suggested that following the talks in the hall we should have meetings with smaller groups. He then told me that they were in touch with the head of the Egyptian Academy of Science, Abu El-Azam, and with his Israeli counterpart, Aryeh Dvoretzky, trying to organize the following month a meeting of the heads of the three academies, but the Egyptians were stalling. He saw no contradiction between that proposed meeting and our proposed symposium. Finally, he asked me to send him an official request from Israel, which he would bring to the Academy for official approval. I could not have expected more than that. Upon my recommendation over the phone, President Ben Shahar called Philip Handler, the President of the US Academy. He was more hesitant than his Foreign Minister, because of the plan to get the three academy presidents together, but said that if Cairo University would join us or if Ambassador Ghorbal would recommend Egyptian speakers living in the US, he would be willing to consider positively giving the Academy's auspices to the planned symposium.

Assousa's suggestion for the next visit was the Smithsonian, where we would meet Farook El-Baz, one of its high officials. The name sounded familiar to me, and Assousa explained that he was the brother of Osama El-Baz, chief advisor to President Sadat. Farook El-Baz was an American citizen and an advisor to President Sadat on scientific matters. A meeting was set, not before I noticed that El-Baz attempted to keep the meeting away from public eyes. I started by telling him about our Peace Project and about our efforts to reach Arab scientists, especially in Egypt. He then interrupted me by asking: Why are you not using your short distance to the colleges in the West Bank and especially to Bir Zeit? Assousa then explained that he had tried to form such contacts with Bir-Zeit College, but failed. I said that I fully understood the difficulties of the West-Bank scientists, and added that I too have psychological difficulties because of the asymmetry, namely, because we were politically in an advantageous position. My positive and sensitive approach as well as my description of our efforts apparently softened El-Baz, and the atmosphere warmed up.

When I started to describe our proposed conference in Tel Aviv, El-Baz interrupted me again and asked: Why won't you hold the conference at the University of Cairo? This will enable about 200 Israelis to meet the whole Egyptian society. My response was that a conference in Tel Aviv would enable about 200 Egyptian scientists to meet the Israeli society, but I had no objection to holding the conference in Cairo if the Egyptians could organize it; and in fact, holding the conference in Cairo would enable Israeli and Palestinian scientists to meet as equals, with the Egyptian host being the moderators. His face showed that he liked the idea of the Egyptians being hosts and moderators. He considered the question further, and added: Because of the various sensitivities today, perhaps we should not talk about Israeli and Egyptian scientists, rather about Israeli and Arab scientists. El-Baz then asked me to supply him with information on the field schools in the Sinai, and added that this information was needed if we wanted the Smithsonian to be in charge of them, and in that case, Israeli and Egyptian scientists would be able to work together under the auspices of the Smithsonian. After we parted Assousa said that the meeting was a success, and suggested that a report should be sent to the Egyptian ambassador to the US, Ashraf Ghorbal, to President Ben Shahar, and to the A.I.D.

David M. Abshire, the Director of the Center for Strategic and International Studies (CSIS), with whom I had a long talk, liked the idea of a symposium in Washington, and offered to host for us a breakfast on Capitol Hill. He suggested adding an Egyptian from his staff to the list of speakers, not in order to have a political debate, but to add a cultural-economical dimension.

My friend Bud Asia from Seattle suggested that I ought to meet one of the most influential people on the Senate staff, Richard Pearl, who was the chief advisor to Senator Henry (Scoop) Jackson[6], the Senator from the State of Washington. I prepared myself psychologically to meet this influential person in the Senate of the most important power in the world. In the Senate building I was told where his office was, and upon approaching it, I wondered how big and roomy it would be. I knocked on the door and entered a room with 12 typists. One of them pointed at a desk in the corner of this crowded and noisy room at which Mr. Pearl was sitting. I was surprised to see how egalitarian this great democratic country was. Mr. Pearl was very warm and helpful and offered his help in organizing anything we planned in the Senate. Senator Joseph Biden's secretary, whom I visited next, was also very helpful, and said that the senator, who was talking about a Marshall plan for the Middle East, would be interested in holding a breakfast for us on Capitol Hill. Her comment on the A.I.D. was interesting. These people, she said, had already received 5 million dollars to help collaborations in the Middle East, but had already used most of it for their own activities. She added an advice: for the success of your activities in Washington, I would advise you not to involve the Jewish establishment.

6 Years later, as a Neo-Conservative, Richard Pearl became a deputy defense minister.

From Capitol Hill I went to the White House to meet Joyce Starr, a friend of Tamar Avidar, the Attaché for Women Affairs in the Embassy. Ms. Starr was coordinating the activities of the Task Force, which was appointed by the State Department, and was herself sent to the Middle East last summer in order to investigate the budding economic cooperation there. She told me that she had been getting a huge number of reports from a variety of American organizations, and we would get a copy of the Task-Force report in January (1979). She suggested that in the symposia we should not plan to have speakers from Washington, but only speakers from Israel (and possibly Egypt), since in Washington at that time, the various agencies wanted only to listen and learn. *What a great opportunity for us to spread our ideas,* I thought. She asked me to send her information and specific requests, and she would try to help.

Hannan Baron, our charge-d'affaires in Washington, was very interested in the report of my activities in Washington, and also very helpful. He said that even if the talks of the politicians would fail, we should hold our symposia to show that Israel was constructive. He advised against involving the embassy in our activities, to keep them as apolitical as possible. I noted that I had received somewhat similar advice at Senator Biden's office. An official at the embassy approached me in the corridor of the embassy and advised me not to trust George Assousa, because he had not had the courage to stand up at a meeting of the American Arab Organization in the US and speak against the PLO. *What a strange advice, and an even stranger explanation,* I thought.

My last meeting in Washington was with Herman Pollack, one of the five American directors of the American-Israeli Bi-National Fund, and a reviewer for the A.I.D. of the 5 million dollars, which they had received, for the encouragement of Egyptian Israeli cooperation. He had visited my office in Tel Aviv a month earlier, after which he wrote a report mentioning the Peace Project several times.

Next I flew to New York, but my visit there was not as exciting as the visit to Washington, and was mainly devoted to meetings with leaders of Jewish organizations such as the Anti-Defamation League and the American Jewish Committee. They were ready to help financially and with the organization of the symposia, I also learned from them that Senator Hatfield of Oregon intended to propose the establishment of Peace Academy, similar to West Point, the war academy. I recalled my attempt at the University Senate to establish the Institute for Strategic Studies as a war *and* peace institute, which met with opposition in our Senate, and the eventual, but late establishment of the Research Project on Peace.

I then phoned Stanley Hoffman and Herbert Kelman, and both liked the idea of holding a symposium at their University, Harvard. Hoffman asked if we would agree to have Walid Halidi as one of the speakers, and I said that we would gladly have him.

****

The following is a summary of my reports on my trip to President Ben-Shahar and to the Management of the Peace Project.:

1. In my second visit to Washington I have strengthened my belief that Washington has the special qualities which are important for the Project's activities as well as for the fund-raising by the President. Washington has a continuously increasing interest in what is happening in the Middle East, and the various agencies are actually competing with one another in their attempts to support activities related to peace there. I mention this important point, because financial support in Washington will mainly be from governmental sources, whereas up till now most support has always been from Jewish sources in the big cities. In Washington, I did not find much influence of the other Israeli universities (The situation is different in New York and other big American cities). In particular, I learned that Tel Aviv University and our Peace Project are well known there.

2. As for my trip, I can say that most of its goals have been achieved. I have established new ties with governmental and academic bodies, and I have successfully investigated the question of having symposia, mainly in Washington, Boston, and New York. These symposia would aim at three kinds of audience which interest us: the academic (mainly in Boston), the governmental (mainly in Washington), and the financial contributors (mainly in New York).

3. In view of my findings, I recommend that the President and the Friends of Tel Aviv University in the United State should now concentrate their

efforts in Washington, specifically in the Governmental and public institutions there. The advent of the signing of the Israeli-Egyptian peace accord and the growing activity and plans of the Peace Project strongly call for such an effort soon. I should add that opening new sources of support and gaining more influence in Washington also has some national value for Israel.

****

Having completed the assignments by the University President in the proposed Center and the investigation of possible financial and political support in the United States, I could devote 100% of my time to the Peace Project. This mainly meant running the infrastructure (Management, Steering Board, and Research Committee), putting in motion the new programs, which I will soon describe, and meeting with academic staff and public leaders. I will now mention briefly three of these meetings.

Professor Dan Michaeli, the chief doctor of Zahal. His main reasons for coming to see me were the following: to inform me of what is going on in the region concerning international collaborations in medicine and international plans; to warn me about the danger of transmitting secret information on medicine and microbiology, which the Egyptians might use to develop biological weapons; and to advise me of the preferred mode of operation in these disciplines. He said that we could safely collaborate in the study of epidemiology, Bilharzia (a very common disease in Egypt), the Rose of Jericho, and the Rift Valley Fever. In his opinion, the best mode should be the following: We and the Egyptians should work independently of each other, and then we should hold conferences to compare and transfer information. *Professor Mori Sokolovski* expressed similar opinions, and suggested collaborations also in agriculture.

Amiram Sivan. As the Director General of the Treasury, he came to my office to suggest that the University takes care of the collection of information on Egypt, perhaps by expanding the activity of the Shiloah Institute. He mentioned several specific important subjects, and suggested getting in touch with the director generals of the corresponding ministries. The Treasury had a budget allocated for that. The Treasury itself wanted us to do research especially on the following subjects: 1. An urgent and secret interdisciplinary study of the mutual financial claims of Egypt and Israel.

For instance, the Egyptians demanded 100 billion dollars for the oil we had been extracting from the Sinai since 1967, and we had a claim for our loss on the development of the Rafiah Bay (Pitchat Rafiah); 2. The Egyptian expectations. They had mainly fears, but expectations as well, and we should know what they are; 3. The possibilities of establishing in Israel regional centers for international companies.4. The cultural and economic consequences of the expected peace on Israel.

I brought these suggestions for discussion with the University experts. They liked the last three projects, but said that the first one, that of the mutual financial claims was not a suitable subject for academic research, and we should not be responsible for such a project.

US Ambassador Sam Louis. He was invited by us for lunch at the University. I used the opportunity to brief him about my meetings in Washington with governmental, public and academic people, and described the Peace Project's activities and plans. I then thanked him for the Embassy's help, and asked him to suggest trilateral collaborations (American, Egyptian, and Israeli) and help us get them. He said that he was impressed by our activities and plans, and promised his help.

A Third Trip to the United States (March 1979). The University president appreciated the new possibilities, which I investigated in Washington and New York, and therefore asked me to go again to Washington, three months after the previous visit, on the eve of the formal signing, at the White House, of the Israeli-Egyptian Peace Treaty. He decided to come to Washington for a few days later, and join me in some of the meetings that I would arrange.

At a meeting in Tel Aviv before the trip, we decided that it would be advisable to find a neutral and influential "third body" who would agree to get us together with relevant Egyptians in order to talk about collaboration. Professor Shimon Shamir suggested that a senator or an A.I.D. official could be that third body, or even David Rockefeller. A head of an American academic institute was also a possibility. We decided to try to convince the people whom we would meet that it was important to have Israeli-Egyptian cooperation, or even a tri-partite cooperation, but that a bi-partite American-Egyptian cooperation without Israeli participation at that time would not be helpful, because it would weaken the Egyptian readiness to cooperate with us, *indeed a very delicate point,* I thought. Our feeling was that the mood in the region was still grim and confused, and might stay so even after the signing of the Treaty. The infrastructure of the Peace Project could be an asset after the signing of the Treaty, which could make it easier for us to start academic collaborations, because we entertained a hope that the Egyptians might then be more agreeable than before to collaborate with us. We concluded that all these considerations supported the need for the President and me to go to Washington.

With the belief that the clout of senators would be sufficient to convince Egyptian academicians and politicians to start scientific collaborations with us, I used my first days in Washington to try organizing a business breakfast on Capitol Hill. I was hoping that senators such as Jackson or Stone would agree to be the hosts, and invite for breakfast business people such as Rockefeller and Aboud, American statesmen and academicians such as Joseph Sisco and Herman Polack, Egyptians such as Ambassador Ghorbal and Farook El-Baz, and Israelis such as Ambassador Evron and professors from Tel Aviv University. One of the goals of the breakfast would be to set up a tri-partite study group to look at all the aspects of Egyptian-Israeli academic collaborations. Another immediate goal would be to get financial and political support. I also wanted to use the break-fast to let President Ben-Shahar meet influential senators such as Senator Church, the Chairman of the Senate Foreign Relations Committee, Senator Jackson from Washington State, and Senator Stone from Florida., as well as the heads of the A.I.D., the A.E.I., Brookings Institution, and CSIS.

In my visits to the Senate and my talks with the aides of senators Church, Jackson, Stone and Biden, it became clear that the senators would be ready to help with legislations in the Senate, with financial allocations, and with recommendations or even pressure on the A.I.D. and even on foundations such as Ford. However, there was a precondition for that, namely, that all these actions would be in support of existing bi-lateral (or tri-lateral) Israeli-Egyptian (or Israeli-Egyptian-American) collabora-tions. Dr. White of the A.I.D. stressed that such collaborations were the only condition for their support. So we were back to square one; namely, not being helped by the Senate to get collaborations, rather getting col-laborations (perhaps with the help of American academic institutes), and only then ask for and get American governmental support. In a way, we found ourselves in a Catch-22 situation. The only way out of this situation was to get help from an American academic institution, so I recommended to President Ben-Shahar to meet with the president of Harvard.

The Brooking Institution. When President Ben-Shahar arrived in Washington he suggested visiting together the Brookings Institution, and talking to a friend of his, Joe Peckman. After consulting with the management of the Institution, Peckman suggested to carryout a tri-partite survey of the various possibilities for Israeli-Egyptian *economic collaboration.* The survey would be done by three groups: six from the Institution, six from the Peace Project, and six from an Egyptian academic body, perhaps the Al-Ahram Institution. He suggested not including the West Bank in the survey lest the Israeli Government would suspect that the Brookings Institution would want to suggest an imposed political solution to the West Bank. His Institution would try to get Rockefeller to provide the necessary budget for the survey – approximately $60,000 – and Rockefeller himself would be invited to be a member of the American group of six. His attitude and suggestion were very encouraging.

A few days later, Joe Peckman informed us that the Egyptian Ambassador Ghorbal was enthusiastic about the proposed trilateral study, and that it was thus agreed that the three groups would be: the Brookings Institutions, Cairo University, and Tel-Aviv University. The Brookings Institution would be leading the study. Ambassador Ghorbal requested that the Egyptian group would not be referred to as Egyptian, but rather Middle Eastern. He suggested further that the meeting of the three groups would take place about nine months after the start of normalization, i.e. the beginning of 1980.

After returning to Israel, in consultations with the Management of the Peace Project, President Ben-Shahar proposed that the study, which Joe Peckman had suggested, would be on "How can the Israeli-Egyptian economic development be best promoted." He proposed further that Professor Dan Patenkin would head the group of 6 Israelis. Several members of the Managements objected to Israeli businessmen being in the group of 6, but not to American businessmen being in the American group. And now back to my second visit to the US.

Professor Ben-Shahar and I held many other meetings in Washington, and discussed various ideas for collaboration and big-scale financial aid. In the report submitted to the White House by the State Department, we received many compliments, and it pointed out that our Research Project on Peace had done more than any other institution to promote Egyptian-Israeli cooperation. We concluded that the signing of the Peace Treaty that took place during our visit opened up new possibilities for the University, even beyond the topics which interested the Peace Project.

****

I will now describe three events in my visit that had special personal meanings to me.

1. A ticket to the signing of the Peace Treaty. Tamar Avidar, the attaché at the Embassy for women affairs, invited me to a party at her home in the eve of the historic signing of the Israeli-Egyptian Peace Treaty, to be held on the lawn of the White House. She also gave me a ticket to the ceremony. I was pleased since very few people were invited to that ceremony. During the party, I was introduced to an impressive lady; Ruth Dayan, the former wife of Foreign Minister Moshe Dayan. She told the people at the party that she had not been invited to the ceremony. I felt that with all my efforts, Ruth Dayan had done more than I for peace. I approached her, introduced myself as a former teacher of her daughter in the Hebrew Gymnasium in Jerusalem, and gave her my ticket. I told her that the reason for my giving her my ticket was that I had important meetings scheduled in the Senate, which had an element of truth in it.

2. A meeting with Senator Jackson. I had had several meetings with Richard Pearl, the influential staff member of Senator Jackson in the Senate. Pearl was a Jew and a great supporter of Israel. Senator Henry (Scoop) Jackson from the State of Washington was also known as the Senator from Boeing for his support of the Boeing Company. The Senator was highly regarded in Israel for his traditional support of the country in military and other matters. In the early nineteen seventies, together with Congressman Charles Vanik, he introduced in the US Senate a law, which made all ties with the Soviet Union conditional on their opening of their gates to emigration of Jews to Israel. On the other hand, Senator Jackson was a member of the military lobby in the Senate, and an influential leader of the Military Industrial Complex. He was also one of the enthusiastic supporters of the bloody war in Vietnam, to which I objected strongly. I visited Vietnam in 1967, during the war, and saw the terrible destruction inflicted by the war on that country and its people as well as on the American people, and described what I had seen in my book "The Rape of a Country". I therefore came to his office with mixed feelings

President Ben-Shahar and I arrived at Senator Jackson's office after a short meeting with Senator Stone, who promised his help in the Senate and with our requests from the A.I.D., again with the condition that we first get Egyptian partners. The meeting with Senator Stone was very formal and lasted 15 minutes. I expected that the hawk, Senator Jackson, would be even more formal. Instead, he received us at 18:00 very warmly and asked if we would object to him taking off his shoes and jacket. He then sat down, put his feet on his desk, and asked the most welcoming question, "How can I help you?" We talked in his office for a whole hour. He gave us a lot of advice, suggested whom we should talk to in the Administration and in Congress, and whom we should not talk to. Then he said that he would do all he could to help us in what we were doing. Finally, he asked us not to hesitate to turn to him in the future with specific requests. Undoubtedly, this was not the hawkish senator I had expected to meet.

3. A conscientious academic dilemma. The last night in Washington I spent by myself thinking and worrying. I was satisfied with my achievements for the Peace Project and for the University. I knew that if I continued along the path I was going I stood a good chance of collecting funds for the Peace Projects, and I also knew that much more financial support would come to the University as a whole. The reader could now ask, "So where was the problem?", and this is where my worrying began. With the money that I expected to pour in, I would get much political clout at the University, since I would have much influence on how that money would be spent. But – and here was my conscientious dilemma – from my experience in academia I was sure that I personally would have objected if another faculty member used his efforts for the University to gain political power for himself. Such behavior went against my beliefs of what academic ethics should be. And here I found myself, unintentionally, in such a position. A year ago I volunteered to form the Peace Project in order to promote research on peace and collaborations with Arab academicians, not in order to gain political strength at the University for myself. Moreover, the University had a vice-president for research, who should be the one in charge of incoming funds and their distribution for research. Having considered this ethical academic problem in all its aspects, I reached a conclusion. I called President Ben-Shahar, who had returned to Israel and told him that I believed that the political and financial matters should be handled by Professor Mori Sokolovski, whom the President had chosen as his vice president for research and development, and not by me. I promised the President that upon my return to Israel I would transfer all the information I had to Professor Sokolovski, and would help him as much as he required to advance the matters that I had handled for the University.

Did I make a mistake in strictly following my academic conscience? Such a question is usually answered by the statement "only the future will tell". In this case I can clearly say that the future proved that I made a mistake. Upon returning to Israel I transferred all the information I had to Vice President Sokolovski, as promised, but no item of the ones I handled in Washington was advanced further by him. What a pity![7]

****

Being, by and large, ignorant of what was going on in Egypt, but very eager to learn, I was pleased to meet, in my office, a group of ten young Americans, representing several student groups of various political persuasions, who had just visited Egypt. They told me very excitedly that they had discovered that the poverty and even hunger in Egypt were much more serious than they had expected. The Egyptians they had met wanted economic development, which would be the real test of success for the peace. These Egyptians believed that the United States, and not Israel, would be blamed if peace would fail. In this group's opinion, about fifty percents of the Egyptian leaders whom they had met were interested in cooperation with Israel, and they expected to get from Israel help in the fields in which Israel had the greatest expertise. The Egyptian leaders talked more about aid than about collaborations. The chief of the ruling party actually told them that the man in the street would gladly get help from Israel. He mentioned the improvement of agricultural harvests as a first such aid.

---

7 *Today, many years later, I still wonder if I made the right decision. I will not try to answer the cynics who would say that they do not believe that somebody would give up power because of academic reasons. Those cynics would get another chance later to doubt my motives. But there are others, myself included, who would wonder if I did right being so dogmatic, and sacrificing all my important achievements, since I was all but certain that the Vice President would not advance what the President and I had achieved in Washington.*

****

Not everything progressed smoothly. During one of the meetings of the Project Management I was told by a member of the Management that Professor Aryeh Dvoretzky from the Hebrew University and the Head of the Israeli Academy of Arts and Sciences was very angry with us. His stated reasons were that we kept our activity secret and initiated contacts with the Egyptians without waiting for the Egyptians to come to us first. People from the Hebrew University even went to the Head of the Ministry of Foreign Affairs, Joseph Chechanover, to complain about our actions. I responded that this was a legitimate opinion, but an official anger of this sort befitted only a totalitarian country. I should have reminded my colleagues that this kind of jealousy could have been avoided if the Project's Management had agreed with me to collaborate with the Hebrew University. Instead I said that if we had something wrong, it was not by what we had done, but with what we had not done. I then related to the Management the various ways by which we had passed information about our actions to the other institutions, one of which was a workshop held in Zichron Yaakov, organized by the Technion in Haifa, and run by Professor Shalhevet Fryer. It dealt primarily with the consequences to the country of peace. A resolution at that workshop recommending the policy of laisser-faire, namely that each institution should go it alone was passed there by a large majority.

A conference in Cairo. This conference was the first time that a group from Tel-Aviv University met with Egyptian academicians, and therefore it deserves an expanded description. Al-Ahram Institute invited the Shiloah Institute to a conference in Cairo. I suggested to Professor Shimon Shamir to propose to the hosts of the conference the following:

- To hold an Egyptian – Israeli meeting on "The Economic Aspects of Israeli-Egyptian Regional Cooperation and Participation of the Palestinians in the Process".
- To invite Dr. Boutros Boutros Ghali, the Egyptian Minister of State for Foreign Affairs, as a speaker to the opening session of our planned international conference, in which an Egyptian artist would be invited to perform..
- To invite someone from the Al-Ahram Institute to visit us for a few weeks, incognito if necessary.
- To invite several teachers of Arabic to our University.

I also gave Professor Shamir the names of six professors from Tel-Aviv University who were willing to travel to Egypt to give seminars in: astrophysics (Giora Shaviv), nuclear physics (Avivi Yavin), economic cooperation (Zeev Hirsch), solar energy (Guy Deutcher), heart diseases (Henry Neufeld), and hematology (Bracha Ramot).

When they came back from Cairo, Professor Shamir gave the President and me the following report: There was an atmosphere of a paradox during the whole conference. On the one hand, the Egyptians were tough, even unfriendly, but there were also some signs of good will towards Israeli academicians and towards Tel-Aviv University. The host was Al-Ahram Institute, which was the center of opposition in Egypt to peace with Israel. In fact, 15 members of the Institute resigned their membership because of that. The departure of non-Egyptian Arabs from the country because of the expected peace was much noticed, and many empty houses could be seen because of that in Cairo.

Dr. Ghali, a member of the Institute, was very bitter in the beginning, because Israel had not shown any gesture of good will, not appreciating the enormous difficulties of Egypt in the Arab World because of the peace. He said that every new settlement sent a wave of tremor to the Egyptian public. Shamir held a short discussion with Ghali and Tahsin Basheer, his assistant for the normalization issue. Ghali was first against collaborating with Brookings, and said that Ambassador Ghorbal was not realistic, but apparently changed his mind a little after Shamir had suggested that we should work together on the sensitive Palestinian Issue, and this could be done best if Egyptians would come to our international conference. Shamir felt that although the discussion was cool in the beginning, it warmed up a bit. Because of the general attitude, Shamir said that it was not the right time to introduce to the Egyptians my four proposals or invitations listed above.

The Tel-Aviv University Peace Papers. Acting on Professor Shamir's proposal, the Project's Management decided to hold a series of lectures by distinguished people on peace issues, and publish each one of them in a booklet in three languages: Hebrew, Arabic, and English. Professor Judah Eisenberg was chosen to head a committee, responsible for the project, and Connie Wilsack was chosen as the editor. M. K. Abba Eban agreed to give the first lecture. The title of the lecture was "Israel's International Relations in an Era of Peace".

The lecture was scheduled for May 20, 1979, two months after the signing of the Israeli-Egyptian Peace Treaty, and was held at the Bar-Shira Auditorium, which could seat more than 500 people. It was open to the general public. The first rows were reserved to specially invited guests such as Jewish and Israeli-Arab public leaders, members of the Diplomatic Corps, and local as well as foreign reporters. A few people, including a Government minister, the speaker, the University President, and the Egyptian Ambassador to Israel, were asked to meet in a nearby office before the ceremony. We were all very excited. A diplomatic scandal was luckily avoided. When the Egyptian Ambassador was delayed for some reason, the Government minister attempted to be noticed or funny, and whispered, "We can start without the clown". Fortunately, no reporter was present[8].

When I entered the Auditorium my spirit was high, but I feared a crisis. I looked around and saw that the Auditorium was packed. In my short opening words I mentioned the Research Project on Peace, and spoke about the Peace Papers, lectures and booklets. I ended by saying, "The booklet, in three languages, will be distributed around the world. In this way we hope to increase the public awareness of all aspects of peace in order to strengthen the foundations of the peaceful relations between us and our neighbors." I then repeated my introductory words in Arabic, a language I had not used in thirty five years, starting by calling the Peace Project's name in Arabic, "Mashru Abhas As-salam". The audience sensed my tension, and applauded me when I successfully finished the Arabic part. The repetition in English was obviously much easier. The following is a summary of President Ben-Shahar's introductory speech:

"There is nothing that is worth more public support than the striving for peace. The blood-covered pages of history teach us how frequent this sacred striving is frustrated. Up till now, Israel and the Arab countries have fought four wars, which are always followed by a state of mutual hatred. The public in the region believes that this process is inevitable, but the annals of history is full of criticism of the 'impossible" and the "inevitable". For instance, until the beginning of the twentieth century people thought that the atom is indivisible, but we all know today that the atom is made up of many parts. Einstein's theory of relativity is another example of how the human mind can change fixed ideas.

8 *This ugly story is presented here just to show the attitude towards Egypt, at that time, by part of the Israeli public. The situation is undoubtedly much better nowadays.*

"The situation in the Middle East presents us with a similar challenge. Already in 1976, we started to think of the possibility to meet the challenge. This was the reason behind the establishment of the Research Project on Peace. We hoped that in the state of no-peace, the Peace Project would be able to find ways to reduce the tension, and after peace is established, the Project would have the means to strengthen and consolidate it. The visit of President Sadat to Jerusalem proved that both our doubt of the inevitability of putting an end to wars and the establishment of the Peace Project were the right things to do. It is now clear to us that, at the present stage, the Peace Project should concentrate on contacts with Egyptians, and later strive to establish contacts with other Arab countries, and then also with the Palestinians. The Project has to develop, analyze, and suggest various solutions for situations, which will precede the actual events, at least by one step, so that the leadership will have these analyses and alternatives when they come to make quick decisions. It is for this reason that the University gave the Project's activity high priority. The series of lectures that are starting here today is one of these activities that the Peace Project has initiated in order to advance the understanding of all aspects of the peace process."

Following the President's speech, and before introducing the main speaker of the evening, I described briefly the Research Project on Peace, its history, its activities till that time, and its plans. This in short is what I said;

"Although some uncoordinated research activity related to peace had existed at the University prior to the establishment of the Peace Project, two dramatic events brought many professors in the nine faculties of the University to coordinate and increase their activities, and the Research Project on Peace was thus formed. The dramatic events were the shock of war, the Yom Kippur War of 1973, and the shock of peace, which the country felt when President Sadat announced last year his intentions to visit Jerusalem, and ended his announcement by promising "No more Wars!" In its reaction to the challenge of war in October 1973 as well as to the challenge of peace in November 1977, Israel – the country of the People of the Book, the people who was famous for its contribution to free and creative thinking – failed badly where it was expected that it would excel. We in academia are at least partially responsible for the intellectual complacency that resulted in such uncritical thinking, completely devoid of imagination. The Research Project on Peace was formed in order to try and correct these deficiencies.

"If we ask ourselves what characterizes intellectuals such as Rene Descartes and Albert Einstein, we will soon discover that they were blessed with courage and ability to doubt, as well as with the ability to think methodically and use their imagination. I hope that our Project will be blessed with the same abilities vis-à-vis the challenge of peace. The Peace Project encourages academic research on all the various aspects of peace in the Middle East. Our research projects can be divided into three groups: 1. the peace process in all its aspects; 2. plans for regional cooperation; 3. the consequences of peace for Israel. The research projects are carried out by members of all the nine faculties of the University, as well as by people from other universities in the country, and by non academic people. We are now making special efforts to include Arab researchers in our studies, and hope that important Arab universities will eventually be full and equal partners in the Peace Project. Our main efforts in the near future will be in holding an international conference, whose title will be "Toward Peace in the Middle East". The conference will deal with transitions from war to peace, with plans for regional cooperation, and with the question of how to stabilize peace, once achieved.

"The lecture this evening, the first in a series, represents another building block in the activity of the Peace Project. We will concentrate tonight on the expected foreign relations of Israel in the near future. It is therefore only natural that we turned to the man who is known around the world for his brilliant thinking and for representing Israel's policies, who is often referred to as "the Voice of Israel". I am therefore asking M.K. Abba Eban to speak to us on "Israel's International Relations in an Era of Peace".

Abba Eban received a long standing ovation. He opened his talk with blessings in both Arabic and English, and then spoke in Hebrew. I will not present here the talk for the following reason: The long and scholarly talk was published in its entirety in Hebrew, Arabic, and English in a booklet by the Research Project on Peace, and can be found in all the important libraries. Here I will only mention the various sections of the talk: 1. Jewish-Arab relations in the past, 2. Israel's concern with security, 3. the recent negotiations between Egypt and Israel, 4. relations between Egypt and Israel after the Peace Treaty, 5. Egypt within the Arab World, 6. Israel's international relations after the Peace Treaty, and 7. the role of intellectuals in the peace process.

Professor Judah Eisenberg and Ms. Connie Wilsack worked hard and got the talk translated into English and Arabic, and the translation was approved by Mr. Eban. We prepared a list of about one thousand persons and institutions in Israel and abroad, including quite a few institutions in the Arab countries, and then sent a copy of the booklet to all of them, in direct or indirect ways. We know that it reached the Arab World.

Unfortunately, no other three-language booklet was published by the Project afterwards, but one booklet was published only in English, (and this was done after I had ended my term as the Project's Director, and had left for Paris for a Sabbatical leave from the University, in the summer of 1980). This booklet describes two symposiums held at the University, and attended by Mustafa Khalil, then the Foreign Minister of Egypt, and Dr. Boutros Ghali, Minister of State for Foreign Affairs, as well as Israeli professors and public leaders, mostly economists. A third booklet entitled "The Palestinian Problem - Selected Topics" was also published by the Project, but only in Hebrew.

Toward Peace in the Middle East – an International Conference. The conference was planned for mid-June 1979, and was supposed to represent an end to the preparatory work as well as a beginning of a new, more meaningful phase in the Peace Project's activity; and not just another theoretical conference on how to solve international conflicts. In the conference, we intended to cover all the subjects pertaining to peace process in the Middle East, and in particular plans for regional cooperation. Our intention was that following the conference we would hold symposia and workshops on specific topics, and the proceedings of the conference as well as the accounts of the following symposia and workshops would be published in a book called "The Peace Book", which would be presented to the regional governments and to their public. Our hope was that the Peace Project would continue with the publication of Peace Books every two years, and that they would be used as indicators of the degree of progress of the peace process. Great plans! Great hopes!

A committee in charge of the program, headed by Professor Zeev Hirsch, former Dean of the Faculty of Management, was appointed by the Project's Management, and its work started months before the planned date of the conference. The full program of the conference is presented in Appendix

VIII. Many distinguished scientists and intellectuals from around the world accepted our invitation to lecture at the conference; among them we will mention just a few: Alfred Grosser from Paris, Herbert Kelman from Harvard, Lawrence Kline from the University of Pennsylvania, Edward Morse from the State Department, I. William Zartman, T. Meron and Ingo Walter from NYU, E.L. Feige from the University of Wisconsin, Steve Cohen from CUNY, Joseph Peckman from Brookings Institution, Eli Kedourie from London School of Economics, and Graf Von Baudisin from Germany.

Together with our friends in the United States we had tried very hard to have Arab scientists from Egypt, other Arab countries, and the Occupied Territories participate in the conference, but only George Assousa, a Palestinian with American citizenship, came. A few hours before the opening session, we had an unexpected visit. An assistant professor from Bir-Zeit College in the West Bank came to the University President's office and asked us if he could listen to the lectures. We clearly agreed, and added that we were willing to let him give a talk, and were even ready to change the program for that, but he declined our offer. We were unhappy about his refusal, but felt shame when he described to us in detail the humiliating conditions of students and teachers alike in his College, which was basically under siege by the Israeli Defense Forces. This sad description strengthened my conviction that my activity in the Peace Project was in the right direction, and could help both Arab and Israeli academia.

Was the conference a success? Did it achieve its goals? I am afraid that my answer to both questions is "no", and here is where we failed:
Although we had many distinguished lecturers from abroad, and most of the lectures were very good, we did not succeed in bringing lecturers or even passive participants from Egypt and other Arab countries. This is a sign of the degree of cooperation, or the lack of it, three months after the signing of the Egyptian-Israeli Peace Treaty.[9]
We had hopes to hold such conferences every two years; but in fact, this was not only the first but also the last conference held by the Peace Project. The proceedings of the conference were not published, and therefore there was no Peace Book; a hope that did not materialize. The reason for not publishing the proceedings is that most lecturers did not submit the copy of their lecture in writing, as requested.

9 *I have recently learned that about ten months after our conference another conference was held in Israel on "Self Views in Israel and Egypt". A few Egyptians did participate in that conference, and the Egyptian writer, Hussein Faouzi, as well as Mr. Gomah the first secretary the Egyptian Embassy in Israel actually gave talks there.*

Finally, I will now present several anecdotes related to the conference.

1. Almost every one we invited was glad to come. My only disappointment came from the president of the country, Itzhak Navon, who was asked to give the welcoming address and refused, without giving any convincing reason.

2. I had another "failure", an amusing one. We wanted to give the conference an international flavor, and decided to invite an African leader to give the keynote address. As I was friendly with a French scientist who was related by marriage to a famous African leader and philosopher, I asked my friend to help me convince this leader to come to the conference. When my friend heard my request, he said that he would not help me in the attempt to invite "that crook", as he called him.

3. Among those lectures, which were submitted also in writing, was one that was rejected by our committee, because the referee said that the article's scientific level was not high enough, and should not be published by us, unless the author made quite a few changes. This happens in many conferences, and I would not have mentioned it if it had not been for the fact that this author received the Nobel Award in his field a few months later.

4. One of our professors volunteered to have his home and garden as the venue for a party for all participants, but set one condition, namely, that Professor Assousa would not be invited to that party. He did not explain the reason for this outrageous request. I tried hard to convince him to relax that condition, and emphasized that Professor Assousa was not only our guest, but also the only Arab at the conference, but in vain. I then told him that unless he changed his mind, the party would be held in a different place, and then he yielded.

My beliefs. On 23.6.1979 I was interviewed by Abraham Peleg, a reporter of the daily Maariv, who requested the interview. In the beginning I told the reporter that I would draw the line between my beliefs as a person and a scientist, which will be brought in the beginning, and my opinion as the Director of the Tel Aviv University research Project on Peace. This interview is presented here since it represents a sort of a mid-term progress report.

Who are you Professor Yavin? I am first of all a person, a member of the human society, and then a Jew and an Israeli. I am also a physicist. As a scientist I have the responsibility to think, to ask tough questions and to check, and most of all to stay away from prejudices, even when the large majority of the public accept them as truths. In this respect I am a student of Rene Descartes and Albert Einstein. I am clearly also a staff member of Tel Aviv University and the Director of the Research Project on Peace of the University.

What is your personal history? I was born in Israel in 1928. My father, David Mondjak, immigrated to the country in 1920 by himself at the age of sixteen, and married my mother, Yemima Brauner, the daughter of the pharmacist of Zichron Yaakov. In his last years, until his death in 1943, my father was the commander of the 4th (out of 6) district of the Haganah in Haifa. I am a graduate of the Hebrew Reali School in Haifa. I was in the Scouts, in the Haganah and the Palmach, and participated in the Defense of Jerusalem in the Israeli War of Independence, serving in the Moriah and the Beit-Horon Battalions. I received my M.Sc. degree in physics, mathematics and philosophy from the Hebrew University in Jerusalem in 1954. I then studied physics in the University of Washington in Seattle, where I received my Ph.D. degree in 1958. I then joined the University of Illinois, which I left in 1970 with the rank of professor. In the years 1960-1962 I was temporarily in the Israeli Atomic Energy Commission in Soreq, trying to get a national nuclear accelerator for Israel. In 1967 I was invited by Professor Yuval Ne'eman to come from Illinois and build the Department of Nuclear Physics at Tel Aviv University. In the years 1971-1976 I served as the first dean of the Faculty of Exact Sciences at the University. In the beginning of 1978 I was asked by President Ben-Shahar to establish and direct the Research Project on Peace.

What convinced you the physicist to accept the position of the Project's director? I will start by saying that many physicists have recently been involved in peace work, perhaps because of their guilt feelings for the development of the atom bomb. As a physicist I learned from people such as Galileo Galilee and Max Plank to beware of popular concepts and consensus. I saw how intellectual complacency was a major factor leading to the disaster of the Yom-Kippur War as well as to the shock of peace a few years later.

Let me bring a few examples from other peoples as well about the danger of a national consensus. The Arab world was jubilant when President Nasser reached an agreement with King Hussein in 1967, but the Six-Day War proved that this agreement, praised by the whole Arab World, brought them nothing but a disaster. A second self defeating example of the danger of a consensus is the notorious "Three No's of Khartoum". The third and most striking example is the unprecedented unity (a consensus!) in the United States, when 98 out of 100 senators and all the 435 congressmen in Washington voted to let President Lyndon B. Johnson launch the disastrous bloody war in Vietnam. Finally I will point out the shameful vote in the United Nations, when this organization voted to accuse Zionism as being racial.

What is the main difference between a politician and a scientist or an intellectual? The political leader strives for a consensus in which he will be in its center; while the scientist and the intellectual should always check all the consensuses.

Why is a scientist involved in politics? I am not dealing in politics, but in the search for the truth in all fields. We do not take sides, but check all opinions, and suggest what these facts say. If you are talking about political issues, I would say that we are not dealing with politics but with political science. I do however wish to add that from a moral point of view as a human being, a teacher, and a father, I feel that I have to do my best to prevent a situation in which young people, including my students and my children, will be killed or maimed.

What do you hope to contribute as a physicist? I have already mentioned the doubt, which a physicist brings to any thinking or deliberation. Another important concept, so popular in physics, is the concept of symmetry. One should look from the other side of each situation, and not only from his side; and ask "what would I do if I were in the position of the opponent. In Judaism there is a wonderful saying related to this, namely, "Do not judge your friend until you will be in his situation". The symmetry concept helps us distinguish between what is good for us and what is really just. Let me give you an example: I assume that if I were a German in the nineteen forties, I would have been anti-Nazi; therefore, my rejection of Nazism does not stem from me being Jewish, but from moral principles. On the other hand, if I were a member of an Arab family who owned the land of Sheikh Munis, I would most likely not think that the land belonged to Tel Aviv University. Therefore, our ownership of that piece of land is perhaps good for us, but not necessarily morally just. As a man of academia I have to understand and clarify to me and to others all aspects of every subject in order to reach good solutions to all the problems. In other words, as a scientist I am required to think on all aspects, and do it also in subjects related to peace as well as bi-national and regional cooperation.

And what do you wish to achieve as a human being? If I let myself dream for a moment, I will say that I hope for peace to come to our region; that the vision of peace in the future, with many across-the-border collaborations, will diminish strongly the image of non-passable obstacles as well as of other present problems; that a solution to the so-called Palestinian problem, which will bring with it harmonious relations between them and us as equals, will be found; that Zionism will thrive and immigration to the country will increase; and that the Israeli society will develop freely without fears and wars.

And now to the Research Project on Peace; how and why was it formed? When President Sadat announced that he was ready for peace we all were astounded. On my part, I was ashamed that the announcement found us, scientists and intellectuals, completely unprepared. I therefore invited ten senior professors to my home to see what we can do for the country. The president and the rector then appointed a committee headed by retired general Aharon Yariv to consider how the University could contribute to the forthcoming peace. One of the recommendations of that committee, which had worked very hard for many weeks, was to set up a university body that would coordinate and encourage peace activities at the University, and this is the Research Project on Peace. We have built the infrastructure, formed a few committees, and at the moment we are trying to enlarge our Israeli Steering Board and make it international.

Can you define the goal of the Project in one or two sentences? Our main goal is to encourage the University staff as well as the whole Israeli society to think deeply, with no bias, and with imagination, on peace and cooperation between us and the Arabs. Another goal of ours is to investigate the possible positive and negative ensuing consequences to our country from peace.

What have you accomplished up till now? We have already approved 16 research proposals, and more proposals are now being looked at by our Research Committee. We held a workshop with the participation of the Government and several national leaders in an attempt to establish a national authority for Israeli-Egyptian, or even Mid-Eastern cooperation. We are now starting a series of lectures, which will be distributes in the region and the world, in Hebrew, Arabic, and English, as Peace Papers; the first such lecture was delivered by Abba Eban. Our last major project was the international conference which we held this month, in which first-line scientists from around the world participated and lectured.

What is unique in your Project? The new thing about the Project is that it is open to the University staff from all departments and faculties. Actually it is open to the public, even to those who are not on any university staff.

Do you have contacts with other academic institutions in the country? In the beginning I suggested to form one national project for all the universities in the country, but my suggestion was not accepted. To some extent, we coordinate our activities with the other universities, mainly in the committees of the heads of those institutions; and as I have said, members of other universities, such as the Hebrew University and Bar-Ilan University, have already submitted research proposals to us, and several such proposals are being financially supported by us.

Do you have any contacts with academic institutions abroad? Our strongest tie now is with the Brookings Institution in Washington. We also have institutional ties with Harvard University in Massachusetts and with the University of Pennsylvania. These ties are especially important to us as long as we do not have bi-party ties with Arab scientists. The main idea is that the institution abroad will form a bi-party collaboration with each side separately; in the second stage the two research project will fuse together into a tri-party research project. We hope that we will eventually be able to form bi-party projects with Arab groups without the help of a foreign "mediator".

Do you have any ties with leaders of the economy in the country? We have strong ties with the Minister of Finance, and upon his recommendation we received a grant from the Knesset. We also coordinate our activities with the director generals of the Prime-Minister's Office and of the Foreign Office; in fact with the director generals of all the ministries. As for the private sector, we have ties with the Manufacturers Association and with the Histadruth.

Have you succeeded in forming ties with the Arab World? Here our success is still small; until the signing of the Peace Treaty with Egypt there were almost no ties at all with scientists from the Arab World. Even after the signing we are moving slowly, since there are many obstacles, and we know that we might fail with hasty moves. There have, however, been a small number of mutual visits. I can sum up the situation by saying that the Arab scientists are waiting for the normalization of relations, and we are also waiting, trying to understand their difficulties. One of our main goals is to think and do research together with them. Personally, I need collaboration for my own research projects in nuclear physics. I assume that we will start the cooperation in non-controversial fields in which we will compliment each other. I hope that at the end of the process the scientific borders with scientists from all neighboring countries will also open up. It is worth remembering that the political détente between the United States and the Soviet Union started only after American and Soviet scientists cooperated with each other, often with no permission from their governments. With us, unfortunately, the politicians beat us.

What are your closing remarks? We have started with the Peace Project, because it is our duty to ourselves and to our society as academicians. We are looking forward to a similar action by the Egyptians, hopefully even to the formation of a Research Project on Peace by an Egyptian university. My personal dream is that we will get rid of our mutual fear through scientific collaborations, and

CHAPTER 4.
THE FIRST VISIT TO EGYPT

An invitation to visit Egypt. My life-long intention to visit Egypt was first attempted in August 1967. Before leaving Illinois for a Sabbatical year in Tel-Aviv University, I asked Tabark, my Egyptian student, how I could get an invitation to give a seminar talk at the Cairo University. She did not answer, and from the look on her face I realized that she thought that I had lost my mind. Years later I received from her a letter to Tel-Aviv University, asking if I could send a letter of recommendation for her to Professor Mohamed El-Nadi at Cairo University. I gladly sent that letter. In the following years I received from her several letters in which she asked if I was willing to certify that her work with me at the University of Illinois on analog states in nuclei had never been published by another student, and I gladly sent the written certification. Later I was asked if I would agree to serve on her Ph.D. Committee, and again I agreed. All this correspondence between me in Tel Aviv and her in Cairo was done via Illinois. All the attempts by President Ben-Shahar, Professor Shamir, and me to visit Cairo right after our international conference in June 1979, three months after the signing of the Peace Treaty, failed.

A month later I traveled to Vancouver to continue my research at TRIUMF, the Canadian national accelerator. There, eight years after our last contact, I wrote Tabark a letter from Vancouver, telling her about our activities on peace, and mentioning my hope that I would finally be able to visit Cairo. Her excited and exciting letter is presented here in full, since it is an important building block of my future activities.

Cairo July 23, 1979
Dear Dr. Yavin

I received your letter today and I was really so glad to hear from you. I wanted very much to write to you, but I did not know your address.

Last week, Ali and I were talking about you, and guessing what would be your feelings after the peace treaty. We got the answer today from your letter and your peace project. We wish you the best of luck and success.

About me, I got my Ph.D. degree in 12/1973 from Cairo University. Since then I have been working in the Atomic Energy Establishment. Actually, I did not do much research work, since our Van-de-Graff accelerator is now in a bad shape. So I am doing now activation analysis on some geological samples, using the reactor.

Ali is now working on the project of the first nuclear power plant. He will be going to Karlsruhe, Germany, on a management-training course, starting September 2, 1979, and lasting 11 weeks. The course is arranged by the IAEA. My daughter Sonia is 15 years old, going to her second year of high school. My son Magid is now 10 years old, going to his 6th year of primary school.

We are all anxious to see you, and Ali hopes that you can make it to Cairo before he leaves for Germany. However, you are certainly welcome to Egypt all the time, and I look forward to seeing you. Please let us know about your detailed plans and date of arrival. My best regards to you, Rivka and the family.

Tabark.

I called Tabark from Vancouver and she sounded very excited when she heard that Rivka and I would soon come to Cairo. From Tel Aviv I called Ali in Cairo, and he told me that he and Tabark would come to Cairo Airport to meet us, and that they would reserve a room for us in a hotel. Fortunately, our visas to enter Egypt arrived on time.

I consulted with many people at the University and in our Foreign Ministry, as well as with physicists in Israel, the United States, Canada and Europe, who had expressed a desire to help any Israeli-Egyptian collaboration in the future. I also talked to the journalist Uri Avnery, who had visited Egypt. Some of the people whom I was advised to meet in Cairo were: Professor Mohamed El-Nadi (the most senior Egyptian physicist), as well as his two sons, Professor El-Bedewi (the Head of the Department of Physics in Ein-Shams University), Dr. Sayyid Yasin (Head of Al-Ahram Institute), Professor Saad Eddin Ibrahim (a sociologist in the American University in Cairo), Dr. Boutros Ghali, Tahsin Basheer (from the Foreign Ministry), and Professor Hassan Ismail (the Head of the Egyptian Academy of Sciences).

In my talk with President Ben-Shahar, before my departure for Cairo, he informed me that the Peace Project had been promised 3.5-million Israeli Lira, mainly from the Treasury and from two banks. We also received smaller contributions, one of them from the 169th Battalion to commemorate their dead. President Ben-Shahar asked me to give Dr. Sayyid Yasin copies of all the papers submitted to our conference as a sign of good will, and to tell Dr. Yasin that we were trying to help the Bir-Zeit College to open up and to have contacts with Harvard University.

Arriving in Cairo! The detailed account which follows is based on the detailed accounts that Rivka and I wrote throughout the visit and after it, and is presented as a logbook. As well as facts, it will deal with personal experiences, feelings, quandaries, and thoughts. I decided to do so because of the unique nature of this visit in a city, which had been a subject of my dreams almost all my life until then.

Rivka (29.8.79): We are in Athens Airport, as there are still no direct flights from Tel Aviv to Cairo. Two Egyptians are sitting on the bench behind us. We tried to talk to them, but when they heard that we were from Israel, they kept quiet. The same happened with an Egyptian woman sitting next to us. A disappointment! I told Avivi that I doubted whether all the stories about the friendship toward Israelis in Egypt were wrong. We decided not to be surprised if we encounter a similar cool reception by our hosts Tabark and Ali.

It is now 08:00 the following day. We are in the sixth floor of the Shepherd Hotel in Cairo, on the bank of the River Nile. The view from the terrace is magnificent. We are facing the Sheraton, and to our right we see the Cairo Tower. I have not expected such a terrific view.

Let us go back now to the troubles of yesterday. The flight from Athens to Cairo was uneventful except for one interesting event that stemmed from differences in culture as well as from human rudeness. One of the Egyptian passengers called the flight attendant by clicking two fingers, as was the custom in Egypt. The TWA flight attendant took it as a personal insult and screamed at him, "Don't you do that! Don't you ever do it again!" The passenger blushed and kept quiet. I wonder whether this American woman would have dared to insult a passenger this way if it had been in the United States.

We landed at 20:00, and exchanged $150 for Egyptian liras, as requested, and walked to the big reception hall, where we had to place our passports in a big pile. After half an hour we were called to a small window, where two officials were sitting. When one of them called Gabriel (a Jew?) saw that we were from Israel, he seemed excited. The other official extended his hand to greet us and said, "Shalom". So far so good. We moved on, stayed in line for another half an hour until another official came out of an office with our passports and asked, "Who is David?" We said that David was either our son or my husband's late father. He went back to his office, and we kept waiting. After a long while they started to turn the lights off in the hall, and we realized that we were left alone there. A TWA official brought us our suitcases and went home, leaving us perplexed and worried. One of our worries concerned our hosts. Were they still waiting for us outside? Perhaps they thought that all the passengers had left, and so they too left. We wanted to send them a message, but a grim-faced official told us to wait. Finally an officer came out from his office, and called, "Israel; come!" It was not clear whether he called Avivi by his middle name, or called the name of our country. He stamped our visas with a smile, said "Shalom", and wished us a pleasant stay. We had one more interesting little event. We had to pay L3.6 (3.6 Egyptian liras). Avivi gave the cashier a L10 bill, and got back L7.4. Avivi tried to tell him that he was mistaken. The cashier was insulted, repeated his calculations, and got the same answer. Avivi then gave him one lira, and the cashier smiled; he either understood his mistake, or thought that it was a tip.

We left the terminal and walked along the fence. There was no sign of Ali and Tabark. "What should we do?" I asked Avivi, and before he could answer they appeared from around a corner. We were very excited, and they either could not hide their excitement, or did not want to. They told us that they had been waiting outside the terminal for four hours. They did not know that the flight was delayed, and there was no way for them to find it out in Cairo. They checked the passenger list and saw that we were on the plane, but when the lights were turned off in the hall they started to worry lest we had left with the other passengers without them noticing.

We got into their car, and Ali drove us through modern Cairo, and then through its center. We then got our first impression of the traffic in Cairo; no rules and no priorities. We reached the hotel at 23:00, 20 hours after we had left home. I was excited like a little girl. Our hosts were wonderful. They had reserved a room for us, paid for one night, without knowing for sure that we would arrive. On parting they told us that they both were at our disposal for the next three days, until Ali would leave for Germany. They would come tomorrow (that is today) at 14:00 for a tour of town, and we would have dinner at their home in the evening.

We went up to our room and from there to the terrace, I with a glass of fruit juice that I found in the room, and Avivi with a glass of whisky from the bottle he was carrying. "A dream came true!" he said, lowering himself down to sit on a chair, and then jumping up screaming. I looked at his chair and saw a huge nail sticking upward. Fortunately, the nail was not at the center, so Avivi luckily did not sit on it. It was then that we realized for the first time that the Shepherd Hotel was not any more the famous five-star hotel. Since we could not fall asleep because of the day's excitement, we went out for a walk along the Nile.

Rivka continues (31.8.79): We have already slept two nights in Cairo. Yesterday morning we decided to see a bit of the city before Tabark and Ali arrived. Dressed like tourists, we went to Tahrir Square (the Liberation Square), which is the main square of the city. Many people greeted us by saying, "Welcome", and when we said we were Israelis, the reaction was a bit cooler, but always friendly. We crossed a bridge and walked to Cairo Tower; the view from there was beautiful.

The Shepherd Hotel was considered luxurious, and charged L30 per night for a couple (about $50). The room was nice, but the furniture almost fell apart. At 13:00 we went to the dining room, which could serve 150 people, but we were only three there. We were served by five waiters, each in charge of a different thing. Upon entering we were met by a waiter in black pants, a white shirt, and a yellow jacket, who brought us to our table, and gave us the menu. Another waiter, dressed in black pants and a white shirt, came to our table with a basket of bread. A waiter dressed like "the Thief of Bagdad" put an empty plate in front of us. Ten minutes passed by and nothing happened; except for twelve waiters in various clothes wandering back and forth doing nothing. Then the Thief of Bagdad came and replaced the empty plates with other empty plates, this time slightly warm. I used all my self control trying not to laugh as I knew that the fate of our marriage depended on that. Two new guests came in and were seated. Finally, The Thief of Bagdad came with some steaks. The waiter with black pants and a white shirt followed him, holding a bowl of potatoes. The maitre d', dressed in a black suit and wearing a white shirt, watches them all from a distance. I felt sorry for the hotel owner because of the scarcity of guests, but I learned later that the Egyptians ate their lunch between 15:00 and 17:00.

Tabark and Ali came after the meal and took us for a visit of the old city. We visited the Al-Azhar and Hussein mosques, we toured the suks (markets), including the famous Al-Khalili Suk, and looked for gallabiyas (the Egyptian national white gowns). We returned to our hotel tired but very satisfied. We noted that people in the places we visited treated us the same way they would treat any tourist

Avivi adds: The visit to the mosques was interesting, and at times even dramatic. The impressive Al-Azhar building, as well as all the houses around it, was old. Inside the mosque there was no clear center, and people were sitting in its corners. We left the mosque, walked a little, and arrived at a small dark house. Ali found somebody who opened its gate. We walked into a beautiful old mosque, but deserted and full of dust. Its windows were colorful and beautiful, but cats climbed on its walls. Ali felt bad and said that his people did not appreciate their historical treasures.

The last visit was to Hussein Mosque. Hussein was the Prophet's grandson. Ali and I walk in through the men's entrance with our shoes in our hands, while Rivka and Tabark waited outside. The big hall was full of people, praying and studying in groups. We entered a room where Hussein was buried and went around his tomb. Ali warned me not to talk so that no one would know that I was not a Muslim. We exited the Mosque and came in again with Rivka and Tabark through the women's entrance. This time they recognized me as being non-Muslim and started to shout and to threaten us. Ali told them that I was a Muslim – so he later told us - but they did not believe him and accused him of "harram". Ali was not scared and invited the three of us to go together around the tomb. Only later he told us that we were in a real danger.

Ali came to our hotel in the evening to take us to their apartment for dinner. They owned a beautiful and roomy apartment. Ali told us that the monthly rent for such a furnished apartment was $1,000, while a professor's monthly salary was about a third of that. Those who rented such apartments were usually "Arabs", as Ali scornfully called the people from the rich oil countries. He said that their politicians terminated their relations with Egypt, but their businessmen continued to come, mainly to have a good time.

Rivka adds: Their daughter, Sonya, was 15 years old. She looked like Tabark, slim, beautiful, delicate, intelligent, and with good manners. She asked for our advice what to see in Israel when she would visit it. Their son, Maged, was ten years old. He read with excitement the letter from our daughter Mimi. The kids opened our presents, and the excitement kept growing. They liked the shirts we brought them, since there were none like them in Egypt. They liked the paddles too, and said that they had them in Egypt, but they used tennis balls not small hard ones as in Israel. They played the disc of Ester Ofarim, and they all said that they liked it. Tabark and Ali were excited about the book on Israel which we brought them, and fought over who would be the first to read it. The food was tasty and consisted of a soup, meat, chicken, pasta, rice, squash, chips, vegetable salad, and fresh fruit. The atmosphere was friendly as if we were members of their family. We all told jokes, and Avivi asked the kids some riddles. Tabark started the evening very tense, but finally relaxed, and even agreed to call Avivi by his first name and not Dr. Yavin.

Avivi: Following the meal we went out to the balcony, and a political discussion started, over coffee and cakes. Both Ali and Tabark were critical of the "Arabs" and doubted whether Khomeini would maintain his control over Iran because of the economic and social difficulties there. I asked what would happen in Egypt if the people there would be disappointed with Sadat, since the economy was in a bad shape following the departure of most of the "Arabs". I asked whether the popular unhappiness and economic hardship could lead to the cessation of the peace process. "No way," said Ali, "We are done with wars with Israel. The Arab pressure will diminish, and Sadat's initiative will not change."

I inquired about the Egyptian physicists El-Nadi, El-Bedewi, and Osman. Tabark promised to take me to Professor El-Nadi in Cairo University, and Ali would try to connect me with Professor El-Bedewi in Ein Shams University. They invited us to their shooting club for lunch on Saturday two days later. What a warm and friendly hospitality!

Rivka continues (in the evening of the following day): In the morning we went for breakfast. On the way we met Ralph Alberg, a travel agent for

Paltours from Haifa, who offered to take us with him to the pyramids in his rented car. Alberg had been born on Egypt, and spoke Arabic with an Egyptian accent. The chauffeur took us first to a village where they made and sold hand woven carpets and gallabiyas. We touched, bargained (as expected), and bought lots of things.

We continued to the pyramids where the chauffeur got us a guide with three camels, each led by a different person. We were dressed in gallabiyas, and they took pictures of us, with me crowned the Queen of Sheba. Alberg and Avivi were requested to take off their sun glasses, as "Sheikhs do not wear glasses." We marched in line on four camels, feeling great. Behind us we could see the Mina House, where the political talks were being held. We were very impressed by the huge pyramids and kept wondering how they had been built. On the other hand, we found the sphinx smaller than what I had expected, but looked more beautiful than in all its pictures that I had seen. After the required picture session the guide suggested to Avivi to exchange his camel for Avivi's camera, and Avivi smiled and said that he could not think of a more practical vehicle in Tel Aviv than a camel. Kids were trying to sell us souvenirs, and inquired about the exchange rate. We distributed some Israeli coins among the kids, and they in turn asked us to exchange them for Egyptian money.

Next we visited a papyrus store. They described there in detail how the papyrus paper was made, and then showed us pictures drawn on such paper. We bought a picture of the creation, which showed the goddess of the sky being supported by the god of the air, with the gods of the creation on both sides of him, and with the goddess of the earth below them. Avivi decided to buy this picture, since it reminded him of the four elements of the Greeks. Each time I called Avivi by his name the girls giggled, since to them it sounded like Habibi (my sweetheart). They all said that they supported peace, and a young fellow declared that he wanted to visit Israel, because he heard that the Israeli girls are pretty. Avivi later said that their friendship could be genuine, but could definitely not represent the feelings of the Egyptian people, because the feelings of people in the tourist industry in any country did not necessarily represent the feeling of the general public in that country. We finally tipped the guide, and later learned that Alberg had also tipped him, together the tips totaled a one month salary. Alberg then said, "Let it be a contribution to peace between our peoples."

Avivi (Saturday morning, 1.9.79): Last night we went out for dinner with Ralph Alberg, in the commercial center of Cairo, i.e. near Talat Harb and Casser A-Neel streets. We walked to the famous restaurant of Hassan Ali, crossing on our way dangerous streets full of rushing cars, and walking in crowded sidewalks full of friendly people. We watched the display of beautiful shoes in the many stores. We asked a young man for the way to the restaurant, and he insisted on walking with us when he heard that we were Israelis, since it was his first encounter with Israelis. He declined our invitation to come in with us, and said that he was a clerk in the central bank.

We returned to the hotel full of pleasant experiences, and discovered that there were two more Israelis in the hotel. We left them a note, and a few minutes later we heard a voice in Hebrew, whispering "Open up quickly!" The two young Israelis walked in quickly, and started telling us their story, which was very different from our pleasant experience so far.

The two of them were born in Egypt, and were members of a kibbutz in Israel for the previous 20 years. They came to Egypt to look for their relatives: siblings, a mother and cousins. They were held at the airport for 6 hours for no obvious reason. They had to pay their hotel in advance for seven days to secure the room for themselves. They were constantly scared, and for fear, talked only English with each other. Cairo appeared to them in a worse state than 20 years earlier, when it had had only three and one half million inhabitants, in comparison with eight million, or ten million, if Giza was included, at present. They had been unsuccessful in their search for relatives. Albeit one of them found a sister who was married to a Muslim, but her attitude toward him was cold. They also found the few remaining Jews in poor economic status. They visited many Jewish homes, including those of medical doctors, and found them in very bad shape. The sister, who was married to a high government official, was living in a dark apartment, almost completely devoid of windows. His nephew was a young engineer, who was earning 30 Egyptian liras a month, while his father was earning seven times that much. They also told us a somewhat funny story: they were very satisfied when they succeeded in buying a train ticket from Alexandria to Cairo. They paid the cashier a "baksheesh" (a tip) of two pounds and got a reserved seat, soon to discover that they were not the only ones who paid a baksheesh for the same seats.

It is possible that this meeting brought us back to a more realistic world, with more dimensions; or was it possible that they were an exception? We debated the question of what should be our behavior in the street; should we move in total freedom and with no fear, or should we hide our being Israelis as much as possible. We decided to continue with freedom and no fear, but not demonstrate unnecessarily our being Israelis.

This morning we went with Alberg to the Eastmar Travel Agency, Paltour's partner. Mohamed El Dorri, the deputy manager, received us warmly and said that he had taken part in two wars with Israel. Already in 1956 he and his friends in the front wondered why they were fighting the Israelis. In the October War (1973) his Palestinian neighbor became rich but refused to contribute a penny to the war effort. Like Ali, he too spoke against the "Arabs". In his opinion, the united Arab front against Egypt would collapse, and then he added, "Any donkey can make a war, but only a strong and wise man can make peace." He invited us to three organized tours, and refused to take any payment. We were impressed by his warm and friendly attitude, but did not rush to generalize it to the Egyptian attitude, since he was in the tourist business, and it was possible that his opinion was not that of the average man in the street. In France I got the impression that the average Frenchman's attitude toward Israelis was better than toward Palestinians, not for the love of Jews, but for the hatred of Arabs. I wondered whether here I discovered a similar phenomenon; namely, that some Egyptians hated the "Arabs", and perhaps the Palestinians too, more than they hated us. The truth was that up till then we had not found hatred towards us, but we had not yet met the scientists and the intellectuals, and were looking forward to investigate this point in future days.

From there we went to the central synagogue in Adli Street. The Jews there, in a very small number, received us with warmth, and asked us to help them get the yet unfulfilled promise to visit Israel with no pay. They all complained about their economic situation.

Rivka: Ali and Tabark arrived in the hotel soon after we had come back from our visit to the synagogue, and took us to their club. The club's grounds were not taken care of, and everything looked untidy. The food was reasonable, not more than that. However, Tabark and Ali were great as before. Following the meal we drove to the Citadel, which had been built to protect the city. It is a beautiful structure on top of a hill, and looks like a naïve picture drawn by kids. The famous Mohammed Ali Mosque is located inside the citadel. We took off our shoes and walked inside. The walls are made of marble, but not kept in good care. It hurt Ali to see the negligence in their historical monuments. While Ali was talking, Avivi stepped on a broken piece of glass with his bare foot, and the foot was bleeding badly. Tabark started to cry. Someone gave Avivi a bottle of iodine and a band-aid. We continued to Sultan Hassan Mosque, and again it was clear that it was not well taken care of.

Next we went to the beautiful Al-Rifai Mosque. It had been built one hundred years earlier to compete with Sultan Hassan mosque. Unlike other mosques, this one was well taken care of. It was built with beautiful marble, had many copper items, with thick doors full of carvings, and beautiful ceilings. Many important people, including King Farouk's uncle, were buried in this mosque. We were then driven to our hotel, where we said good bye to Ali, who was to leave for Germany.

Avivi: This morning was finally devoted to the reason I had come to Cairo, namely, to try and get collaborations between our professors and Egyptian ones. I took a cab to Tabark and together we tried about twenty times to call Cairo University, but with no luck, a typical experience in Cairo those days. We decided to travel to the University uninvited, and fortunately met with luck. Professor Mohamed El-Nadi, the senior Egyptian physicist, the former head of the Atomic Energy Establishment, and the Vice President of Mansura University, was willing to see me in his office.

In the room I also met the young Professor Omar Badawi, who was also working at CERN, and young Dr. Sheriff. On the wall, over the head of El-Nadi, hung a large picture of Nasser, but there was no picture of Sadat in the room. El-Nadi started by apologizing for not coming to a meeting in Frankfurt organized by Professor Walter Greiner, who had attempted to introduce El-Nadi to me and to Judah Eisenberg. He said frankly that he had sent a request to the then prime minister, and received a letter saying that it was too early for such a meeting. He then went one step further in his frankness, by admitting that he had received the letter I sent to the dean in 1975, and then too he was not allowed to respond to me. His frankness set the tone for our discussions.

He asked me for the reason of my visit. I described the various experiments we were doing, mainly in Los Alamos, in France, and in Switzerland, as well as our plans for work in Vancouver. I told him that we had many ideas and the necessary budget, but lacked the necessary manpower to start new experiments. El-Nadi, who was listening attentively, interrupted me by saying,

"We will send you people, but not yet to Israel. The best way for us to work together is abroad." I was very pleased by his comment because not only were we talking on the desired collaboration for the benefit of both sides, but also because the suggestion had come from him. He said that as far as he was concerned, the problem at the moment was only financial. I then told him that we had in Tel Aviv the budget for two new positions in physics, and it was possible to offer one or even two to people that he would choose. He said that it was essential that the offers would come from a third party, to which I said that it could be arranged. He then said that he had a good candidate to work with us in Vancouver by the name of Osman, who was finishing his Ph.D. work. He added that he had received letters from Germany and Scandinavia, telling him that they too needed people, but I beat them by coming to him in person. My radiochemical experiment in Vancouver, in which we produced pions by bombarding bismuth and isotopes of lead with protons, seemed to him a good candidate for the first collaboration, if they would get an invitation from Vancouver. I knew already that this would work, since my collaborator in Vancouver, Dr. John D'Auria, had already told me so. El-Nadi then invited me to visit their laboratory.

In his lab there were about 20 students, almost half of them women. They were all introduced to me, and they showed me the microscopes and the emulsions which they had received from the Soviet Union. The emulsions had been irradiated by alpha particles, with energy of 4.2 GeV per nucleon. There was one Iraqi student in the group, and several of them said that they would soon travel to Saudi Arabia to work there. Tabark noticed my surprise, and told me that professors and students kept working in the Arab countries in spite of the breaking of relations caused by the peace agreement. I was then invited to tell them all about our research. I approached the blackboard, a fulfillment of a twelve year old dream, and started to lecture. I described our experiments in the various laboratories in Canada, the United States, France, and Switzerland. They listened very attentively and asked good questions. At the end El-Nadi said that the radiochemical experiment and the one about detecting neutral pions with a spectrometer seemed most suitable for them. I left with them the list of my group's publications, and promised to send them reprints and preprints. They promised to prepare for me a list of their people and research projects. I suggested to them to call me in my hotel, but did not suggest meeting again, leaving them the option to withdraw from the offer of collaboration if El-Nadi had done so only out of politeness. In summary, the visit was successful, and El-Nadi looked like a charming and constructive person, befitting his international reputation. I started to believe that a scientific collaboration in the near future might be possible.

On the way out Tabark told me that they were unable to buy books or journals for their libraries by the order of the country's president, and this was the reason that they had asked me to send reprints. She told me further that studying in Egypt was free throughout the university, and that the government had to supply jobs to every university graduate.

On the way to my hotel Tabark said that she would never forget that in June 1967 I came to her by the lab door in Urbana and said, "Our peoples are in a political and a military conflict, but we are human beings, and therefore we will continue working together," and asked me if I too remembered the event. She added that when we came to her house her children thought that I was strict and unfriendly, but after I told the first joke and played the first game with them they liked us. I asked Tabark if she was interested in working soon with us for one or two semesters. She first wanted to know if there was a possibility for a long term or even a permanent position. As far as she was concerned, she might want to work with us next summer, and might want to come to Israel with her children if conditions allowed it.

Back in the hotel I made a few phone calls. I called the cardiologist, Professor Atiya, and he told me that he would go the following day to Haifa, and would meet with Professor Henry Neufeld. The sociologist Saad Eddin Ibrahim from Al-Ahram Institute set a date to meet me at the American University. Tahsin Basheer, the diplomat and advisor to the president, would come to my hotel for lunch.

Tabark and her children came to the hotel for dinner. I discussed political issues with the mother and her daughter. The daughter Sonya was very intelligent and went to a school run by nuns. The following is a selection of her expressed views:

"In Israel there are extreme doves, extreme hawks and dove-hawks; I prefer the third group, because the pure doves are too soft. The best way to proceed politically is the Sadat-Begin way. You may not like what I am going to tell you, but I believe that you should know the facts. In Egypt too there are three groups. The first group supports peace, but wants to cut down the size of Israel; the second one too believes in peace, because it believes that Israel will eventually dissolve; while the third one wants another war. I admire Geula Cohen, mainly because she had the courage to stand up in the Knesset and object to Begin's policies. In Egypt every member of parliament always applauds the rais (the president)"

At the end of the evening she said that the ones who wanted a war were mainly the "Arabs", but there were not many Egyptians in that group. By and large the Egyptians were not very sophisticated, and they easily changed their minds between wanting peace or war. When I said that this worried us, she answered, "If all will go smoothly, there would be no need to change. The people are interested in peace." In the beginning of the evening Tabark asked why we did not want to live in one state for the Jews and the Palestinian Arabs. They admired Begin, had respect for Dayan. Tabark then told me that Tahsin Basheer, the very intelligent diplomat, once came to Urbana and lectured there. He was apparently the representative of the Arab League, whom I confronted when he forbad the Arab students to talk to the Israeli ones. Tabark recommended to me to meet with him.

I decided to write down a few political observations already at this early stage of my visit, and see if and how they would change at the end of my visit:

Until now I have not heard one good word about the Palestinians, or even a criticism of Israel for not solving the problem. When the Palestinian problem was raised, it was mostly done by me. Scientific relations or relations in general with the gulf countries are taken for granted, and they practically continue in spite of the breaking of official relations. Contrary to my expectations I have not found any inferiority feelings vis-à-vis Israel, and there is a good reason for that; although the poverty and dirt are more pronounced than in Israel, the people, by and large, look very smart. In spite of all the wars, the image of the Israeli here is identical to the image they have of the Jews in Egypt, namely, that of a rich merchant. It will be interesting to see how they will be impressed by the average Israeli in his country when they visit Israel. (My friend Judah Eisenberg told me later that they would be shocked). In summary: at the moment I would say that the average Egyptian seems wiser or smarter than the average Israeli, perhaps more mature; while in my eyes, the Israeli is faster or more dynamic.

Rivka. I went on a Paltours tour of the pyramids of Memphis, Sakara, and Giza. The following day I took the tour to Hassan Mosque, and Avivi joined us. The guide advised us to photograph the Citadel from the Mosque, since this was the only place from which it was allowed to do so, because the Citadel was a military zone. We then visited the famous Museum of Cairo, in the center of the city. Like many other public places, it is run down and dirty. We got explanations, but were left with the feeling of "more". We saw the mummies, and said hello to "our" pharaoh, Menephtah, although some experts said that Ramses was our pharaoh.

Avivi adds: The Egyptian guide was a husky fellow with a moustache. Rivka told me that in the first day he was both hostile and embarrassed, and did not say a word to her. In the second day he was cool to me too. However, throughout the tour we felt that he was devoting more time to us in his explanations than to the others in the group. He tried to show us special things such as the Star of David in the center of the dome in the Mohamed-Ali Mosque. At the end of the tour it was he who asked me to take a photo of him and Rivka. When we parted we wanted to give him a tip, but he refused to take money from us, since now we were at peace. I tried to tell him that accepting the tip would be a sign of normal relations, but he did not understand what I was saying or did not want to understand. He hugged me with tears in his eyes and said that we were his guests, and said that I would honor him by agreeing to him not taking the money. His warming toward us appeared natural, and I guessed that our respectful and friendly attitude toward him was one of the reasons for that. As a response to my question he said that he respected General Ezer Weizmann more than all other Israeli leaders.

Rivka: We had breakfast in our hotel room with Ralph Alberg, who had returned last night from a visit to Alexandria. He found the city run down and dirty. The place had changed so much that he had to go through the street several times to find the house which had belonged to his family. The villa where he had lived became a dirty house with several rented apartments. After breakfast, Avivi left for the American University and Ein-Shams University.

The tour today was to the so-called Oasis of Fayum, a tourist town on the way to Alexandria. The road was rough, and there were old wrecked cars on its sides. One episode is perhaps worth describing. The only thing a tourist could really buy there were baskets made of hand-woven raffia. They asked for 3 lira for a basket, but could be bargained down to half a lira. A young British couple appeared, carrying a large pile of baskets to our bus, and laughing. They bought a basket and gave the vendor a large note. He did not have change, so he gave them all the baskets as the change.

I came back to the hotel in early afternoon, dirty and looking forward to a well needed shower. On my way to my room I knocked on Alberg's door, and when he opened it I could see two young Egyptians behind him. They said that they were young faculty members from the Physics Department of Cairo University, and that they came to see Dr. Yavin. I invited the three of them to my room, and ordered Coca Cola for all of us. We talked about various aspects of peace between our countries. One of them, Dr. Sheriff, who looked tougher, said that in Egypt people thought that Prime-Minister Begin was too tough. He then asked if Jews from Arab countries suffered discrimination in Israel. I said that officially there was no discrimination, but there are problems caused by the difference in background, education, culture, and customs. I said that we were constantly looking for solutions, but integration was a long process. I then added that our situation was similar to that of Cairo into which many people from the country were continuously flowing. His younger friend said that I explained these matters very well. Sheriff then asked about our marriage customs, particularly about financial arrangements before the wedding. He asked if Jewish parents would agree to their children marrying Arabs. I did not have to answer, since the telephone rang. It was Avivi on the line. I asked him to come quickly to the hotel.

Avivi: Yesterday I felt that I was perhaps starting to understand Egypt and to see the way to scientific cooperation. At 10:00 I came to the office of Dr. Saad Eddin Ibrahim at the American University. It was Herbert Kelman from Harvard who had advised me to see him; "it will be good for him", was the way Kelman had put it. The discussion took place in the office of the department head, an American who had spent two years in the oil countries and now eight years in Cairo. I gave Ibrahim copies of papers that had been submitted to our conference. He said that they would be interested in translating them into three languages, and to publish them as one of their publications, simultaneously with us; "but not together", he added. He said the same about the talk by Abba Eban. He promised to send some of their material to my hotel; I doubted that he would do so. He told me that 80% of the people in Al-Ahram Institute were against Sadat, not so much because of his intentions but because of the way he was going, distancing Egypt from the Arab World. Also, some leftists object to Sadat's attempts to get closer to the US. He was doubtful about the likelihood of collaborations. I gave him the phone number of my room in the hotel, hoping that he or his university president, Peterson, would call me, but doubted that it would happen. Some nagging questions started to bother me: Was Al-Ahram the right institute to work with? Was it possible that we were just wasting time and efforts on them?

I traveled next with Tabark to Ein-Shams University. Six people were in the room of the Department Head, Professor F.A. El-Bedewi. He introduced them all to us. They did not shake my hand, and turned their heads away, not saying a word to me. Not a very warm welcome. They continued with their discussion in Arabic for a long time, while we were seated in their midst. One of them asked me quietly what my field of physics was. Five of them left after 30 minutes, while one woman stayed, arguing angrily with the Department Head. Tabark explained to me later that the woman had just returned from teaching in Saudi Arabia, but her husband stayed there. She wanted to go back, but the Head refused her request.

When the woman left El-Bedewi ordered coffee and started talking about Pugwash meetings and about Shalhevet Fryer, one of the Israelis there, who had talked about Israel's security, contrary to the previous agreement. I suggested to talk about physics, but he insisted that the scientists' role at that time was to help Sadat, and that collaborations would come afterwards. He also insisted that all the Arabs wanted peace, and we could count on that. A strange statement, indeed. He did not pay much attention to the possible optimistic future which I described to him, and the meeting ended with him saying that it was important that people like me would take part in the next Pugwash meeting. I did not tell him that I had tried to do so, but the Israeli representatives rejected my candidacy, most likely because I was not part of the Israeli establishment.

When we left Tabark asked me if I was disappointed. I said that I was, and asked her to explain what had happened. She started her interesting explanations by telling me that one of the six participants had been a teacher of hers. He had told her quietly that he would be interested in working in Israel, but at present it was not possible. She said that unlike El-Nadi who was only interested in physics and was open and secure, El-Bedewi was involved in politics, and at that time was trying to please the establishment. The students in the universities were one of the main centers of opposition to Sadat. Still, most of them wanted peace, but were afraid of what might happen after Sadat. The import of physics books and scientific equipment had stopped seven years earlier. All the money was used to buy food and weapons. She emphasized again that there was pressure from below of most scientists, who wanted peace and cooperation with Israel, but they worried about their personal safety. "Are you not afraid because of my visit and talks with you?" I asked. "No" she answered, "because you were my former advisor in the US". I then asked her if there was any difference in views and behavior between scientists and intellectuals, and she said that in her opinion there was no difference. She added that the Egyptian scientists and intellectuals did not have a problem traveling to and working in the oil countries in spite of the peace with Israel.

On our way home I asked her again if she would want to work with us, for instance in Switzerland. She said that she would, but she would first have to stay and work in Egypt for a while because of her recent trip to Moscow. She said that my suggestion appealed to her, because in Egypt she would have only three unattractive options: Research with old equipment, teaching, or traveling to the oil countries to make money. There was no chance, she said, to do advanced research in Egypt. Finally she stressed that whatever she or any other nuclear physicist plan to do needs the approval of El-Nadi.

In her home she felt more at ease and told me the following bizarre story: When she came to her lab in the Atomic Energy Establishment and told her friends about my visit, they were all astounded. They listened to her attentively, but no one wanted to speak. She knew that they all were interested in meeting me, and later some of them actually told her so. I said that I was interested in a frank and open discussion on all topics with professors and students, clearly with the knowledge of El-Nadi. She said that she would try to have a meeting in her home on Saturday evening. When she heard that I was scheduled to leave on Sunday she was very disappointed.

Since there still was no formal Israeli representation in Cairo, I decided that the American scientific attaché would be the closest one to an Israeli representative at that time. I therefore took a cab to the American Embassy. It turned out that Addison Richmond, the attaché, had in the past been one of the five American directors of the Israel-American Bi-National Fund. He was very friendly, and asked me what he could do for me. I told him that Ibrahim Badran, the president of Cairo University, did not seem to be interested in meeting with me. He said that he was surprised to hear that, and would speak to his friend Badran, trying to arrange a meeting with me and possibly also with my university president, Ben-Shahar. He also offered to help me meet other Egyptian scientists. I excused myself and called my hotel room, and

Rivka told me to come quickly to meet with two Egyptian scientists in our room, Dr. Sheriff whom I had met in El-Nadi's office, and Dr. Mohamed Abdel Harith. I then rushed to the hotel.

In the hotel, Abdel Harith told me that he had worked both in Egypt and in East Germany in low energy inelastic scattering of protons and neutrons, and was chosen by El-Nadi to cooperate with us in research. I was surprised because El-Nadi had mentioned another name, Osman, and wondered whether he had already assigned two people for the collaborations. When Abdel Harith heard that we were talking about collaborations in Los Alamos, Vancouver, and Switzerland, he could not hold his excitement. Like Tabark he said that he would need travel and living expenses, and said that he would be ready to leave already in November, hopefully for a long stay, and would like to take his wife and young daughter with him. He emphasized that El-Nadi was the one who would make the final decision about candidates. He then offered to take Rivka and me to visit the children village.

As they were leaving I had another visitor waiting by the door, Professor Ahmed Osman. After introducing himself, he said that he had been in favor of collaboration with us for a long time, and that he was applying pressure in this respect on his friend, Professor Hamdi, who was being sent to As-Siyut University to suppress the student uprising there. He told me that the Muslim Brothers at the University had sent President Sadat a tough letter, and Sadat in turn cancelled the elected student council and appointed 5 students and 7 professors in their place. He added that Dr. Sheriff was the leader of the Muslim Brothers in Cairo University and that Abdel Harith too belonged to them. He added that Sheriff was an extremist who wanted to separate the women from the men in class. He claimed that the Muslim Brothers opposed Sadat's actions only with respect to Jerusalem. When I asked him how come Muslim Brothers wanted to cooperate with us, he said that science was a special issue, and stressed again that the Muslim Brothers were not against peace. He too repeated the statement that they all would do what Professor Mohamed El-Nadi would say. This barrage of statements was hard to swallow, but I kept listening very politely. He then talked mainly about himself, and this in brief is what he said:

He was interested in having Professor Judah Eisenberg from Tel Aviv University and Professor Avraham Gal from the Hebrew University come to visit him, each for two weeks. He would also prepare a plan for a scientific conference in Cairo, soon after the normalization of relations between our two countries. Almost everybody there was for peace and cooperation, but they were afraid. The coming summer was expected to be politically hot following the opening of the universities. He spent his life till then as a bachelor in several countries, about two years in Hungary, four years in Kuwait, and so on. He, like many other Egyptians, did not see himself as an Arab, and had contempt for them. The Arabs, in their traditional clothes, were sitting and drinking all day long in the lobbies of the big hotels. He was glad that their number had recently diminished somewhat. He intended to travel to Frankfurt for a year or two to the laboratory of Professor Greiner. He also wished to spend some of that time in Tel Aviv University.

When we told him that we had to leave at 22:30 from El-Bourg Hotel, he sounded disappointed, since he intended to take us to the club in the Sheraton, where the best Egyptian belly dancer appeared every night, and added that Henry Kissinger had wanted very much to see her."

Osman said that he lived in an apartment whose area is 150 meter square, and paid 24 liras per month, out of a monthly salary of 120 liras. In Kuwait he earned twenty times that salary. In summary, he was very warm and hospitable, perhaps too warm. I told Rivka that I wondered whether there was another reason for that apart from hospitality.

I decided to write at this point some of my initial thoughts about my mission, and this is what I wrote: It is perhaps advisable, for the immediate future, to cool down our efforts (particularly those of the Shiloah Institute) with Al-Ahram, and perhaps also with the whole group of these intellectuals. The probability for collaborations with them is very low at the moment, so we should not waste our time and efforts on them. (I was also told by an Israeli reporter in Cairo that the Egyptians thought that the Shiloah Institute was an agent of Israeli intelligence). It is not advisable to apply pressure on presidents of universities and on academic administrators; instead, we should concentrate our efforts on developing plans for collaborations with a selected group of scientists. It is advisable to start the collaborations abroad, and move them to Israel and Egypt if and when they are successful.

I went again to see Addison Richmond in the US Embassy. He told me that Hassan Ismail, the former minister of science and the head of the national academy, had told him that it was too early for him to meet with me, because he was part of the establishment. We went to see the representative of the USAID. He had a low opinion of the Egyptians, and said that Egypt was a third class country, and that the people were eager to get help from the US, but they were very inefficient.

Christine Monroe, whom we visited next, was dealing with the economic and financial matters in the Embassy. She started by saying that people from the Al-Ahram Institute had told her in June that they were still in doubt whether to collaborate with us through the Brookings Institute. They would soon publish a book in Arabic and English, whose title would be Military and Economic Consequences of Peace. The first part would deal with military aspects, the second part with the relations of Egypt with the Arab World after the peace with Israel, and the third one will deal with the possibilities of collaboration with Israel. There they would concentrate on what is important for Egypt. In their opinion, agriculture in arid regions could be a plausible candidate.

Richmond and I then went to see William Roux, a senior person at the Embassy. He said that there was indeed hatred and contempt in some circles in Egypt toward the Palestinians and the Arabs, but the Egyptian people are rich in opinions and attitudes. He was more pessimistic than I in considering our chance for collaboration, and was therefore surprised to hear about my experience since my arrival in Egypt. Considering the Al-Ahram people, Roux said that most of the people there were put in the Institute because President Sadat did not want them to be a center of power, and hesitated to arrest them. They were an opposition which could one day control the government; however, if Sadat succeeded, they would join him.

I returned to the hotel to wait for Tahsin Basheer, who was supposed to be an intelligent diplomat. I waited a long time in my room for his phone call from the lobby or for a knock on the door, but there was no sign of him. After about an hour an envelope was pushed under my hotel door. It said the Bashir came a little late, rang my room several times, and when I did not respond he left. We checked and discovered that when one rang my room from the lobby, my room phone did not make any sound. I called Bashir's home and told him what had happened. His only reaction was, "Egyptian inefficiency!" He said that he had to leave immediately to go to Manchester, and we both expressed sorrow. Tabark later said that not meeting him was unfortunate, because he was the right man for me to meet.

Addison Richmond came to the hotel and apologized for not letting me see the Embassy doctor after I had cut my foot in Mohamed-Ali Mosque. He said that the doctor was only allowed to see the Embassy people or American citizens. However, he was happy to tell me that he found a solution for me. Together we went in his car to his friend, Dr. Kamil Kamel, who was a graduate of the University of Michigan, and therefore had a stock of medicines used in the USA. Dr. Kamel then gave me a booster shot against tetanus. Back in the hotel Richmond told me that he had arranged a meeting for me with Dr. Shaharabander, and promised to have a drink with me in a later day. His care and warmth impressed both Rivka and me.

In the Evening we went to Dinner at the Sheraton with Ahmed Osman who insisted on paying for the dinner. Then in the club we saw the belly dancer "preferred by Henry Kissinger". Back at the hotel I called Tabark, and she sadly told me that she had learned that it was too early to meet people from her lab at her home to talk about collaboration. There could have been a misunderstanding between us, since I had not meant to talk only about collaboration, but her story was another indication of the difficulties I was facing.

Avivi again (a couple of days later): Abdel Harith came yesterday morning to take Rivka and me to Cairo University to meet Professor Omar Badawi (El-Nadi was in Alexandria). On campus I took a couple of pictures of the famous clock, which I used to hear on Cairo radio. A student jumped on us from nowhere and said that taking pictures on campus was forbidden (apparently for security reasons). We visited the lecture halls in the physics building and found them run down. A young student who had just received his Ph.D. described the experiments he had done in Dubna, in the Soviet Union. It was clear that the Soviets let him use an old accelerator and very old measuring equipment, similar to the equipment I had used 25 years earlier in Seattle.

Together with Professor Omar Badawi we went down to see Dr. Samir Alam's mass spectrometer. Badawi told me on our way that he been active in the ruling party of Abd-El-Nasser, but El-Nadi convinced him to be involved only in science. He asked me to talk to my friend, Albert Messiah, the head of physics in the French Atomic Energy Establishment, and ask him to accept Egyptian researchers, chosen by El-Nadi, to work in Saclay. Dr. Alam showed me his mass spectrometer, which was used for the investigation of ionization and breaking down of molecules. Although the spectrometer was old, the results were beautiful.

In Badawi's office we agreed on the following actions, which we should pursue: Abdel Harith, who was apparently chosen by El-Nadi to be the first one in our collaboration, will join us in any laboratory abroad which we would choose. For that, El-Nadi would need a letter of invitation from that laboratory's director, in which Tel Aviv University would not be mentioned, and he would take the letter to their University management for approval. We then agreed on the details of the financial support for Abdel Harith from both Egypt and our group. I said that I accepted the nomination by El-Nadi of E-Harith, but asked him to tell El-Nadi that as her old teacher, I would like Tabark to be the second choice. If El-Nadi agreed, I would find the place and financial support for her. As for theorists, El-Nadi had a good young candidate to work with Judah Eisenberg; and he added that if Ahmed Osman wanted to collaborate with Eisenberg, El-Nadi would have to approve it.

Rivka and I left a CD of Yehoram Gaon in the library for Osman, thanking him for his hospitality, and inviting him to be our guest in Israel. When Abdel Harith heard about the agreement I made with Badawi he was very pleased, and I added that if he came to Vancouver, I might be able to find a job for his wife in radio-chemistry with John D'Auria.

In our room Rivka asked me if I did not feel offended by the request that our name should not be mentioned in the letter of invitation. I admitted that at first I was offended, but then I thought about it further, and decided that the one who should feel bad, if at all, was El-Nadi, and I admired his courage to go against the general attitude of the politicians in their academia. I then added that in spite all the difficulties, it appeared that I was on the right track of scientific relations, following El-Nadi's suggestions, with no politics involved, but with being sensitive to the difficulties of the Egyptian scientists. I felt that this was only the beginning, and as such, I should expect all kinds of obstacles, but if successful, it could be expanded.

Next I went to meet Professor Peterson, the president of the American University. He had no difficulty to meet with Israelis, and in fact wanted to meet President Ben-Shahar in Cairo or in Tel Aviv. Like Badawi before, he too said that when the Americans write to the Egyptians, they should not mention the Israeli counterpart. He suggested the following subjects as candidates for collaboration with his university: Desert research, Arabic, English, administration, and sociology. He added that they, in his university, were week in science, and suggested to us to collaborate with Egyptian academicians in medicine, since there were good doctors in the country. Finally, he offered the following personal advice: "Rather than sending your best scientist for collaboration, send the person with the right attitude." I later discovered how right he was.

Rivka and I went to visit Rashad, a Hebrew speaking official, working at the airport. He had met there Shimon Shamir, but was not working when we arrived. He and his family were very excited to meet us. He had told Shimon Shamir that he would be interested in continuing his studies at Tel Aviv University, so I told him that the dean of liberal arts at Tel Aviv University had asked for his diplomas to see if he could be admitted. Rivka and I worried that Rashad might face some difficulties in getting adjusted to studying at an Israeli university. I decided to recommend to the Peace Project to establish an absorption unit for arriving Egyptians, dealing with social absorption as well as the problems of language and housing.

Avivi continues: This morning I had two meetings at the American Embassy, arranged again by Addison Richmond. The first one was with Dr. Salah Shahabandar, the dean of the Egyptian national institute on cancer and an advisor to three ministries. His father was a Syrian prime minister who was murdered in 1940. He emphasized at the outset that our meeting was unofficial, because for official meetings we had to wait for the decision of the politicians, a statement I had heard many times in the last days. He told me that he was embarrassed each time he received an invitation from Israel, because he could not come or even respond in writing to these invitations. In his opinion medicine in Egypt was at a high level, and his institute, which dealt with research, teaching, and treatment of patients, was the biggest in the Middle East. When I told Richmond about my talk with Shahabandar he was a bit surprised, saying that Shahabandar was more formal than he had expected, perhaps because of his formal duties. Richmond then suggested that Professor Matot, the Israeli hematologist, should invite Dr. Namet Hashim, the physician of Sadat's children and a good friend of Mrs. Sadat, to visit Tel Aviv University.

A while later another man came in and was introduced to me as Hassan Hafez, the head of the department of wild animals in the zoological gardens, who used to be the director of the Cairo zoo. He said that he would be interested in having Professor Felix Mendelssohn from Tel Aviv University visit him, and was also very friendly and informal throughout the whole meeting. I was therefore curious to hear him make the following critical comment: Why can't Israelis be more sensitive to the customs of others? For instance, a group of Yohai Bin-Nun's institute, which included a woman, stayed together for several nights in the same tent, next to stunned Bedouins.

Avivi continues: Addison Richmond came and took us to his home for drinks. He and his Moroccan wife lived in a beautiful apartment facing the Nile. The daughters of Sadat lived in the same building. With a smile, he told us the following interesting story: President Sadat spoke to students, and at the end he told them, "I gave you democracy; now you should be good children and do what I tell you to do."

We traveled next to Tabark's home, where she gave us presents for our daughter Mimi. Together with her brother and his wife we traveled 15 kilometers southwardly to see the rich and beautiful residential district of Ma'adi. The brother was a retired colonel and a mechanical engineer. He was a very pleasant and intelligent man. (I imagined that he was one of the brothers who had been lost for a while in the Sinai during the Six-Day War). He said that he was a Muslim, and claimed that Cairo and El-Azhar were still the center of Islam. The Islam was a liberal religion, so he claimed, especially the real Islam and not that of Syria and Iran. Women in Egypt had equal rights with men; in fact. He answered all my questions, but did not seem interested in Israel; in fact, he never uttered the word Israel. He was unhappy when I inquired about the use of the term "Arabs", and said that in his opinion, the term also included Egyptians.

My talk with Tabark started a bit tense. She was unhappy when I told her that I would accept El-Nadi's recommendation to pick Abdel Harith, and not her, as the first collaborator. I reminded her that she had emphasized several times that El-Nadi was the one to make all decisions concerning nuclear physics. I added that we were only in the beginning of the hard route toward cooperation, and although I listened to all requests, I had to accept El-Nadi's decisions, that even she had said that I should. When I told her that I had told El-Nadi that I had a commitment to her as a former student of mine, she calmed a little down. She then admitted that in Urbana Illinois she had known that I was Israeli when she had applied in 1967 for a job at the cyclotron, but she had hoped that the subject would not be brought up.

In the following morning I came to Richmond's office to meet Dr. Mahmud

Bahram, the manager of the consulting office Alsabash, who used to be the director of the oil institute. Richmond opened the meeting, which turned out to be long and very interesting, with a critical remark. He said that it was not wise to have shown Sadat the tomograph in his visit to Haifa, because this was a very expensive piece of equipment. I said that the reason for that was perhaps to convince the Egyptians that together we could sell it to the developed countries including the USA. On his part, Bahram mentioned the advantage of cooperation between Israel and Egypt, since Egypt had human wealth and Israel had great strength in technology and world financial markets. I pointed out the social danger of plants where the managers and engineers were Israelis and the blue-color workers Egyptians. He said that this did not worry him, and that Egypt needed very badly industry which used a lot of manpower. He suggested energy as the best field for cooperation. He knew that Israel was very advanced in solar-energy research, and said that in Egypt there were two committees looking at energy sources, one for solar energy and the other for renewable resources. He added that their expectations of help from Israel were small, but from the US they were huge. He himself wanted the US to act mainly as a catalyst. He recommended further the following subjects for cooperation: education, agriculture, medicine, and tourism. He was not afraid of Egyptian disappointment from the peace, and added that we should not wait for the official normalization. Specifically he recommended having a conference on energy or technology transfer, and holding half of it in Egypt and half in Israel. He himself wanted to be involved, and suggested that Richmond would appoint the Egyptian participants after getting the okay from Sadat. Richmond welcomed the idea, but said that he should not be the one who decided on Egyptian participation. It appeared that Bahram was intelligent and knowledgeable, free and effective, and apparently with influence. I was glad that the suggestions for cooperation were his, and did not come from me.

Before parting Richmond allowed himself to add two additional critical comments, this time directed at me. He first said that we should have selected a less political and less pretentious title for the international conference which we had held in June, whose title was: Toward Peace in the Middle East. I asked him if he meant that we should have talked about Israel and Egypt and not the Middle East, and he said that this was not what he had in mind. He thought that in considerations for the sensitive relations between Egypt and the Arab World, we should have used a technical not a political title. His second critical remark was that the preparations for the conference were only ours rather than 50% Egyptian and 50% Israeli. I then told him about our efforts to involve the Egyptians in the conference and about my offer to El Baz to give the Egyptians more than 50%, and added that all our efforts had failed.

Rivka: Dr. Abdel Harith took us to the S.O.S. children village for orphans, in the patronage of Mrs. Jihan Sadat. The place could be described as legendary. There were thirty clean houses in the village, surrounded by green grass, and in each house there was "a mother" and about nine children of all ages, who lived like a family. They anticipated some difficulty when a mother left, for instance for marriage. In order for the children not to experience a second (or a third) orphanhood, each house had "an aunt", who was prepared to replace the mother when she left. There were two nursery schools in the village, and the bigger kids were driven to a nearby school until the age of 14; then the boys would continue in a high school, while the girls would stay in the village until they got married or became "mothers" in the village. The village was supported by donations from abroad, and often a family from another country would adopt, or rather sponsor a kid for 10 dollars a month. In the children's files we saw pictures which they had drawn on peace, and pictures which they had received from 10-12 year old kids from Neveh Magen in Israel. Some of the Israeli drawn pictures showed guns and tanks shooting flowers.

The traffic in Cairo deserves a special description. The Egyptians are not aware of the existence of traffic laws, or do not care about them. A red light may sometimes mean stop, other times it means 'go", and nobody can tell you when it means what. Each driver should "feel" it, and a driver who stops at a red light when the "healthy sense" tells him to continue, will regret his stopping when the car behind him bumps into his car. The two systems, cars and traffic lights, coexist, independent of each other. In fact; there exist two more independent systems, that of the pedestrians crossing the streets, and that of the traffic police. There are no turning signals in the cars and no traffic lanes, and when a gap, even a small one, is formed, several cars would try to move in. The only aid the driver has is his horn, which when blown announced "I am here". For this reason almost all the drivers move with their hand constantly on the horn. Crossing a street is a work of art; still, very few pedestrians are hurt. Why? Only god and the Egyptians can tell you. Parking in Cairo is another unique phenomenon. The Egyptian driver will park in any open space, even if it is in a narrow alley or in the middle of the main street. There is almost no car in Cairo which is not scratched or dented, but there are few fatal accidents, mostly because the Egyptian drivers are very good. Making turns can be done from any place on the road, even if the driver is going, say, on the left of a broad one-way street, and wants to turn to the right. It is amazing that nobody gets nervous or screams. When the borders between Israel and Egypt will open, the trip by car to Cairo will be very inexpensive, but body and paint work afterwards will be more expensive than a flight, even through Athens. The solution for the Israeli driver will have to be the finding of parking lots outside Cairo, and coming in with busses. Busses in Cairo are another curious phenomenon. The density of people inside and outside most busses, with people hanging outside, is something to see in order to believe.

Avivi adds: The four independent or non-interacting traffic systems which Rivka describes – the traffic lights, the cars, the traffic police, and the pedestrians – remind me of a container with four noble gases, whose atoms do not interact with one another. I recall a case in which we wanted to cross a street by foot in a marked pedestrian crossing. We waited for the correct light (red for cars moving in the street we had to cross), and walked along with a policeman with a whistle. He whistled and lifted his hand to tell the cars to stop for us. No car stopped or even slowed down, but miraculously we were not hurt.

****

Following the advice of Richmond I went to the National Academy of Science to meet Professor Mohamed Abdel Hady, the head of the institute for remote sensing. He had received his Ph.D. in civil engineering from the University of Illinois in Urbana in 1963. He was a citizen of Egypt and of the United States, and had an appointment in the Egyptian Academy as well as in Oklahoma State University. Richmond told me that he was very influential in Egypt and had very good relations with the minister of education and science.

Abdel Hady was very friendly, and our relations warmed up more when we realized that our laboratories in Urbana had been next to each other. At the outset he expressed interest and readiness to exchange information and to collaborate with us as soon as possible. He told me that they were dealing in remote sensing for many practical reasons in various disciplines such as: fighting the desert, soil properties, reclamation of the soil, water under the surface of the land, natural resources, dynamics of various coasts, environmental pollution, and agriculture. The resolution of his equipment was 80 meters. He could also penetrate with his equipment 20 meters below the surface of the sea, a capability which is important for fishing. We decided to suggest to both President Sadat and Prime Minister Begin that remote sensing would be one of the first candidates for collaboration. He said that Sadat knew him and had even visited his laboratory accompanied by his wife. He said that he was interested in having a meeting soon in Cairo, in Tel Aviv, or in the United States, and suggested having the meeting attended by three Americans, three Israelis and three Egyptians, even before the expected normalization agreement. The purpose of such an early meeting would be to discuss the collaboration, which should start soon after the signing of a normalization agreement. He hoped that the American N.S.F. would support us financially. He expressed strong interest in getting our publications, and gave me a lot of written material. He was also interested in teaching students of ours in his laboratory.

He took me for a tour of his center, which included a modern computer, enabling him to see various areas in the world. He told me that he had received his modern equipment from the United States with the recommendation of President Sadat. The UN recognized his lab as a regional center for remote sensing. Finally, he told me of something that puzzled him. He showed me a photograph taken from the air. In the photograph I could see a clear line along the international border between Israel and the Sinai (the so-called Green Line). The line extended for 10-20 kilometers from the sea southwardly. He then told me that he had gone there with a jeep, and could not see any line on the ground, and asked me whether I knew the explanation for the puzzle. I did not know at that time, but promised that I would try to find the answer for him.

My last meetings convinced me that upon my return home I should meet with Prime Minister Begin in order to suggest to him to talk with President Sadat on the advisability of starting some pilot projects of collaboration even before normalization. Remote sensing appeared to be a good candidate for the following reasons: Abdel Hady had dual citizenships; he was known by both President Sadat and his minister of education and science; he was (apparently) a good scientist and was interested in collaborating with us. Moreover, his equipment was better than ours, so that in the collaboration with him the Egyptians would be more advanced than us, which was a rare case.

Avivi: Last night we packed our suitcases and went for the last tour of the city of Cairo. It was sad to leave, as we got attached to the city. In general, we were treated nicely whether or not they knew that we were Israelis. We found the Egyptians to be smart, warm, and non-aggressive. In spite of the heat and density of people in the streets, we hardly saw any aggression. We were treated properly in the hotel too. The only difficulty there was the low efficiency. For instance, every day we were promised to have a TV delivered to our room, but we had no television till we left. The same happened with the Herald Tribune. As a rule, the word "no" does not exist in Cairo; it is replaced by a promise, even if there is no intention to fulfill it. For instance, in the hotel dinner the waiter told us that for dessert we would get a pudding. We asked if we could get a fruit instead of pudding. He said 'yes", but brought us a pudding without offering any apology.

At the airport we passed security and passport checks, but our suitcases did not move on the carrousel. I got the message, and gave the TWA agent a tip, and the suitcases started to move. Similarly at the gate, the policeman with a bayoneted rifle did not let us in before we tipped him. I left with the feelings that I had learned a great deal about our chances for scientific cooperation, and basically knew how to proceed.

****

Avivi (in the plane to Athens): Now, when we have left the Egyptian territory, I will add a few words about security. We did not want to write on this subject while we were in Egypt, because we were not sure that our belongings were not searched, and that Big Brother there did not read our papers.

As for personal safety, we felt very safe throughout the whole visit. I believe that we were a bit negligent by not paying enough attention to our safety. For example, we took pictures every where, even in places like bridges, in which – a fact we learned afterwards – it was forbidden to take pictures. Also, we always identified ourselves as Israelis. In contrast, in the Taxi, Tabark did not identify us as Israelis, but just said that we were Jewish. The only two times in which I did not feel safe were when I took pictures at the University and when Ali and I were visiting the Hussein Mosque. All the Israelis were put on the same floor in the hotel, apparently for our own safety as well for the ease of watching us.

Some Egyptians we met brought up the security issue. For instance, Professor Ahmed Osman warned me that Professor Omar Badawi was working "outside physics", and was connected with security bodies. He said, "Badawi is not only the head of the experimental group, but also the head of the Muslim Brothers on campus, and gives orders to them and to people such as Dr. Sheriff." Osman's whole behavior was strange if not suspicious. Soon after he had heard the interest of Judah Eisenberg and Avraham Gal in talking to him, he appeared by our hotel door and invited us to dinner; the following day he invited us to a night club; and he insisted on paying in both places. There is a possibility that all this stemmed from his being very hospitable. Then, throughout the dinner and in the night club he kept saying that we were his guests for our whole visit (why?), and kept talking about cooperation and against the "Arabs". The following day he disappeared, and never called us although we had left him a record and several messages. This behavior can have many plausible, mainly personal explanations; it is also possible that he worked for a security (or intelligence) body, and obeyed their orders, as was hinted to me by El-Nadi.

It is curious that the following day Omar Badawi himself told me that he was in the ruling party (and not in the Muslim Brothers), and left all political activity on the advice of El-Nadi. I wonder: who lied to me? It appears that there is tension between Ahmed Osman and El-Nadi's group. I recall, in this respect, the tension, or competition, between Tabark and El-Nadi's group and the tough discussion at Ein Shams University between Professor El-Bedewi and the woman who wanted to go back to the oil country. These examples basically stem from a common cause; namely, the scientific suffocation which is felt by the young scientists in Egypt and their healthy desire to go out to the scientific world, causing them to compete strongly with one another on any offer from the outside. This observation taught me one lesson: There could be many candidates for collaboration with us among the young scientists, but I should be very careful not to find myself involved in internal struggles.

The Rashad story is also curious. He met Professor Shamir at the airport when Shamir arrived for the meeting at the Al-Ahram Institute. Is there a security reason for him, a man who talks Hebrew fluently, to work at the airport, or just a touristic reason? In his home he told me that he had been interrogated by security people who had asked him why he had always brought Israeli tourists to the Shepherd Hotel. Then he added that nevertheless he was not afraid. He took us in a cab back to our hotel, but asked us to get out of the cab one block away, not to be seen by security people, so he said. When we parted, he promised to bring me his diplomas to the hotel, and that we would meet again in the hotel or at the airport, but we never did. Why? Is it possible that our visit in his home hurt him in his job? As it happened with Osman, it was he, not I, who raised the security issue. Was it done in order to gain our trust? Is it possible that both he and Osman wanted to hear my reaction? Or is it possible that I am unnecessarily suspicious, and they both told me the truth? I don't have answers to these questions.

It is interesting that Tabark asked me not to call her home from Tel Aviv before the start of the normalization, and that her friends in the lab were afraid to meet me (or were ordered not to do so). Soon after we had arrived in Cairo I asked Tabark if I could visit those parts of her lab that visitors could visit in order to see what she was working on. A few days later she informed me that the lab was closed for visitors. Professor Badawi, on the other hand, said that he could take me there, but it would take him a month to get the permit. Remote sensing too has security aspects, but Professor Abdel Hady did not mention them, as expected. All the above are only thoughts, wonders, and questions, but there is no doubt that the security issue added interest and tension to our visit.

In Athens we learned that our troubles were not over. One of our suitcases was missing. Two weeks later, when it did not come to my home in Tel Aviv, I understood that it might have been confiscated by security at the Cairo Airport. They might have seen the scientific papers, which were given to me by the people I had met, looked through them without understanding, and decided to confiscate them along with the suitcase. Many of the items which we bought in Cairo were in the "lost" suitcase. I was sorry mainly for losing the copy of Tabark's Ph.D. thesis, which had a personal dedication to me.

****

Back in my office I decided to look back at our visit to Egypt and draw some conclusions, mainly on what to do and what not to do. The main purpose of my visit was to investigate the various aspects of cooperation with Egyptians scientists and academicians; specifically to identify the fields which looked most promising for cooperation, and the best ways to achieve these goals. Other considerations were related to timing, i.e. when to start collaborations and in what order. My intention had been to come as a tourist, to keep my eyes and ears open, and to make acquaintance and form ties, mainly with scientists and engineers; and not necessarily with newspaper men and politicians, who had been met by most Israeli visitors before me. I carried with me a number of questions, some of which got their final shape only during the visit. The following were the questions:
- Do the Egyptians want peace, and what do they mean by peace?
- In general, are the Egyptian intellectuals against the peace with us?
- Is there a difference in attitude between the scientists and the intellectuals

with regard to cooperation with Israel?
- Is the Al-Ahram Institute a good candidate for planning the peace?
- Is there a difference in attitude between the scientific administration and the individual scientist?
- Is it possible and desirable to agree on or even start collaboration in nuclear physics before the start of normalization? If so, how to do so?
- Who are the other (non-scientific) immediate candidates for collaborations?
- Are there inferiority or superiority feelings in Egypt vis-à-vis Israel, and if so, where and for what reasons?
- What do the Egyptians expect to get from the cooperation with Israelis, and in which fields?
- In case of disappointment, who will get the blame?
- In general, how does the Egyptian in the street and in academia view the Israelis?
- What is the feeling of the Egyptians toward the Palestinians?
- How has the Arab boycott affected Egypt?

In all my meetings I tried to get answers, even partial ones, to these 13 questions. I was especially pleased when the Egyptians volunteered their answers without me asking the questions. Whenever I received an answer, I checked it with others, and was greatly helped in this and other matters by the American scientific attaché, Addison Richmond. Tabark and her family too were of great help to me in this analysis. I did not meet any Egyptian politician; Boutros Ghali was in Cuba during my visit and Tahsin Basheer came to my hotel, but somehow did not reach me, as I explained above. Several fields appeared to be good candidates for early cooperation: experimental and theoretical nuclear physics, mass spectroscopy, cardiology, remote sensing, agriculture, and wild animals:

I had reached several decisions as to what I and the Peace Project should and should not do; some of them were the following:
Not to apply pressure on the academic and scientific administrations; they have instructions from above to say "no", at least until the beginning of the normalization.
Whereas there is more inclination to collaborate with us among natural scientists (including also physicians, agricultural scientists, etc), I should not stop trying in a later time in the humanistic disciplines, but not through the Al-Ahram Institute. To establish the necessary infrastructure for sending professors and students to Egypt and for accepting their counterparts at Tel Aviv University.

Most importantly, in my various talks with Egyptian scientists, including students and young professors, I discovered a new dimension, which was either not known to us, or at least not emphasized enough. We had always talked about pressure in Egypt *from above* against cooperation with us. The scientific and academic administrators (university presidents, deans, and heads of departments) pressed their professors largely because the government applied its pressure on them to wait, at least until the start of normalization; while the religious and political leaders (especially the Nasserites and the Muslim Brothers) were against any cooperation with us at any time. The new thing I learned in my visit was that there is another pressure in Egypt, this one *from below*. This is the pressure from scientists who want to break out of the scientific strangulation of not buying books and modern equipment, and working in old-fashioned laboratories in Eastern Europe and in the Arab countries. The possibility of breaking into the modern scientific world attracts them, and we could be the doorway for that if we acted properly. This hitherto unknown fact could become a pressure on the scientific administration in Egypt to allow cooperation with us at an early stage. This fact had not received much attention in Israel, and this was why the possibilities (and dangers) imbedded in it had not been investigated.

Scientists deal with facts, but like other people they sometimes dream too. I wish to add a question that I asked myself while sitting in my office in Tel Aviv and thinking about my first visit to Egypt: *My visit might introduce new dimensions and new emphases to the work of the Peace Project. There is some hope that we might soon enter a new era of active cooperation with Egyptian scientists. And I wonder: Will my next visit be to Cairo, Bir Zeit, Amman, Damascus, or Riyadh?*

CHAPTER 5.
SUBSEQUENT ACTIVITIES

I reported my findings to the University leaders and to the Peace Project. Many bodies outside the University asked me to tell them about my visit and impressions. The reason for the great interest was that very few people had visited Egypt before, and those who had done so had not reported their impressions to the public. Also, mine was the first visit of an Israeli scientist in various scientific institutes in Egypt, attempting to form scientific cooperation. I gave my written report to Defense Secretary Ezer Weizmann, who was one of the architects of the peace agreement. I hesitated in presenting my reports to bodies outside the University for fear of premature publicity, because I had promised the Egyptians hosts that our talks would not be publicized unless we agree to do so. The reason for the sensitivity in premature publicity, even just the fact that the talks had taken place was the Egyptian fear that it might hurt them in their country as well as in the other Arab countries in which they used to work. I kept my promises and have not publicized these talks now for thirty years. In my various appearances in Israel I used to omit names, and asked the audience not to publicize my stories. I am pleased that I have never heard any complaint from the Egyptians about this issue, although I have heard many complaints about extensive publicity by other Israelis who visited Egypt.

The Field School in Santa Katharina. I got involved in this issue because of national reasons; similar to the reasons for my getting involved in the question of the National Authority for Economic Planning. I did not do it as a director of the Peace Project, because I myself was not sure that the Project should be involved.

The Field School in Santa Katharina, called Tzukei David (David's Rocks) after the dead son of Minister Shmuel Tamir, was a center of research and training activities, and was a base for desert tours. The Society for the Protection of Nature as well as scientists from the various Israeli universities used it extensively. Since the Sinai was going to be given back to the Egyptians, the various users looked for ways to keep some of their activities there. Since the place was going to be run by the Ismailia University, our scientists were looking for ways to cooperate with them, and actually held conferences with their Egyptian counterparts about this subject. I got involved when the director of the Society asked me if Tel Aviv University would be willing to take charge of the Israeli activities in the Field School. Professor Shimon Shamir's advice was not to accept the responsibility because of the great sensitivity of the Egyptians in all issues concerning Sinai. Retired general Abrasha Tamir too had reservations concerning the many plans that our people had for Santa Katharina. He claimed that our people had not yet fully understood that the Sinai was to be given back to the Egyptians.

A Campaign in Canada. When it became clear to the University President and Management that the peace issue was hot and that we had a good reputation in the US as well as in Egypt, I was asked to bring to the University president a suggestion as to how to use the peace issue in the University's campaigns. The reader may recall that some members of the Peace Project's Management saw money collection as the main goal of the Project, and even congratulated me for promoting such a good campaign tool. I later realized that this was one of the main reasons for the opposition in the Management to join forces with the Hebrew University. I have to admit that the congratulations offended me; helping the University financially was fine with me, but in my eyes, collecting money was definitely not one of the Project's main goals. Still, there was definitely nothing wrong in helping the University financially.

I described to the University president and rector how to use the Project's good record in the University's campaigns, and suggested to make the subject of peace the university's main campaign subject for that year. My suggestion was presented at a broad meeting of the University leadership, and all participants supported the idea except for Vice-President Sokolovski, who almost always opposed all my suggestions. He said that Professor Heimkeh Shaked had told him that the world was mocking us for becoming the "University of Peace". It is curious how the praise, which we received from the White House, the State Department, the American Academy of Science, as well as from distinguished universities such as Harvard and from senior scientists in Egypt, differed so much from Heimkeh's "learned opinion". I decided not to comment on Sokolovski's story, and so did the rest of the participants of the meeting. The Development and Public Affairs Division of the University welcomed my suggestions and decided that the University's activity in regards to peace would be the main emphasis of the planned campaign in Montreal, Canada. I soon realized that I was facing a Catch-22 situation. Campaigns which used our activity related to peace required some sort of publicity, while the success of the proposed collaborations with the Egyptians required discreetness at that time. Moreover, excessive discreetness might, at times, appear as fraternalism.

Remote Sensing. I continued my meetings with various faculty members, but I will not present their nature here unless they had meaningful consequences. Among the possible collaborations suggested in my visit to Egypt, the subject of remote sensing, along with nuclear physics, appeared to be the most promising candidates for an early start. Fifteen faculty members in the University were candidates for collaboration with the Egyptians in this field. According to Professor J. Joseph, they could be divided in two groups: those who were interested in the remote sensing technique, and those who were interested in using the technique in their research. Joseph volunteered to write a proposal to be submitted to the Egyptians. I discussed the matter with Rector Abarbanel, and he said that he worried that the Egyptians were interested in working with us on remote sensing in order to learn some of our security secrets. In his opinion, we should mostly be interested in this technique for crop detection and desertification, and least interested, for security reasons, in coastal studies and resource monitoring.

The following subjects for collaboration were proposed: Geology and oil, fields in which the Egyptians had expertise; ground survey; marine biology; and pasturage. As I had done before, I informed Dan Patir, an advisor to Prime Minister Menahem Begin, and later of Prime Minister Itzhak Rabin, on the interest here and in Egypt, and asked him to help us with Prime-Minister Begin in advancing the planned cooperation in remote sensing.

Dr. Mahmoud Badr. Dr. Badr was a professor in Cairo University, and used to be president of The Egyptian Urology Society. I met him in our rector's office where he said that he had heard about our Peace Project and wanted to talk to me about it. I invited him to my home, where we held a long, interesting, and friendly discussion. He told me that a year and a half before he had been invited to a medical conference in Israel, but his university president, Ibrahim Badran, had not allowed him to go. This time he got the permission from Badran to come, because some Israeli urologists

130

had talked to Sadat's wife, Jihan, about it.

I described to him our activities in the Peace Project and told him about my visit in Cairo. It turned out that we had common acquaintances: Dorri, Shahabandar, and Addison Richmond, who was a close friend of his. He spoke about the wish of most Egyptians to live in peace with Israel, and about the many ties that he had with Jews in Egypt and the United States. Together we watched the Arabic program on Israeli TV in which he was interviewed and said that many Egyptians, including several urologists, had told him that they would like to visit Israel. I suggested to him to tell his colleagues in Egypt about our Peace Project, and to suggest to them to get in touch with me, especially if they were interested in collaborations. He said that he would gladly do so. Dr. Cero Sarvadio, the urologist and general manager of Beilinson Hospital, together with his wife, joined us later in my home. Sarvadio told Badr about his suggestion to hold a conference on urology in March in Tel Aviv, with a possible continuation in April in Cairo.

A few days later, the Servadios held a cocktail party at their home to which they invited several people, mostly physicians. Dr. Badr told me there that following his appearance on Israeli TV he received several calls from old Israeli friends whom he had known a long time ago. He then suggested that we two would be liaisons for all things concerning medicine. He promised to prepare for me a list of medical people in Egypt who might be interested in collaborations, and suggested that the correspondence between us would be through Addison Richmond.

Nuclear Physics – Medium and High Energies. Since Professor El-Nadi and Professor Omar Badawi from Cairo University were interested in collaboration in nuclear physics, I started to look for foreign laboratories where this would be possible. Three European laboratories seemed to be good candidates. Dr. Fredie Friedman from the French CNRS, a collaborator of ours, who was working at Saclay in France and at CERN in Geneva, came to my office and said that he was in touch with Badawi, trying to help him get a position in one of the laboratories in which he was doing research. Also, Professor Gideon Alexander of Tel Aviv University invited Omar Badawi and me to join his group working in the big accelerator DESY in Hamburg.

I traveled to the national Swiss laboratory SIN near Zurich, where one of the three medium-energy proton accelerators (meson factories) was starting its operation. I spoke with Professor Blaser, the director of SIN. He said that he would be willing to write a letter to El-Nadi inviting a student of his to work at SIN, and added that he would start the letter by writing "At the request of Professor Yavin…" He then added that they would not be able to support that student financially. I called El-Nadi and Badawi and described to them all that I had done. They were very pleased and thanked me for that. El-Nadi added that he was considering sending a man younger than El-Harith, and suggested starting the first collaborative experiment at SIN in the summer. My next challenge was finding funds to support the Egyptian student, either in Tel Aviv University or elsewhere.

George Assousa. My secretary told me that she had received a strange inquiry about Assousa from Yossi Ben-Aharon from our Foreign Office. I talked to him over the phone, and he told me that in the Office he was in charge of everything concerning the PLO. He then said that he had heard from our Embassy in London that Assousa had met European businessmen in Europe, some of them Jewish, and had asked them to invest in the West Bank, for which – according to Assousa – the Saudis were establishing a 400-million dollars investment fund. He knew that Assousa had met many Israeli political leaders, and asked me if I knew what Assousa's motives were. I told him that I had no expertise in such matters, and asked him why the Foreign Office had not helped Assousa a year earlier when I had asked them to do so. He dodged the question by saying that it was generally known that the Foreign Office was not a serious office. It appeared that our government had been suspicious of Assousa for quite some time then, but I did not know if it was for security or political reasons.

I called Assousa and after hesitations he confirmed the information that had been given to me and said that the ball was in the Israeli hands. He added that he was trying to organize a seminar in central Europe, to which three Egyptians would come, and would also invite an Israeli leader. I informed him that there was progress concerning the request of the Palestinian cardiologist Dr. Shhada Hareb to give advanced training to some of his people in Ramallah in an Israeli hospital.

The interest on campus and outside in the activities of the Research Project on Peace and in contacting Egyptians through our Project was steadily growing at that time (the beginning of 1980). My office was always busy with visitors who came to report on their activities in Egypt or to ask for help in their plans concerning Egypt. I kept my word and never publicized the details of my own meetings in Egypt. I learned that the highly publicized and noisy visit of Yossef Tekoah, the president of Beer Sheva University, received negative reactions in Egypt, while the Hebrew University decided to freeze their activities until the official normalization takes place.

Ford Foundation. On November 22, 1979 my office received a call from two representatives of the Ford Foundation, who said that they had heard about us and wanted to talk to me. One of them was Ms. Ann Lesch, the Foundation's director for the Middle East, who had actually been to my office before on the recommendation of Steve Cohen. The other one was William C. Carmichael, the head of the regional office for the Middle East. They informed me that they had a fund of $500,000, and that up till then they had been supporting Bir-Zeit University in the West Bank, an Israeli foundation run by Danny Shimshoni, and the efforts of Joseph Peckman of the Brooking Institution to get three-way cooperation. Their support of Peckman was only in seed money until he got a grant from AID. I described to them our goals and activities, and Carmichael suggested that we ask for a grant for the Peace Project as a whole as well as for some specific research. He himself had the power to approve a grant of up to $25,000; but if we wanted to ask for a bigger grant, it had to receive the approval of their board. He then described to me the other foundations where we could ask for grants. They told me that they were very impressed by our plans, activities, and actions. I reported to Professor Ben-Shahar that I felt that we would get support from the Ford Foundation of at least $25,000.

A week later I wrote a letter to Carmichael including two alternative requests for aid from the Ford Foundation, one for $25,000 and a more expanded request for $50,000. The requests were for support of mutual visits between Egyptians and Israeli scientists, of small collaborative projects, and for efforts to get larger grants from governments as well as larger foundations. The following is a part of my letter:

As you know, many members of the nine faculties of Tel Aviv University participate in the activities of the Research Project on Peace, which is perhaps a unique experience in academia. Two of the major factors that contributed to this response were the shock that Israel experienced during the 1973 war and the shock of Sadat's visit to Jerusalem in 1977. The latter event presented a unique challenge to our faculty, which was totally unprepared for a peace initiative, and induced me, a nuclear physicist, to devote the greater part of the last two years to the establishment of the Research Project on Peace.

I added to my letter a document, which I called Promoting Academic Regional Cooperation (See Appendix IV). In this document I described in detail the activities of the Peace Project in the country, in Egypt, and in the United states, and ended it with the following section:

Although phase II, that of establishing academic cooperation with Egyptian scholars and institutions, has not yet officially begun, the Research Project on Peace is already preparing itself for the next phase, that of cooperation with other Arab academics. In the last year we have established some contacts with professors and administrators of the three major colleges in the West Bank. Due to the sensitivity of the parties involved and the political inequality between them, conditions that are not conducive to the establishment of normal academic relations, we have been very cautious in pursuing these contacts. Yet, the heads of the West- Bank universities are aware of our interest in developing normal academic relations with their institutions, and we expect that progress in establishing such relations will continue. Relations with academics in other Arab countries are more problematic than relations with Egyptian academics, and will most likely have to await progress in the political arena. Unfortunately, the scholars of the region have not learned from the American-Russian experience, which demonstrated that academic détente can, and perhaps should precede political détente. Still, the Research Project on Peace is preparing itself for wider academic regional cooperation, utilizing the experience acquired in the Israeli-Egyptian case.

I included in my letter the following list of the twenty five research initiatives which had by then been approved by our research committee. (The approval of the ones marked with * was conditional on the participation of an Arab partner):

- Possible and Desired Border Adjustments in the "Green Line" in Judea and Samaria – Geographical Aspects, by M. Braver (Department of Geography).
- Spatial Alternatives in the Planning of the Autonomy in Judea and Samaria, by E. Efrat (Department of Geography).
- The Perils of Peace: Domestic Influences on Israel's Security Policies in the Transition from War, by Z. Gitelman (visiting from U. of Michigan).

- The Role of Multinational Corporations in Promoting Economic Cooperation in the Middle East, by S. Hirsch and T. Agmon (Faculty of Management).
- Trade Relations between Israel and Egypt, by S. Hirsh (Faculty of Management).
- Reciprocal Legal Relations between Israel and Egypt, by A. Shapira (Faculty of Law).
- A Survey of Animals and Plants in the Negev (Towards the IDF Withdrawal from the Sinai and the Establishment of New Settlements in the Negev), by H. Mendelssohn (Faculty of Live Sciences).
- The Palestinian Issue: Electoral Behavior, Coalitional Aspects, and Probable Tendencies in Its Operational Environment, by S. Mishal (Department of Political Science).
- Israel as a Regional Financial Center? By Y. Orgler (Faculty of Management).
- Institutes of Higher Education and Scientific Research in Egypt, by E. Rekhess (the Shiloah Center).
- Einstein – Peace and Israel, by G.E. Tauber (Department of Physics).
- Intermediaries and Arab-Israeli Relations – Past and Future, by S. Touval (Department of Political Science).
- The El-Amarna Tablets in the Cairo Museum, by A.F. Rainey (Department of Archaeology).
- Archaeological Dig at the Qal'at Al Nakhi – the Main Station in the Road to Mecca (Hadj) in the Sinai, by S. Tamari (Faculty of Arts) *.
- Study of Host Defense Mechanism against Schistosoma Mensoni (Bilharzias), by M. Aronson and J. Lengy (Faculty of Medicine) *.
- Study of Dust Storms and Deposited Surface Features from Satellite Imagery and from the Ground, by J. Otterman (Department of Geophysics) *.
- Cooperative Studies of LANDSAT Imagery, by J.H. Joseph et al (Department of Geophysics) *.
- The Bedouin Society in Southern Sinai, by E. Marx (Departments of Sociology and Anthropology) *.
- A Seismic Study of the Earth Skin and Outer Layer in Southern Red Sea, by A. Ginzburg (Department of Geophysics) *.
- Archaeological Excavation of Ancient Sites in the Delta, by R. Giveon (Department of Archaeology) *.
- Marine Natural Products of Desert Plants – Potentially Active Constituents, by Y. Kashman (Department of Chemistry) *.
- Religious Courts in Peace Time in Israel, in the Territories, and in the

Arab Countries, by A. Kirshenbaum (Faculty of Law).

- Productivity of Desert Ruminants: Water Economy, Food Utilization, and Nitrogen Metabolism, by A. Shkolnik (Department of Zoology) *.
- Study of Pion Scattering and Absorption Reactions, by D. Ashery (Department of Physics) *.
- Tolerance and Intolerance in Israel – Its Scope, Target Groups, and Sources, by M. Shamir (Department of Political Science) *.

Following an exchange of letters with Carmichael, and as a result of my second visit to Egypt, which is described in the following chapter, we were notified by the Ford Foundation that we were granted a fund of $35,000 for three purposes: Financing one research project in my supervision, seed money for the encouragement of other fields of cooperation, and travel money and administration. In a telephone conversation, Ann Lesch stressed that they had approved the grant to me, because they trusted me personally.

CHAPTER 6.
THINK-TANKS

I have always been of the opinion that a university has more duties to the society than just teaching and research, and that the most important among them is independent thinking and independent checking of consensuses. This is true for any field, especially the security, the political, and the social ones.[1] I therefore believed that the Peace Project should look into this task of independent thinking and checking of the public opinion or consensus with regard to peace, especially since the Israeli society failed so badly in preparation for peace with Egypt. I felt that we should learn from that failure about future challenges.

Soon after the establishment of the Peace Project we held preliminary discussions on the need to form a variety of think tanks. Up until that time we had basically worked in the Project from below; namely, discussed and supported the suggestions and work of individual researchers. The main goal of the think tanks would be to add "thinking from above"; namely, to initiate the investigation of topics, which we thought, were important to the country and the society.

In December 1979 I offered Professor Yakir Aharonov the responsibility for the formation of think tanks and their functioning as part of the activities of the Peace Project. Professor of physics Yakir Aharonov was known as a deep and original thinker (and later became the first Israeli to receive the prestigious Wolf Prize, and a serious candidate for the Nobel Award). He had already done some voluntary work with Professor Horn on solutions of vari-

---

1 *Among the early think tanks at Tel Aviv University on specific interdisciplinary subjects I will mention the following: In 1970 President Yuval Ne'eman asked a group of us to look into the contribution the faculty could make to security. I broadened it to include all fields. In 1973 I proposed to the Senate of the University to appoint a think tank whose task would be to study how to prepare the University and the nation for a possible mass aliya (immigration) from the Soviet Union. In 1978 Vice-president Sokolovski appointed the Yariv Committee, following Sadat's declaration of "no more war". The workshop on the national authority for economic planning was another example of such a think tank.*

ous tough security problems, which required critical and creative thinking.

We agreed on a list of six candidates for topics for our think tanks, which seemed appropriate, because they had the following characteristics: Each topic was important, insufficiently investigated by independent bodies, and was such that we could deal with it:

Possible scenarios for the development of cooperation between Israel and Egypt.
Consolidation of the peace with Egypt.
Formation of academic ties with Egypt.
The Palestinian problem and/or the relations between Israel and the Autonomy.
Peace with Egypt, and what next?
 Social, psychological, and educational repercussions of peace on Israel.

We agreed further that faculty members and students would be invited to participate in the think tanks as well as outside experts or rather free thinkers. It would be advisable to add Egyptians, and in any case, to send the information to Egypt with the hope that the Egyptians would form similar think tanks. We thought that the end result of a think tank could be specific recommendations; one of them could be the suggestion to form other think tanks. We realized that some work had already been done in various university bodies, such as the Center for Strategic Studies, and the result of such work could be used as an input to the think tanks that we would form.

The first meetings of the people we selected for the think tanks were held in my home in the first weeks of January 1980. The following people took part in some or all the meetings of the group: The professors Yakir Aharonov, Yair Aharoni, Yehuda Amir (from Bar-Ilan University, Eitan Berglas, Uriel Dan, Judah Eisenberg, Yair Evron, Joseph Gross, David Horn, Yair Orgler, Itamar Rabinovitz, Nadav Safran, Amos Shapira, Uriel Tal, Aharon Yariv, and Avivi Yavin. Other participants were Moshe Keren, Simcha Soroker, Dov Yisraeli, and Drora Beit-Or, who was also in charge of handling the protocols. Other people joined us later. The list above includes some of the most senior people of the University as well as distinguished guests.

Just as I did before in presenting the thoughts and deliberations of the Yariv Committee and the workshop on economic planning in some detail, I will do so here for the think tanks of the Peace Project. It will give us an account of what the intellectuals and scientists in the group thought, hoped, and feared, thirty year ago. However, large as the group was, I cannot claim that it actually represented a real cross section of views in Israel, and some of the views seemed bizarre even thirty years ago. Still, the reader is invited to compare these hopes and fears at the dawn of the era of peace with Egypt with what has actually taken place in the last thirty years, and draw his/her conclusions from that. The following is the text of Aharonov's opening remarks in the first meeting:

The idea of forming interdisciplinary think tanks on various problems of peace and war was first raised five years ago, soon after the Yom-Kippur War. We organized then a think tank at the University, which included professors such as David Horn, Eitan Berglas, Avivi Yavin, and me, as well as students and people from the public and private sectors. Its goal then was to help the political and defense systems by basic and methodical investigation of subjects which seemed to us to be important. As an outcome of that activity, a smaller group made some suggestions, and some of them were actually implemented. The effectiveness of the group was high because its members were independent thinkers from various disciplines, and not official security or political experts. This enabled us to raise and investigate problems from various angles, which were not affected by inertial thinking of those who dealt with them on a daily basis

One of the interesting and important subjects for our think tanks here is the possible scenarios for the future development of the cooperation between Israel and Egypt. We should present a series of scenarios, from the most pessimistic one that says that after the return of Sinai the state of belligerency will return, all the way to the most optimistic one of a continuous growing of the Egyptian-Israeli cooperation. I believe that our government is only reacting to the fast developing events, without possessing any long term plan. The government does not have the time or manpower to consider long-range planning, and a think tank such as ours can be of great help. Our group, at least in the beginning, does not have to get input from well-defined sources; on the contrary, apart from some well-known facts, its main tools should be common sense, free thinking, and the readiness of its members to devote time to the investigation of the various aspects. Moreover, the idea is to bring a whole spectrum of ideas and perspectives, which will enable a global view of the subject. For instance, we could assume that we were Egyptians intellectuals, and look at the positive and negative aspects of the cooperation with Israel.

Let us then assume that there is a consensus against (or for) the formation of a Palestinian state in the West Bank, and the government is about to follow this consensus, the contribution of the think tank could be to present the advantages and dangers of following this public consensus, and point out alternative ways.

At the end of Aharonov's presentation I said that a public consensus is sometime the twin brother of the notorious "conceptia", which got its notoriety in the Yom-Kippur War. There are cases in which the government, consciously or unconsciously misleads the public and itself into a consensus, and it would be up to the think tank to point out where such things take place. One of the participants added that the advantage of a think tank is in its ability to analyze the generally known facts and their meaning without filtering them through preconceived political views.

The next meeting was devoted to the question of the motivation of Egypt in entering the peace process. The following are some of the ideas which were presented by various participants: 1. the whole process was the biggest hoax of the century (similar to the opinion of Chief-of-Staff Motta Gur), apparently on the advice of the Soviets, following the Egyptian failure to defeat us militarily; 2. President Sadat is interested in entering the annals of history, and such a leader is not likely to plan a long-term hoax, that might endanger his life. In fact, it is possible that Sadat is actually constructing a monument to himself; 3. A red light might be the crossing the Suez Channel by the Egyptian Army; 4. Changing the leader should be taken as a yellow (warning) light.

The meeting ended by a suggestion to consider two interesting and provocative questions: Would Egypt take part against us in case of a war between us and another Arab country; and should we encourage the Americans to supply arms to Egypt?

The following are summaries of the four documents or working papers, which were submitted to the think tank. They represent various possible scenarios, which do not necessarily represent the opinions of their authors, at least not entirely so. The authors often used strong black-and-white pictures, some of them very bizarre, in order to allow the participants of the think tank to be aware of the whole spectrum of possibilities to its extremes. The reader is invited to compare the views and predictions of each of the papers and of the views expressed in the discussions which followed with what is going on today as well as with what has actually happened in the last thirty years. I hope that these papers will contradict statements often heard, such as: "nobody thought about it at that time". Appendix X presents the full text of the four submitted papers.

Moshe Keren, an entrepreneur, presented the introductory. He suggested several possible reasons for Sadat's peace moves. It is possible - so he said - that the moves were a Soviet-Egyptian or an all-Arab hoax intended to improve the Egyptian position in order to launch a new war against Israel. It was also possible that Sadat wanted to shift his alliance from the Soviets to the Americans, which will help him develop the Suez Canal and his oil fields. Sadat also expected to get economic aid from the Americans. Keren pointed out that Sadat may adapt different options in the future, and therefore it was important to identify signs of change.

Yakir Aharonov presented the next paper in which he elaborated on the possibility that Sadat's move was indeed a hoax, in which only the Egyptian government was involved and not the Egyptian people. This would enable Sadat to go back to the war path. These two papers along with the publicly expressed doubt of the Israeli chief-of-staff as to Sadat's peace intentions indicate the pessimistic view regarding peace of a large portion of the Israeli public at that time.[2]

I presented a paper describing optimistic scenarios (Appendix X). I admit that this paper is not only a chore I volunteer to do, but presented my opinion, or rather my wishes. I believed that if the peoples and their leaders followed my ideas, the Middle East could soon become a pleasant place for all the people and all the nations living in it. However, I did not entertain much

---

2 *Now, thirty years later, a large portion of the Israeli public and some political leader are still pessimistic concerning the likelihood of peace with the Palestinians and the whole Arab World (excluding Egypt and Jordan with whom peace treaties have been signed).*

hope that this would indeed take place, and the last thirty years justified my doubts to a large extent. In my paper that I presented to the think tank, I describe two alternative or rather complementary routes to approach the future in optimistic eyes; I called them the continuous scenario and the optimistic vision as a guide to the present. The first scenario described a step by step progress toward peace and prosperity in the region that could or should take place, while the latter draws a picture of an optimistic future, which helps overcome all the obstacles at that time.

David Horn was worried about the dangers facing Israel in case of a breakdown of the meeting between the Egyptian and Israeli delegation, which was scheduled to take place on May 26, 1980. The meeting was supposed to deal mainly with the issue of the Palestinian autonomy. In his paper, presented in Appendix X, Horn listed the many the dangers for Israel of such a breakdown, and said that the PLO could then form a government in Exile, and the Palestinians in the West Bank and Gaza could then declare independence. Horn suggested that the Israeli Government should consider the dangers seriously before it allowed the meeting to break down, especially because the newly established Palestinian state could be recognized by the international community.

The following are excerpts from the discussions, which followed the four presented papers:

Itamar Rabinovitz[3]: There are three layers to be considered when dealing with Sadat's initiative: His policy since he took power, the important political factors that were then active, and the dynamical processes that keep changing and may therefore change the reasons for his initiative. Sadat has a view of how the Middle East should look like. The Soviet Union is considered by Sadat to be a historical enemy. Israel was an unknown entity for him, and even now he does not count her as one of the important factors. He needs the friendship of the US, and hopes that Israel will help him in that. He emphasizes the "no more war" rather than peace. He believes that he will be able to control what will happen in the territories as well as the pace of the

---

3 *Professor Itamar Rabinovitz later became a rector of the University, and then he was appointed an ambassador to the UN, and headed the Israeli delegations in talks with the Syrians. Afterwards he became the president of Tel Aviv University.*

normalization. His biggest fear now is from the cessation of the return of the whole Sinai. He is emphasizing the Palestinian issue, but this is mainly for internal political reasons.

Yair Aharoni: The first obstacle in the optimistic scenario was already apparent in the discussion of the autonomy, when it appeared that the Palestinians will not agree to have control only over those aspects that are not controversial. This scenario is utopist because it neglects the suspicious nature of the Israelis as well as the characteristics of Begin's government. Moreover, a significant part of the public in Israel is afraid that if the optimistic scenario will materialize, we will lose our identity as a people. On the other hand, the assumptions of the pessimistic scenario are unacceptable, because Sadat wants to get back the Sinai, and therefore will avoid a breakdown of the talks. Actually, Sadat is afraid of losing the improved relations with the US.

Eitan Berglas: Peace talks with Egypt will not stop because of the failure to agree on the autonomy. With our actions in the territories we should prove to the Americans and the Europeans that we are only interested in security and not in ruling the Palestinian population. A clear statement about our intentions in the territories along with a freeze on the settlements could help stop the current anti-Israel swing in the West.

Judah Eisenberg pointed out some of the possible ways to avoid the dangers mentioned by David Horn or at least to protect ourselves from them: He said that the first and obvious danger was that the Palestinian state would be used as an Arab base in case of an Israeli-Arab war. The Palestinian state would therefore have to be demilitarized, and frequent checks by Israel and an international body would have to verify their compliance. A proper distribution of lands (gerrymandering) like the Alon Plan would help. Also, if many Palestinians would stand to lose appreciably from a war (their ties with Jordan, a port in Haifa, etc), they might object to being part of such a war. Illegal infiltration to Israel would undoubtedly increase, and a good fence could help to avoid it.

Uriel Tal: In all our discussions we have to take into consideration what could happen if a Palestinian state is not formed. There are basically four options for this case: 1. the present situation will go on. 2. An autonomy ala Begin or Sadat-Carter will be formed. 3. In some way, Jordan will control the West Bank. 4. Israel will annex the territories. These are the main arguments which were presented, in our meetings as well as in public discussions, against the Palestinian state: The Palestinian state will encourage and aid the enemies of Israel. It will be a firm base for those Israeli Arabs who want to separate from Israel. It will endanger Israel militarily ("tanks approaching Netanya"). It will serve as a base for terrorist actions against Israel. It will become a Soviet satellite next door. Because of its weakness it will be an incubator for all kinds of troubles. On the other hand, the minute Israel will start discussing the possibility of a Palestinian state, the outside pressure on her will decrease, allowing Israel more diplomatic and psychological maneuvering. It is ironical that the minute Israel will consider this option, its supporters in the Palestinian camp will be confused, and may even discard this option. Moreover, all the dooms-day predictions in Israel are guesses and our experience always shows that things do not happen this way. Any way, Israel will be much stronger militarily and economically than the Palestinian state.

All the members of the think-tank took part in the discussion, which culminated in the need to consider seriously the pros and cons for Israel of the formation of a Palestinian state, even before dealing with the other problems of the Israeli-Egyptian developing relations. Moshe Keren, who had presented the introductory paper, discussed the reasons against the formation of a Palestinian state: the PLO covenant stated specifically that their goal was the destruction of the State of Israel; the Palestinian state would become a Soviet base; and economically, Israel stood to lose its cheap labor force. On the other hand, Dov Israeli (a well known lawyer) argued that Israel stood to gain from the establishment of a Palestinian state, politically, as it will improve its image in the world; economically, as Israel would free itself from caring for the million and a half Palestinians in the territories; and militarily, since Israel could then make peace agreements with its Arab neighboring states. I expressed a fear that if Israel refrains from discussing seriously our control of the Palestinian people, we would soon face a Palestinian revolt, and not later than in 3-5 years[4].

Following the discussions, Aharonov said that the think tank had started with our relations with Egypt, present and future, but soon realized that the Palestinian problem is more critical. Moreover, the absence of a solution prevented real progress in our relations with Egypt. Since very few people, or groups,

4   *The reader is reminded that the deliberations took place years before the first Palestinian intifada and more than a dozen years before the Oslo Agreement.*

or organizations were treating this problem sincerely and seriously, we spent a great deal of time on it, and felt that we had to come up with several solutions, or even with a preferred one.[5]

****

Before looking for a possible option that would be accepted by Israel and by the Palestinians, we decided to hear the opinions of respectable politicians: for M.K. Meir Pail for a Palestinian state and M.K. Itzhak Rabin against such a state. Their lectures, which included answers to questions by the members of the think tank, will now be presented.

M.K. Meir Pail

Israel will have to retreat from the West Bank and Gaza and allow self determination to the Palestinians because of the following reasons: the conflict has been going on for a long time, the Arab consensus, demographic problem (3 million Jews and 2 million Arabs west of the Jordan River), and international pressure. It is therefore preferred to act from our own initiative rather than from external pressures and dictates. Israel should come out with a declaration similar to the Balfour one, namely "The government of Israel views favorably the establishment of a national home for the Palestinian people, side by side with the State of Israel". Such a declaration should be conditional on the readiness of the Palestinians to live in peace with us. On her part, Israel will commit herself to withdraw from the West Bank and Gaza.

The Palestinians will then be faced with three options: Forming an independent state, or cooperating with Jordan, or cooperating with Israel. Israel will negotiate with the appropriate factors on the details of the chosen option: Security arrangements, police, control of the Jordan River, economics, work, energy, water, development, etc. East Jerusalem will be under Palestinian control, and there will be two municipalities in Greater Jerusalem as well as a super-municipality, but there will be no border between them. Starting with just autonomy for five years is also acceptable. The main obstacle to the whole plan is the Israeli public, which will have to be convinced by the government of Israel.

---

5   *Professor Yuval Ne'eman claimed at that time that there are problems, and the Palestinian problem is one of them, which do not have a solution.*

145

There are people who claim that the hatred of the Arabs to Israel is pathologic, similar to anti-Semitism. The truth is that the hatred is the result of the national conflict. Territorial compromises are the best answer to such problems. However, it is also true that in our case there is also religious hatred. My suggestion is to start with Gaza as an experiment.

The military worries should be taken care of by demilitarization of the returned lands, and there should be no airports there except for a civilian one in Calandria, near Jerusalem. There are also several Arab states which will want the Palestinian state to be demilitarized. Israel and Jordan should control the Jordan River together. Exchange of lands should be considered; for instance, Israel would give up Kaffar Kassem for equal area south of Tirat Zvi.[6]

M.K. Itzhak Rabin

The Arab regimes today are totalitarian; therefore, no arrangement with them is similar to those in Europe or North America. The conflict between the Soviet Bloc and the West also contributes to the lack of stability. Even Ceausescu, the Romanian president who is active in mediation, does not believe that there will be stability in our region in a decade or two, even if we sign a peace agreement with our neighbors. The important dilemma for us is to decide which are the security and political balances that have to be included in a peace treaty to ascertain that it will be able to withstand the dangers from various directions after it is achieved. We have to look closely at the security problem of returning to the 1967 borders, especially in our eastern front, and at the political problem of the formation of a Palestinian state. Judging from past experience, and because of the density of population in the center of Israel, the greatest danger to our security is from the east. We have to insist that in any peace agreement there will be guarantees that the West Bank will not become a jumping board for an armored attack on Israel. Demilitarization is not an ideal solution, since history teaches us that demilitarization agreements were violated more often than honored.

Those who do not appreciate the motivation and urge of the Palestinians in the Diaspora to return to their homes, underestimate them unjustifiably. On the other hand, agreement to their return means the destruction of our state. The chance for a realistic political settlement depends on two things: on the

6 It is curious that such an exchange of lands, which 25 years later would be suggested by the right-wing Israeli politician Avigdor Lieberman, was suggested here by the left-wing politician Meir Pail.

likelihood of reaching an agreement with the Egyptians that will lower their interest in a war and on finding an acceptable solution for the Palestinians. This solution should create a cooling-down atmosphere that will eventually satisfy most of the Palestinians here as well as in their Diaspora in Lebanon and Syria. We cannot allow the establishment of a Palestinian state, because such a state will necessarily be controlled by the PLO and his ideology of the destruction of the State of Israel. For these reasons, a Palestinian state in the pre-1967 borders is not a solution because of political as well as security considerations. Such a state will be seeds of calamity, because that state will insist on the right of return of the Palestinian refugees into Israel in order to destroy her from within.[7]

There is a broad consensus in Israel that we need to stop controlling the lives of a million Arabs and at the same time safeguard our security. We should therefore look for a solution that will involve Jordan, perhaps in the form of a Palestinian state on the two banks of the Jordan River having two parts, the West bank and today's Jordan. The Hashemite regime will be able to live with this solution. There is a chance that a Palestinian regime in Amman will be more moderate because of the breadth of lands under their control, and will be able to absorb an appreciable part of the Palestinian refugees living in the Diaspora. However, it is still possible that the Palestinians (not the king of Jordan) will still insist on the right of return to Israel. As for the United States, it is likely that it will go along with such a solution. Having discussed the idea of an eventual formation of a Palestinian-Jordanian state, I should say that making peace is a process of slowly looking for a solution, and not one act. Any attempt to look for an ideal solution now and carry it out in steps is wrong.

Peace with Egypt is more important than the solution of the Palestinian problem. The real question that bothers me most is the likelihood that the Egyptian people will be dissatisfied when they realize that peace is not solving their economic problems. This disappointment and not the debate about the West Bank could change Egypt's policy.

In conclusion, after the Camp David Agreement with Egypt we are faced with two alternatives: 1. To give a full autonomy to the Palestinians in all the

---

7 It should be noted that M.K. Itzhak Rabin was an ardent opponent of a Palestinian state, while the same Itzhak Rabin, as a prime minister thirteen years later, signed the Oslo Agreement with Yasser Arafat that could lead to a Palestinian state, and was assassinated by a right-wing Israeli in November 4, 1995 because of that.

territories except for a few security regions. This is an intermediate arrangement that does not exclude their right to demand a complete retreat to the Green Line at the end of a five-year period. 2. To form a Jordanian-Israeli regime in the territories for a transition period, with a division of duties: They will be responsible for the administration and we for the security. As for Jerusalem, the problem is very complex and it is not worth our while to deal with it now. We have to aim at keeping Jerusalem under one (our) control, and looking for a solution to two problems: the religious problem, by letting the various religions run their religious places and the municipal one by dividing the city into largely independent zones.

****

The Outcome. The think tank was formed in December 1979, mainly because I believed that the Peace Project should undertake to fill up the serious void in the country, the lack of independent, open, critical, deep, and constructive thinking about some crucial problems. I thought that this was a good way to face the future challenges and prevent surprises such as the Yom-Kippur War or Sadat's peace initiative. Dozens of people, from within the University and from the outside, participated in the work of the think tank, which was led by Professor Yakir Aharonov, while Ms. Drora Beit-or took care of the administrative work. The think tank met almost every week, and ended its intensive work in June 1980. It started its work with the problems and challenges of the budding peace with Egypt, but pretty soon it became clear that settling the Palestinian problem was an important condition for the success of the Israeli-Egyptian peace. Many aspects of the Palestinian problem were discussed, and many papers were presented. Outside speakers (M.K. Meir Pail and M.K. Itzhak Rabin) were invited to talk for and against the establishment of a Palestinian state in one form or another. Although some of the participants had several doubts concerning the advisability of the formation of a Palestinian state, and some even had objections to such a formation, it became apparent that the solution of a state or of a full autonomy for the Palestinians became acceptable or even desirable to the large majority of the participants of the think tank, provided that the security of Israel would be maintained.

The reader, who has gone through all the ideas presented in this chapter, and who compared the doubts, the hopes, and the predictions with what has happened in the following 30 years, may obviously wonder what were the conclusions of the study. The reader may also wonder what happened to the conclusions. Was the work of the think tank only a theoretical exercise, or did it have any influence on the Israeli public and the Israeli leaders.

So you are wondering what was written in the report, to whom it was submitted, and what its influence was. The answer is very disappointing. Drora Beit-Or prepared a complete draft of the final report, summarizing the papers, the discussions, and the conclusions. However, this report was never signed or distributed, but found its way to the Project's drawers. I still do not know for sure the reasons for the. I left for a Sabbatical leave in Saclay, France, in July, and Professor David Horn became the Project's director. In November of that year (1980), I was not in the country and do not know the exact reasons for the disappointing result. I can only guess that the main reason was that the report dealt with political questions, mainly the Palestinian problem, which was delicate and controversial. The Project's Management must have decided not to expose the Project to too much criticism, and therefore it decided to keep the information within the walls of "ivory tower". Was it a courageous decision? Was it an intelligent one? I doubt it. It is possible that a courageous and serious analysis of the Palestinian problem and the possible solutions by a think tank of the Peace Project, already in 1980, if made public, could have helped the Israeli people think about this important subject at that time rather than 12 years later, after a bloody Palestinian intifada (uprising), and I regret it very much that it was not done. I recall that the report and conclusions of extensive work in 1973 of the think tank on the immigration of academic Jews from the Soviet Union also found itself to the rector's drawer, with a similar fate to the workshop on national authority for economic planning which was discussed earlier in the book. One conclusion from these failures is that the good intention of academia to get out of the ivory tower and analyze, along with national experts, some burning national problems is likely to be met with deaf ears by the political leadership, unless it is done inside the official political bodies. My other conclusion is that interface between academia and those bodies should be improved.

It could be appropriate at this point to discuss the attitude of various people in the Peace Project and outside to its existence and various activities. I realized from the outset that some public figures saw the Project as a leftist political organization, which it was not, and refused to join even the Steering Committee. Professors from other universities were critical of our activities and successes, mostly out of jealousy, and this is understandable, while on the other hand there were other such professors who got grants from us and took parts in our activities. The reaction in Egypt was more positive than expected and in the US it was very positive and helpful. Some of the fiercest opposition to the Peace Project was within the University and even within the Management, as has already been mentioned. I see the following reasons for the objection of the Project's Management to publicize the work and conclusions of the think tank: some members thought that the Palestinian problem was not so important and actually said so; others objected to the conclusions of the think tank, although they were clearly not supposed to be an official paper of the Project; and some were just afraid to touch a "hot" topic like the Palestinian problem. Whatever the reason, a tremendous amount of work turned out to be in vain, just an exercise in futility, and I definitely regret it.

CHAPTER 7.
PLANNING SCIENTIFIC COLLABORATIONS

Planning a Second Visit to Egypt in March 1980. Six months after my first visit to Egypt I felt that it was time to make another trip. In preparation for the trip met with each of the deans of the nine faculties. Some of them expressed doubts about the scientific level of any collaboration with Egyptian counterparts; others thought that their people who expressed to me interest in such collaborations were not the best people in their faculties. After my telling each of them who in their faculties expressed interest, and about our insistence that the proposed collaborations would be on a high level, they all changed their critiques, expressed interest in helping me, and gave me a list of other people in their faculties who might also be interested in collaborating with their Egyptian colleagues. All the deans were interested in mutual visits, and said that they would support financially visits by their Egyptian counterparts. They all expressed interest in exchange of scientific information such as reprints, preprints, possible sources of grants, etc. Several deans mentioned energy as a good candidate for a conference, while some of them actually knew Egyptian scientists, and asked me to look for them.

Scores of faculty members contacted me, mostly by visiting my office, all asking me to find future partners for collaboration in research or for organizing conferences in their disciplines. The largest groups were from medicine and the exact sciences. I promised each of them that I would do my best, but added that at this stage my contacts were still limited and the duration of my planned visit in Egypt was short. I also added that the political situation was still not clear. I was, however, encouraged by my talks with the deans and the faculty members that there was great interest in our University to collaborate with Egyptian counterparts. I was still not clear about the interest in Egypt, and most importantly, about the attitude of Egyptian government and academic administrators.

It became clear that if my first visit in September 1979 was mainly intended to acquaint me with Egypt and her academia, the second visit would be a working one, which would be helped by the contacts I had made in Egypt on my first visit. These contacts were with professors such as El-Nadi, Abdel Hady, Badr, and others, as well as with Richmond and some Egyptian businessmen. I also talked with Dan Patir, Begin's secretary and with Gomah, the first secretary of the Egyptian embassy. Rivka joined me on this trip too, but the report this time was written only by me. This time I will not report my activity chronologically, but mostly group together all my meetings with each person.

Professor Muhammad Badr. He invited me to his home, where I met the urologist Ibrahim Abdoul Fettouh and the pathologist Abdalla Khalil. The latter told me that the French professor George Mathe from Villejuif was very interested in trilateral (Egyptian-Israeli-French) collaboration in cancer research, and was apparently preparing to do it in his laboratory. Khalil himself was planning to go to Villejuif in June and to visit Israel on his way there. I showed him the proposal for cooperation in cancer research, which the dean of biology at Tel Aviv had given me, and invited him to visit the Peace Project, with all expenses paid.

Badr then asked me to help him get an Israeli visa from the recently opened Israeli embassy, since he was planning to go to a conference in Israel in a couple of days. He then asked me for a list of Israelis, whom it would be worth his while to meet.

On the way to get the Israeli visa we stopped at Cairo University, where Badr hoped to get his dean's permission to travel to Israel. When he left the car he advised us to keep the car's windows closed and the doors locked and not to talk to students, because most of them were extreme Muslims, and could harm us. When he came back he was very nervous, and said that Badran, the University president, was against any collaboration with Israelis, and that his dean was also tough, because of pressures on him from above, but he did grant him the permission to go. He then estimated his financial loss from the Gulf sources because of his visit to Israel to be about 10-20 thousand Egyptian liras.

In the evening he came to my hotel and we spent several hours going over the list of requests for collaborations, conferences, and exchange of visits, which

I had obtained in Tel Aviv. It turned out that he knew many Egyptian candidates for that, some of them close friends of his or even relatives. I then invited him to be the Peace-Project's guest while in Israel and that we would pay all his expenses. He thanked me and said that although he was going to give a talk at the conference in Israel, the meetings with Israeli scientists were of greater importance to him. I could not have asked for a better contact in Egypt in medicine and in the biological sciences than Professor Muhammad Badr.

A few days later he called me and told me that there would soon be a ceremony where they would give honorary citations to the great medical people in Egypt, and this would be the second time that he would not get a citation by Badran's decision, most likely because of his visit to Israel. I told him that his pioneering and courageous actions would get into the annals of history. Later I inquired in Egypt about his scientific competence, and everybody I asked praised him. He was indeed an honest and courageous scientist.

Addison Richmond. In his office he informed me that he had been told in his embassy that because of the recent exchange of ambassadors between Egypt and Israel he should not be actively involved in the creation of Israeli-Egyptian relations. Nevertheless, he promised to try and arrange for me a private meeting in the Suez-Canal University with its president Osman. Richmond then introduced me to the Egyptian deputy minister of agriculture, Hafez, and to Professor Ali Maher, the head of plant protection in As-Siyut University. They both wanted to get information from our experts in their fields, but said that it was too early for open collaborations, mostly because of psychological reasons (former enemies, etc). Hafez knew Professor Yitzhak Vahl from agriculture in Tel Aviv University, and Maher knew Professor Felix Mendelssohn from botany, and these two Israeli professors were praised by the two of them. Richmond then invited Rivka and me to dinner at his home.

Abdel Hady. In his office, Abdel Hady told me that he was organizing an international meeting, which would take place the following year, but he was afraid that the Arabs would boycott it because of Israeli participation. He studied the suggestions that Professor J. Joseph from Tel Aviv had prepared for him and said that three of these suggestions were in his field and he would start working on them right away., and would pass the suggestions in meteorology to the meteorological service. He suggested that we start working right away on proposals to be submitted together to the American AID and NSF and write together a letter to the Ford Foundation. He was willing to come to Tel Aviv and work together with our people on the proposals and the letter, and then he and I would submit them together in Washington. However, Abdel Hady hesitated when I asked him if he would be willing to give an open lecture in Tel-Aviv University. Finally, he added that the Egyptian Academy of Science would have to approve all our plans.

Three representatives of the American AID then came to his office, and told me that they were interested in supplying training material to Abdel Hady's laboratory. They suggested to me that together with Syria and Lebanon, Israel should research the water sources in the north. I was not sure whether they were acquainted with the political situation in the Middle East. Abdel Hady complained to me later that the Americans were supplying expensive equipment worth 3.5 million dollars to the Syrians and were doing so in a strange way. An American plane landed "mistakenly" in Damascus, and the equipment was taken off.

I called Abdel Hady a few days later, and he said that there had been some changes in his plans. He had talked with his boss, Hassan Ismail, the president of the National Academy of Science, who told him to continue working with me on the preparation of the proposals, but added that for the actual execution of our plans we needed the approval of the Egyptian and Israeli governments. For this reason Abdel Hady wanted to postpone his trip to Tel Aviv, but wanted us to continue working on our plans and proposals. He then invited Rivka and me to the Hilton for dinner with him and his wife. I gave him a letter to our embassy, which he would be able to use when applying for an Israeli visa. He told me that the head of the National Academy was very religious, and therefore had refused to meet me in my visit six months ago. He added with a smile that Ismail himself had a collaborative research program with the Israeli head of the Institute of Seas, Yochai Bin-Nun, supported by the American AID. Abdel Hady's next story amused me: A few months earlier they had a visit by Joseph Tekoah, the president of Ben-Gurion University, who left a bad impression on the academy when he arrived with Egyptian guards armed with sub-machineguns. His next story amused all of us: El-Shazly, whom I had briefly met in my visit to the Academy, was a little scared when he met me, and told Abdel Hady afterwards, "We have to behave as we did in the time of King Farouk, when each brother in the family belonged to a different party in order to prepare for any political developments. You, Abdel Hady, will work with the Israelis, and I will maintain my ties with the

Arab countries." Abdel Hady then advised me not to meet scientists only on the recommendation of our foreign ministry; a similar advice to that which I had gotten from Steve Cohen. I noted that Abdel Hady's wife repeated a comment which had been made earlier by Tabark, "If you build settlements, at least do it quietly."

Talks with Critics. In the Shepherd Hotel I met Ehud Yaari, an Israeli reporter. He asked me to tell him about my meetings in Cairo, and I refrained from doing so because of the sensitivity of these talks and plans at that time. He then launched the following verbal questions, or rather attacks: 1. What are the Israelis who come to Cairo looking for? 2. Why are they applying pressure for cooperation on the Egyptians? 3. Why did the Shiloah people, who had been met with a hostile reception, not keep quiet after they returned home? 4. Since the Shiloah people are not professionals, what are their credentials? It was apparent that there was no great love between him and the Shiloah people, perhaps because of jealousy, and for this reason I took his comments with a grain of salt.

I received even greater criticism from another person I met at the Shepherd's club. Dr. Arlosorov, the head of the neurological department in Assaf Harofeh Hospital near Tel Aviv, started with a direct attack on me. "Who are you? The Peace Project is doing nothing with regards to cooperation with the Egyptians." In light of my great but discreet efforts which I was making I decided to keep quiet and not respond to this "criticism"; but I suggested to him to present a proposal with an Egyptian colleague to our research committee and ask for financial support.

Candidates from Cairo University. Professor Omar Badawi came to my hotel room and took me to the University. We talked about my efforts on his behalf in Europe, and he urged me to continue. In the name of El-Nadi, who was still in Abu Dhabi for a couple of days, he asked me to interview two possible candidates for cooperation with us. They had already submitted their Ph. D. theses, and each gave me a copy:

Mohamed Tawfik Ahmed Ghoiem. He did his research on inelastic alpha scattering at 4.2 GeV in Dubna in the Soviet Union. He was married and seemed to be very intelligent.

Mohamed Tarek Hussein. He studied the interaction of negative pions at high energy also in Dubna. He was working in Cairo on El-Nadi's model of the

"Fire Ball", and seemed to be intelligent, energetic and original in his thinking. He was married to a young physicist.

Both candidates looked good although they had no experience with counters, since they worked in Dubna with emulsions; but they had experience in electronics as instructors in third-year electronics laboratory.

Abdel Harith came to me after hearing that El-Nadi had suggested other candidates, and repeated the statement that he was El-Nadi's first choice to collaborate with us. In an answer to a question he said that the reason that many Egyptians joined the extreme Islam is not because of Khomeini's influence, but because of the spread of poverty in the country. As for visiting Israel, many scientists would want to do so, but every one is afraid to be the first one to do so. He told me to expect a visit by a friend of his, Ismail Amin.

Ismail Amin. He appeared in my hotel room and told me that he was a mathematician, whose field was algebra, and that he had received an invitation from Dan Segre from Haifa. He had consulted with El-Nadi who recommended that he accept the invitation, but his dean advised him not to go. His decision was to go, and he was interested in coming for the summer or the fall semesters. He said that they did not get the Israeli literature and asked me to send him copies of the Israel Journal of Mathematics. He was also interested in publishing in this Journal. After my first visit he thought, as did his friend Abdel Harith, that El-Nadi became cooler towards cooperation with us, and did not realize then that El-Nadi apparently became cooler only to the candidacy of Abdel Harith.

Several days later Ali told me that a student from Tabark's laboratory in the Atomic Energy Establishment had already looked for me in my room in the hotel, but I was not in the room. Ali thought that the student wanted to talk to me about studying at Tel-Aviv University or about collaborative research.

Students from the Atomic Energy Establishment. Two students from the Egyptian Atomic Energy Establishment came to my hotel room, Ahmed Azam and Mohamed Shoukry El-Karim; the latter was working with Ali in the Egyptian AEC. They both were working on getting nuclear energy to Egypt. The government had decided to get a nuclear reactor, but the two of them were not sure that it would be built in the location which they had selected. Azam, who was working with Tabark, had gotten his M.Sc in experimental nuclear physics in Cairo University under the supervision of Professor Mohamed El-Nadi and the woman head of the department, also named El-Nadi. I suggested to him to write to the head of The Physics Department in Tel Aviv University and in the Weizmann Institute and ask to be accepted as a Ph.D. student.

Dr. Boutros Boutros Ghali. It looked to me at that point that I could end up with good plans for cooperation, with willing and good candidates, but what might apparently be holding them back was government approval. I therefore decided to try and overcome that obstacle, with the hope that I would find an attentive political leader, who might help me. I decided that what I needed was a contact with a high-ranking government official who was also a scientist or an intellectual. The name that crossed my mind was the Egyptian secretary of state for foreign affairs, Dr. Boutros Ghali.[1] I hesitated for a while wondering whether it was proper for me to call him without being introduced, but decided that I had nothing to lose if I tried. I therefore picked up the phone and called his office. I introduced myself and he immediately said, "Come to my office tomorrow at 19:00."

When I entered his office he came and sat next to me, and except for two short phone calls we talked for almost two hours. I started by saying that meeting him had been suggested by Steve Cohen, Herbert Kelman, and Jack Cummings, but he gestured that introductions were not necessary, and that he had things he wanted to say to me.

Dr. Ghali started by telling me that he was unsuccessful in his attempts to bring Professor Steve Cohen to Cairo to advise him and coordinate all matters of bilateral and trilateral cooperation. He said that the Foreign Office did not have a budget for that, and he could also not find outside funds to finance it. With a smile he said, "It is apparently easier to get ten million dollars than ten thousand." I said that if he was talking about a mutual coordinator, who would spend some time in Cairo and some time in Tel Aviv, we were also interested, and could contribute some money for that.

He talked at length about the political dangers to Egypt from Israeli-Egyptian cooperation, and added that even American-Egyptian-Israeli cooperation is viewed by the Arab countries as part of the same plot. For him, trilateral cooperation with Holland, France or an African country replacing the US is

---

1 Dr. Ghali later became secretary general of the United Nations.

much preferred. He pointed at the building across the street, the Arab-League building, which was empty then because of the peace treaty with Israel, and talked about his country's isolation problem. "Your people should understand it and help us with that problem". I said that I fully appreciated the problem and added that one important element was still missing in his description of the problem, and this would make the problem two-sided and symmetric, but I would explain it later. I asked him to let me describe our Peace Project, which is a unique project, and he agreed; and this is what I said:

> Your country surprised us twice, in 1973 in the shock of war and in 1977 in the shock of peace. The Israeli academic society can only blame itself for its intellectual complacency that made the two sur- prises possible. At Tel-Aviv University we quickly overcame the peace shock, and viewed President Sadat's visit as a new and welcomed challenge. Following intense discussions we formed the Research Project on Peace with four goals: 1. Research, thinking and analysis of all matters concerning peace. 2. Preparing plans for regional co- operation, and not only the Egyptian-Israeli one. 3. Investigating the possible influence of peace on our country. 4. Starting small-scale, scientist-to-scientist collaborations with Egyptian scientists. Our Project is basically new in Israeli academia, possibly worldwide, with professors from all faculties taking part in its activities. For help in the first stages we formed contacts with the business sector in Israel, as well as with important groups in the United States, such as: Sena- tors Jackson and Stone, Rockefeller, the Ford Foundation, the AID, Harvard University and others. We expanded the contacts to include Egyptian officials such as Ambassador Ghorbal in Washington and Ambassador Mortada in Tel Aviv.

Having obtained permission from the Egyptian scientists to mention our contacts, I briefly described to Ghali my discussions with professors Badr and Abdel Hady, and outlined our plans for collaboration. I did not mention El-Nadi, because as he was then in Abu Dhabi, and I had not been able to ask and obtain his permission. I then described our efforts vis-à-vis the West Bank: The meeting of President Ben-Shahar with President Baramki of Bir- Zeit College, our visits in the colleges in Hebron and Nablus, and the courses in Tel-Hashomer Hospital for technicians and nurses from the West Bank. I described at length our attempts to form academic contacts with the West Bank, and the inherent difficulty because of the present political inequality between us and them. I emphasized our efforts, which up till then had been successful, not to give any publicity to contacts in Egypt in order not to harm our Egyptian colleagues and damage the budding peace process. With his permission and encouragement I then turned to the political situation, after emphasizing that these were my personal views, and did not necessarily represent the views of the Research Project on Peace:

Contrary to what has been expected, Israel today is less enthusiastic about the normalization. I detect in my country, even among the intellectuals, a growing apathy concerning important issues such as the fate of the peace, the Palestinian problem, etc. Under pressure of groups of extremists, the Israeli government continues with its policy, which hurts even Israel itself, by building settlements in the occupied territories, allowing the Jewish Hebron to grow, etc. There exists in my country a de-facto agreement between extreme nationalism and public apathy of the majority, and this agreement hurts the peace process. This unfortunate situation is aggravated by the anxiety, mistrust, and even fear in Israel of a hidden Egyptian trick. The Israeli public talks only about what Israel has sacrificed for peace - the retreat from the Sinai, and there is little appreciation for your sacrifice – your isolation in the Arab World. There is also little concern with the danger of explosion in the Arab population in occupation in the West Bank and the Gaza Strip.

From the beginning, the Israeli public believed that Egypt had little direct interest in peace, which you viewed as a sacrifice rather than an opportunity. The negative attitude of the Egyptian intellectuals stems, so the Israelis think, from personal interests and from ideological reasons. The personal interests are clear; namely, the intellectuals and many others are afraid of losing their income from their ties with the rich Gulf countries. Also, they have a psychological difficulty to cooperate with an enemy from the past. The ideological opposition to peace is more profound. In my two visits to Egypt I have learned that the natural scientists are not as strong in opposition to peace as are the intellectuals and the academic people from the liberal arts and social sciences. The natural scientists show greater interest in the opportunity to cooperate with the United States and even with Israel. I believe that the reason for that is that the centers of religion, language, and history, the centers of science are in the Arab World;

while the centers of science is in the West. Regarding science, some Egyptian scientists view Israel as a possible doorway to the Western World.

I admit that I have found here a lot of uneasiness with the recent Egyptian isolation from the Arab world as well as from the policy and behavior of Israel toward the Palestinians in the occupied territories. I have often the feeling that the Egyptians are saying, "We have made peace with you, and you are not behaving as good partners should, so at least leave us alone."

I imagine, sir that you may wish to ask me the following question, "If you, Professor Yavin, understand that the Israelis should leave us alone; what are you doing in Egypt and in my office?" This tough question gives me an opportunity to explain what I meant before when I said that there was a missing symmetric element in your understandable request that Israel should understand Egypt's difficulties, and that this understanding is necessary for the success of the peace.

Peace is a fact, and the normalization of relation is becoming a reality. The question about the normalization is not *if, rather how, with whom, at what pace, and according to which principles?* The dynamics of the new situation, which is unfolding every day, will bring about contacts of Egyptians and Israelis whether or not we want them. Just as is the situation in Egypt, in Israel too there are constructive elements such as Ezer Weizmann, the peace movement, and the Peace Project, but there is also fanaticism which grows on fear and mistrust. If the normalization of relations will fail, the fanatics in Israel will have an upper hand, and most likely in Egypt too. On the other hand, if the normalization will succeed, it will have positive influence in Israel, in Egypt, and in the neighboring Arab countries. The constructing elements in Israel will be able to say to the public, "It is not true that the Arabs always want to throw us into the sea." And you will be able to say to the Arab countries, "You see; it is possible to work with the Israelis." You told me before that we have to consider seriously your difficulties, and you are one hundred percent right. Now I am telling you that you have to consider seriously our difficulties, for the success of the common process. The understanding in Egypt of the difficulties of the peace-supporting elements in Israel was the missing symmetric element I mentioned before. In other words, and borrowing from mathematics, I am saying that the Egyptian political system and the Israeli one are not independent; each one of them depends on the other. We therefore have now one system of two coupled equations, which should be treated or solved together, because what happens in one of them affects the other. We are in one boat in a stormy sea of ignorance and hatred. Unfortunately, no side fully understands that constructive actions by him can affect and change what is happening in the other side, and that such a change can help his own side. People from our Peace Project are trying hard to explain your difficulties to our public, and you can help us quiet some of the doubts and fear in Israel. Let me end by stressing the importance of coordination between constructive people of both sides, who understand the difficulties of both sides as well as the advantages to both of them from the success of the process.[2]

At the end of my long presentation Ghali said that he agreed 100% with what I said. In particular he agreed with the need for mutual considerations which I raised at the end, and stressed that it was necessary to consider the difficulties of Egypt as well as those of the Israeli government, which was attentive to her public's doubts and fears, thus hampering the progress of the whole process. Having said that he stressed again that it was important for us to know that Egypt was in a process of waking up and of dissolution, and he himself, like his people, was in fact torn. In order to illustrate his concern he said, "If an Israeli professor will come to an Egyptian university, his Egyptian host will be in danger; and if an Egyptian professor will travel to Israel, he will be in danger from his students when he will come back." He then added another discouraging remark, "Academic cooperation may perhaps add 20 positive percents to the equation, but may also add many negative percents, and might even endanger the whole process."

---

2 *Those who think that these ideas are trivial and self evident should consider the following: The majority of people in Israel believe that the Oslo Agreement failed although both Prime Minister Itzhak Rabin and Prime Minister Benjamin Netanyahu officially accepted it. However, Rabin understood that we and the Palestinians were in one boat in a stormy sea of 100 years of hatred; therefore we should understand each other's difficulties and we Israelis should try to help the Palestinian Authority. Netanyahu, on the other side, saw us and the Palestinians as being in two hostile boats in the same stormy sea. He was not interested in understanding the difficulties of the Palestinian Authority and in helping them overcome those difficulties; rather he recognized the sea of hatred between us and the Palestinians and the internal difficulties of the Palestinian Authority with the Hamas, the Islamic Jihad, and the opposition inside El-Fatah, and did his best to amplify these difficulties in order to obstruct the Authority as well as the Oslo process.*

"I understand your concern," I said, "and we have to take it into serious consideration; however, we both know that there will be growing cooperation one way or another, and it is, therefore, important to ascertain that the right, that is constructive Israelis, and the right Egyptians will interact in a controlled way and in the optimal pace. It is crucial that the 20 percents will indeed be positive, and will not be negative by the meeting of the *ugly Israeli* with the *ugly Egyptian*."

He then said that he agreed that in spite of the difficulties we had to start with cooperation but do it at a slow pace, and science was a good candidate to start with. Then he said, "I do not object to you continuing with your efforts in a slow pace and according to the principles you have just described; in fact, I even support your doing so". He added that I could send all my recommendations to him in a sealed envelope through the Egyptian ambassador in Tel Aviv. I asked him which way the Egyptian scientists, who are interested in collaboration with us, should follow, and he answered, "Through channels." He then explained that he meant through the ministry of higher education, and added encouragingly that he would then call that ministry and give his support.

Toward the end Ghali summarized the principles for academic cooperation which should be followed: 1. The cooperation should not be given publicity, because any publicity will ruin its chances. (As an example he brought the case of building a hospital in Saudi Arabia. The Saudis were interested that Egyptian would run it, but were afraid that the project would be cancelled if the other Arabs knew about it.) 2. The cooperation should be in pure science or in applied science, because it is easier to do it in the non-ideological fields, since the people in liberal arts and social sciences were afraid to lose their contacts and professional future. His principles and mine were, clearly, very similar.

I asked him if he would agree to come to Tel-Aviv University as one of the speakers in our Peace Papers program. He said that he would be glad to come after the autonomy talks, which would soon be held in Herzliya; but added that he would have to get permission, since not everybody agreed with his ideas and methods, which sometimes appeared to the critics to be too sophisticated. It was okay with him to invite to his lecture professors from other universities and even politicians, but not the press.

His last question was purely political. He asked me why my government made peace, and then kept hold of the West Bank. I said that I would give him my personal opinion, which he might not like. I said that in my opinion, Begin saw the peace agreement as a trade agreement; he gave up the Sinai and got the West Bank for it. I added that in my opinion the majority of the Israeli public did not support the government on that. His next comment was again in line with my ideas. "Unfortunately," he said, "there is de-facto cooperation between the rejectionists on both sides". I responded that this phenomenon was well known, and this was one reason why I was looking for ways in which the constructive elements on both sides could cooperate. We parted as friends, and I felt that it was a very encouraging meeting.

Tymour Kammal. On the recommendation of Amiram Shkolnik from the Department of Zoology in Tel Aviv, I called Tymour Kammal, the head of radio-biology in the Egyptian Atomic Energy Authority. He came to my hotel, and told me that he had worked with Shkolnik in the US, and that they were good friends. He showed me a letter from Professor Howard Johnson from Missouri, who was interested in three-way cooperation: Johnson, Kammal, and Berman (from Rehovot) on poultry. Therefore, Kammal was interested in meeting with both Shkolnik and Berman in Cairo. I gave him an invitation by Professor Shmuel Schorr from Ichilov Hospital to a meeting on tomography and ultrasound as well as an invitation by Professor Dan Michaeli, the general manager of Ichilov Hospital, for Egyptians doctors to get advanced training in his Hospital. He said that he would consult with his friend Mahfouz. I recalled that Badr had recommended to me to meet Mahfouz, a radiologist who used to be the health minister. Kammal said that he was studying camels, goats, and sheep, and was interested in the Sinai. We agreed that together with our people he would submit a proposal to the Ford Foundation and to the AID, but he added that he had to consult on that with the head of the Atomic Energy Authority Effat, who would soon be replaced by Hamouda. A few days later I had dinner with him and Ali at the Shooting Club, and he told me there that he had already talked with Effat, who gave his O.K., but asked that a formal request would be submitted.

A day later Tymour called me and said that he had had another talk with Effat, who repeated his personal approval for collaboration with us, but said that the whole thing should go *through channels,* i.e. we would have to request the collaboration from our foreign ministry, which would then ask the Egyptian foreign ministry. In the meantime he could not give me any written material. I told him that I would talk to our dean of biological sciences, and ask him to prepare a letter to Effat, which would be sent through channels after the cultural agreement would hopefully be signed soon. In the meantime we would not come to visit him in his lab, and he agreed. I suggested that I would write to Boutros Ghali on this matter, and Kammal agreed.

Kammal took me then to the Faculty of Pharmacology, where we were warmly met by Professor Samira Abdel Wahab and by Professor Hilal, the deputy dean, who said that he knew me, and it turned out that we both had studied in Seattle at the same time. The door then opened and in came Professor Shaabana, who had been corresponding with Professor Yoel Kashman, and wanted me to tell Kashman that he was going to send him his additions to Kashman's proposal. He was interested in getting an invitation and would like to come to Tel Aviv for six months, but asked me and his colleagues who were present not to give it any publicity.

Rivka and I visited the Association for the deaf, located in Tahrir Square. We met there the deputy minister Hommossani and Dr. Bonna. They told us that they were responsible for the civilian rehabilitation program in Egypt and that Reuma Weizmann (Ezer's wife) had visited them. They both were interested in visiting Israel and inspect our rehabilitation program.

The President of the Suez-Canal University. Since our experts on desert and on the Sinai were interested in cooperation with the Suez Canal University, I wanted to meet President Osman. Our people had actually met with members of the staff of the University. Richmond tried to call Osman's office in Cairo, but failed. I tried to call his office in Ismailia for three hours, and failed. The following day I was told by the telephone operator of my hotel that Osman wanted to talk to me. I was transferred from one secretary to another, and when he got on the line, I told him who I was, and the line was cut off. Half an hour later the same chain of events took place; namely, a call to me in the hotel, two secretaries involved, he started to talk, and the line was cut off. Several days later I called Osman's office, this time in Cairo. A man answered. I told him what I wanted, and he said that he would pass the information. I asked him who he was, and his answer was, "I am a staff member and there is no need for you to know who I am." I never heard from Osman again. *Was the whole thing a result of political considerations? Security considerations? Personal ones? Or was it just the result of Egyptian inefficiency as happened to Tahsin Basheer missing me in the hotel because of a bad telephone line?* I wondered.

Reflections. I talked with Raymond Baker, an American scientist who was spending an extended period in Egypt in order to study Egyptian society. He felt that the control of the country by President Sadat was weakening because of the failure of his policy of an open door to the West. The gap between the rich and the poor was widening. An example of the government's social insensitivity was the construction of luxurious hotels in El Kornish Street along the Nile, replacing the popular promenade that had been there. Sadat's promise that 1980 would be a year of prosperity was not fulfilled for the masses. I asked him if there was any stabilizing force in the country, and he said that the unwillingness of the people to go to war was perhaps the strongest stabilizing force.

Rivka talked with Amos Eilon, a famous Israeli author and journalist, who had been in Cairo for quite some time then. He told her that the Egyptians were starting to talk about corruption in and around the presidential couple, mainly around Jihan Sadat, who had the last say on every important issue. Large commercial deals and money transactions were done close to her. Their children lived in rich dwellings, and she lived extravagantly, most of the time not with her husband.

These two talks, along with my experience with the scientists and the scientific administrators such as President Osman of the Suez-Canal University, started to worry me. *Are we all living in a fool's paradise and do not understand that Sadat's peace initiative could soon collapse? To what extent does even the Peace Project add to the danger? More specifically, along with the psychological difficulties (contacts with past enemy) Egypt also has real difficult problems with the Arab countries. Every additional tie with us increases the rage in various circles in the Arab World, and they apply pressure on their colleagues in Egypt. This situation badly affects the position of Sadat in Egypt, which is also badly hurt by the declining economy as well as by the increase in the social gap and the corruption. Therefore, cooperation with us, and especially a noisy and publicized one, is embarrassing to President Sadat and might hurt rather than help the peace process. I am therefore faced with the following dilemma:*

On the one hand, as I told Boutros Ghali, cooperation is developing whether one wants it or not, and therefore it is desirable that the first collaborations will be between the right parties such as the scientists. Such collaborations, if successful, will increase the understanding in Israel that it is possible to work with the Arabs and benefit from such cooperation. This is also important for the possibility for Israel of establishing cooperation with Arabs in other countries. Similar understanding will then also grow in Egypt and later in the other Arab countries in regards to cooperation with Israel.

On the other hand, cooperation will also have negative aspects, and could also hurt the support of peace in Egypt, as was stressed to me several times by Boutros Ghali. The conclusion is that one has to look for an optimum, and this is not an easy task. Therefore, I have to move very carefully, slowly and without premature publicity. I should carefully choose the right people and right subjects for first collaborations. Candidates for the first fields of such scientific collaborations are: nuclear physics, remote sensing, the desert goat, medicine and agriculture. Also, we will have to pay attention to Ghali's recommendation not to start in the first stage contacts in liberal arts and social sciences.

Mohamed El-Nadi. He called me in the morning and asked if he could come to see me in my hotel, and I told him that I would be honored. Upon arrival and to my surprise he started talking about the social gap that had existed between our two peoples and about his own bad experience with Jews and with Israelis. For instance, in 1948 he lived with a Jewish man in a rented room in London, and a local rabbi asked his roommate, "How come you agree to live with an Egyptian?"[3] In various scientific meetings he noticed that the Israelis tried to stay away from him. I told him that I was amazed that both he and Dr. Badr had had similar experienced as being repelled by Jews and Israelis, while I had had a different experience. I had always felt that the Israelis had wanted to get close to the Egyptians, but the Egyptians or any other Arabs had stayed away in any encounter abroad. We both smiled and shook hands.

El-Nadi offered Rivka to drive her to the main market or to any other place she would want to visit, and she thanked him, but declined his gracious offer. He then apologized for not inviting us to his home in our previous visit, because his wife had just died. He then told me that he had waited for me for two weeks in February, and had therefore postponed his trip to Abu Dhabi. When I did not come he had to go there to Al-Ein University to deliver a lecture on modern physics at the ceremony marking the completion of the last year of their BA program. I thanked him for waiting for me, and apolo-

3 *Years later I was invited by a Polish friend to come to Poland and help him see if and where there was anti-Semitism in his country. On his invitation I gave a colloquium in Warsaw University on anti-matter. The following day, my friend said to me that there was no need to search further for anti-Semitism, since after my talks some of his colleagues said to him, "Your friend gave a good talk, but why are you a friend of a Jewish physicist?"*

gized for the postponement of my visit due to my difficulties in getting the Egyptian visas.

We then settled down to business and started by discussing the various candidates from Cairo University for collaboration with us. He first commented on the theoretical physicist Professor Ahmed Osman, whom I had met in my previous visit to Cairo. He said that Osman was not in his group, and added that Osman was a strange man with a dangerous personality and opinions. Since we had decided that the cooperation in physics would go only through El-Nadi, we agreed that at the moment Osman was not a candidate. As for the young Dr. Abdel Harith, who was so eager to work with us, El-Nadi had some reservations, mainly because Harith did not get his Ph.D. in Egypt, and El-Nadi was afraid that he might not return to Egypt from the West. We concluded that he would be a possible candidate at a later stage for work at the Weizmann Institute in Rehovot.

As for the two candidates whom I had interviewed together with Professor Omar Badawi, his first choice was Tarek Hussein who was excellent and without children, although Ahmed Ghoniem was also very good. He wanted Tarek Hussein to go to Switzerland to work with us there already in June. For that he would need a letter of invitation from me or from Professor Ashery from Tel Aviv or from the head of the group in Switzerland, Professor Walter, and wanted the letter to be sent from Switzerland. In the letter there should be a promise to pay for Hussein's travel ticket as well as per diem for his two months of stay. El-Nadi then added that he might hopefully get the money for the Tickets in Egypt. We agreed that the question of bringing his wife with him was Hussein's problem, but I told el-Nadi that we might be able to let her join the experiment in the future and might even find financial support for her. To my surprise he then asked if we could send Ghoniem too, and I answered that we should start with one and if successful, he would send the other one, and he agreed.

I raised the suggestion of collaboration in an experiment in Los Alamos, which would start in less than a year, and would last about two years. El-Nadi said that it was fine with him, and added that Abdel Harith would be a candidate for that, although he had another candidate, Ibrahim, who had been his best student, ever, but was then in the army. I said that I would consult with Professor Alster from Tel Aviv who headed our group in Los Alamos and ask David Bowman, the head of the group from Los Alamos, who was visiting Israel at that time, to go through

Cairo on his way back to Los Alamos. We then talked about getting financial aid for our planned collaborations from two possible American sources:

1. The Ford Foundation. We agreed to apply together to them. Since El-Nadi had responded positively to the invitation of Professor Blaser from the SIN Laboratory in Switzerland, he agreed that I would use this correspondence in my application to the Foundation. He worried whether the foundation's refusal to support him in the past would hurt us this time, and I said that I believed that an application for collaborative research had a good chance to be accepted by the Foundation.
2. The AID. El-Nadi said that we had two options to ask the AID for financial help for the planned collaboration in Los Alamos: we can apply for scholarships or ask for a grant from the special five-million-dollar program. Together with Badawi he had once applied through Richmond, but the application was turned down because the decision of whom to support was in the hands of the Egyptian government and not of the American Embassy. He therefore suggested that we should apply together. For Los Alamos, he suggested that Bowman, Alster and he would apply together, and added that they were in need of a written proposal for that.

El-Nadi then told me that at a certain party he and Abdel Hady spoke with their minister of education and the minister was in favor of scientific cooperation. Considering participation in conferences, El-Nadi suggested sending him an invitation through channels, but he guessed that it was probably still too early for him to visit Tel Aviv. On the other hand, he would most likely be able to invite 1-3 members of our people to the next conference in Alexandria. Before parting he warmly shook my hand and thanked me for my willingness to help his people. I told him that my actions were not entirely altruistic, because I expected that the collaboration would advance my group's research. To Rivka I said after he had left, "I have the feeling that El-Nadi and I are on the right track for cooperation with understanding and benefit for both sides."

Professor Muhammad Badr. He came to my hotel in the afternoon to say good bye, and spent most of the time telling me how he was suffering from his connections with Israelis. Nine months earlier he had gotten an invitation to a conference in Indonesia, but the Egyptian authorities prevented him from going, although he was willing to pay the cost by himself. Hamdi Said, the head of the doctors' organization, told him that he had not gotten the honorary citation because of his old age (64), but he did not believe it. As the head of the national organization of urologists He invited Shahabandar, the head of the cancer institute, to lecture in a urologist conference in the Hilton, and he agreed provided no Israelis would take part in the conference, and the organization accepted his condition. Badr did not know whether these examples of negative attitude were due to orders from above or were the result of those peoples' personal attitude, since Mahmud Mahfouz from nuclear engineering and a former education minister had told him that he was in favor of scientific cooperation with Israel. Badr then asked me if we could help him financially if on the way to San Francisco he would go through Tel Aviv, and I said that we would be happy to provide all the expenses for that.

Finally, Badr surprised me by saying that he agreed with his government's request that the Jews leaving Egypt should leave all their money behind, "Because in the United States too, if all the Wall-Street people would want to leave the US and take their money with them, the US government would not let them do so in order to prevent the collapse of the country's economy." I said to Rivka after he had left, "It is interesting that even people with a strong positive attitude toward cooperation with Israel, and are even willing to suffer for that, still possess opinions with a touch of anti-Semitism. I imagine that we will hear such opinions from other Egyptians, as we have heard derogative anti-Egyptian statements in Israel. Our educators should pay much attention to that."

Tabark and Ali. Our friends Tabark and Ali came to the hotel to say good bye. It was an excited meeting for the four of us. They brought presents for our youngest daughter Mimi, and Tabark brought me another copy of her thesis to replace the one that had been lost or confiscated at the airport in our previous visit. They offered to drive us to the airport, and we thanked them for that, but declined the offer. This couple had already done so much for us.

Summary and Conclusions.[4] In comparison with my first visit, half a year earlier, I found Egypt in general more receptive to the idea of cooperation with Israel. Formally, there was one important change; namely, a framework for agreement on cultural cooperation had now been signed by the two governments, although the agreement itself was still waiting for the formal and final signing. Since the instruction from above not to cooperate with Israeli universities was still in power, I agreed with most of my Egyptian colleagues to wait for the final signing.

As for the scientists themselves, I found a whole spectrum of personal attitudes. Side by side with those who objected to cooperation with Israelis because of ideological and psychological reasons as well as fear of losing their ties with the Arab

---

4 *The reader is reminded that the ideas presented here are those of the author, 30 years ago, and is invited to compare them with what has actually happened since then.*

countries, I found a growing interest for cooperation in academic people from the natural sciences. There were some, such as the chemist Shahabandar, the mathematician Ismail Amin, as well as the physicists Tabark, her friend from the Atomic Energy Authority, and Abdel Harith, who were eager to collaborate with us. Last but not least, there were the senior scientists who were very interested to collaborate with us. They were: El-Nadi, the senior Egyptian physicist and his colleague Omar Badawi, the remote-sensing expert Abdel Hady, the biologist from the AEA Tymour Kammal, and the senior urologist Dr Badr.

Socially and politically, I found in Egypt a stronger religious right, notably in the universities, and some weakening of the left and of the Nasserites. The social gap was increasing and the economic conditions were worsening. It therefore appeared that the policy of an open door to the West was not working well. I noticed more opposition to President Sadat than in my first visit, but it appeared that he had still the support and even the admiration of the majority of his people. The desire to have peace, or rather the opposition to war was the feeling of the great majority of Egyptians.

From my own interests, I felt that the visit was both interesting and important. It enabled me to get to know Cairo better and to agree on collaborations with several senior scientists, provided the politicians would not stop them. There were several dramatic moments in my visit, when I had the feeling that the interest in collaboration was fading away, but the situation changed when the rate of visits to my hotel room increased dramatically. In some cases I was on the verge of agreement with some Egyptian scientists on all the details of the proposed collaboration, as were the cases of remote sensing and the desert goat, and then these scientists realized that they had been too optimistic when they received instructions from above. I realized that the road to collaboration might be longer than originally expected even with the most willing and eager senior Egyptian scientists.

From the official and political point of view, I had one important success; namely, my long and good meeting with the Secretary of State for Foreign Affairs Dr. Boutros Boutros Ghali, because it opened the door for us to communicate in the future. Abdel Hady had told me that he would try to arrange for me a meeting with President Sadat, but the meeting did not take place because of illness. I was again greatly helped by Addison Richmond from the American Embassy. Although he had a directive from above to let the Israelis and Egyptians develop their ties by themselves, this exceptional human being and diplomat did everything in his power to let me make first contacts with the Egyptian colleagues.

My luck with university administrators was not very good or useful. I did speak in a friendly way with the president of the American University, but I failed to meet the President of the Suez-Canal University. In most of my meetings it became clear that Ibrahim Badran, the president of Cairo University, was the key person concerning cooperation. Dr. Badr and others with whom I dealt said that Badran was a tough man, others such as Addison Richmond and El-Nadi refrained from commenting on him, while Abdel Hady praised Badran's attitude concerning cooperation. Who was right? It was hard for me to tell, but I noticed that they all agreed that Badran had the last say on the subject at Cairo University, and that his influence on the government on the issues of collaboration was decisive. I decided that I should look for ways to talk to him, with the hope that the arguments I had used in my talk with Boutros Ghali would steer him our way.

Concerning mutual visits, I concluded that I would recommend to our staff in Tel Aviv not to send at that time invitations to their Egyptian colleagues, since the Egyptians had instructions from above not to go, at least until the actual signing of the cultural agreement. Even after the signing, (if indeed there would be one) the Egyptian colleagues would be told that they might expect the severing of their ties with the Arab countries as well as hostile reactions from their students; all in all, not a very optimistic recommendation. As for visits of our people in Egypt, my recommendation would be that they take place after some preparation, and by a selected group of people. I would recommend that there should be a special body at the University, which would overlook this program, and I would suggest that it would be the Research Project on Peace.

CHAPTER 8.
THE THIRD VISIT TO EGYPT

When I returned to Tel Aviv from Egypt I was faced with two major tasks: making sure that the Peace Project continued to work and develop, which mostly meant meeting with people, and trying to advance the most probable collaborations as appeared in my visit to Egypt.

Steve Cohen. Although the request by Boutros Ghali to help him bring Professor Steve Cohen to Egypt seemed strange, I knew that it was important for us to help him financially. I first tried to get a contribution from Raymond Sackler, the chairman of the board of governors of the University. He was willing to contribute $10,000, if his friend the Egyptian ambassador to Washington Ashraf Ghorbal would contribute $5,000. (Later Sackler withdrew his offer, but President Ben-Shahar found another source). In my talks with Sackler he said that he had met Badran in Cairo, and found him very friendly. He said that he would try to arrange for a meeting between our president Ben-Shahar and President Badran of Cairo University (but he never succeeded in that).

I informed Steve Cohen about my talk with Boutros Ghali about him, and said that we were trying to help his visit financially. He too said that while in Cairo, he would try to arrange for a meeting between Ben-Shahar and Badran in his presence. Cohen then suggested not writing to Ghali before the important meeting of the Israeli and Egyptian negotiating teams on May 26, because on that date it would become clear if Ghali's policy and attitude would be accepted in Egypt. He informed me that he had heard from the Ford Foundation that they had been impressed favorably with the Peace Project in their meeting with me.

A few days later I received a call from Steve Cohen informing me that a Palestinian named Professor Anabtawi, who was a member of a group organized by Cohen and Kelman to try to advance Arab Israeli cooperation, was about to arrive in Israel from the US. Anabtawi was a professor of political science in Vanderbilt University in the US, had already been in Kuwait for two years as an active vice rector, and was coming to investigate the levels of universities in the West Bank, mainly of Bir Zeit and Nablus. Steve asked that I would go to the airport and meet him there. I said that I would gladly be Anabtawi's host and that I was hoping to hear from him about the West Bank and about Kuwait, since at that time we knew very little about the academic institutes in these places.

Anabtawi. I called the director general of the foreign ministry Joseph Chechanover, who was very interested in our plans for cooperation and of Steve Cohen's involvement, and informed him about the expected visit of Anabtawi. I met Anabtawi at Ben-Gurion Airport and he told me then that he was in Kuwait replacing the Vice Rector Anan Shihab El-Din, who was spending most of his time in Berkeley. The second vice rector was Professor Isam Naquib, a Palestinian friend of mine, who had been a student with me in Seattle. I learned from Anabtawi that the Kuwait University, with 500 faculty members and 9,000 students, had an annual budget of close to 200 million dollars, and was planning to build a new campus for one billion dollars. The teaching load of an average professor there was three quarters of an hour a day. It was, so he said, one of the best universities in the Arab world, with many Egyptian and Palestinian faculty members and students. They were doing research only in the natural sciences, "because how can one do research in the liberal arts and social sciences when one is not allowed to make religiously unaccepted assumptions and to ask questions."

In Kuwait there were then (1980) about 400,000 Kuwaitis, some of them Bedouins of a low status as well as 250,000 Palestinians and other foreigners. With regards to personal freedom the situation in Kuwait was much better than in Saudi Arabia. They served alcoholic drinks, and young women wore bikinis on the beach. One could watch there all kinds of programs on the TV, including reports from Israel, but the Khomeini influence was gaining momentum.

Anabtawi's stories about Libya were frightening and amusing at the same time. He flew to Kuwait first class in an American plane. He put the small bottles of scotch he received on the plane in his briefcase. When the plane landed to refuel in Tripoli, the Libyan police climbed the plane and asked the passengers who was a Muslim. When he raised his hand, they searched him, and when they found the liquor they started pulling him out of the plane, announcing that they were taking him to the city square to be whipped in public. The American captain saved him from that by insisting that the plane was not a Libyan territory. With a smile Anabtawi said that each summer the Libyan students, who were studying in American universities, were ordered to come back to Libya for "training." When they returned to the US they said mockingly that for ten days they had heard lectures on political science and international law from a bunch of idiots.

Anabtawi told me that the purpose of his visit was to check if there were not too many universities in the West Bank. He told me further about Professor Kelman's efforts to organize an Arab-American-European conference in order to discuss higher education in the West bank. "Israelis have not been invit-ed from fear that they would dominate the conference." The following were some of his political assessments[1]: The peace with Egypt is irreversible; the developments with regards to the Palestinian problem will mostly be affected by what will happen in the oil countries; revolutions in the Arab countries will happen, and the only uncertain parameter is when; perhaps Israel should help the revolutions take place; the people in the West Bank, who are led by the Feudal-Bourgeois families, will not accept the revolutionary heads of the PLO as their leaders. Jordan will not become a Palestinian state, and the Palestinian problem will not be solved this way. Finally, I invited him to be a guest in my home when he returned from the West Bank.

After several days he came back to my home from the West Bank. I first took him to a party for Dr. Eli Reches, a member of the Project's Management and of the Shiloah Institute, where we met other members of the Institute as well as Josh Palmon, who had been Ben-Gurion's advisor on Arab affairs. Among other things, Palmon said that the main reason that the so-called Palestinian Rejectionists such as George Habash and Naïf Huatma were fighting us in their own extreme way was their being refugees from Israel proper and not from the territories. Their being Marxists, and possibly also Christians, might cause them to be rejected by the leadership of the West Bank. He expected that the Rejectionists would continue fighting even if the West Bank would become an independent political entity.

The following is a brief report of Anabtawi's visit to the West Bank: He was

1   *The reader is again invited to compare these assessments, made 30 years ago, before the expulsion of the PLO leaders from Beirut and a dozen years before the Oslo agreement, with what has actually taken place.*

received warmly there. Unlike the Israelis, the West Bankers were proud of their young men who went abroad to study, and did well there, even if they did not come back to the West Bank. The life of the people living in refugee camps was very hard, and they did not believe any more that Pan-Arabism would help them. The West Bankers as well as the majority of the PLO (not the Rejectionists), whose leadership was in Beirut, would agree to accept a Palestinian state next to Israel.

His next report was on the universities or rather colleges in the West Bank: There were three large colleges in the West Bank and one Muslim college in Gaza. Each college wanted to become a university, but there was very little coordination. Eight more colleges were planned in the West Bank. Bir Zeit was the largest and most open and cosmopolitan. Something curious had lately happened. Arab universities were planning to have a conference in the city of Medina in Saudi Arabia. Since no non-Muslim was allowed to enter Medina, the president of Bir-Zeit College Hanna Nasser and Vice President Gabi Baramki would not be able to attend the conference because they were Christians, and a junior faculty member will represent Bir Zeit College at the conference. He was invited to come again to the West Bank for a visit of ten days, at the end of which he would present his proposals. The PLO was expected to support his recommendations, at least partially, perhaps because of the long talk that his colleague Herbert Kelman had held with Yasser Arafat. Finally, I invited him to visit me again after his next visit to the West Bank, and told him that I hoped that he would be able to help us get West-Bank professors to visit us.

Yair Hirschfeld[2]. Hirschfeld, who did his doctorate research under the supervision of Professor Uriel Dan of the history department and the Shiloah Institute, was sent to me by Professor Itamar Rabinovitz to present some new ideas. Hirschfeld was an Austrian citizen, who had gotten his Ph.D. summa cum laude at Tel Aviv University. He and his father knew the Austrian Prime Minister Bruno Kreisky very well. He told me that his father owned a big construction factory in Israel, and Kreisky had offered to give such a factory to Egypt as a present, and that the Israeli Koor company will be involved in the deal. Yair planned to spend a year in Egypt to carry out research there. He was going to submit a research proposal on that to the Peace Project, and to ask Prime Minister Kreisky to finance his stay in Egypt. I told him that his idea seemed good, and contained good elements such as a tri-partite collaboration,

2   *Together with Dr. Ron Pundak Professor Yair Hirschfeld was a key architect of the Oslo Accord in 1993, thirteen years after his talks with me as described earlier in the book.*

with the third party being European and not American. However, I cautioned him not to be too optimistic, since Kreisky and Austria were not liked by the Israeli establishment.

We talked at length about some of his ideas for the tri-partite collaboration, such as disintegrated technology, a hydraulic process which changes cellulose into sugar and the introduction of solar energy to villages in Egypt. He suggested that I come with him to Austria to talk with the Austrian science minister, a socialist from the Viennese pro-Israeli wing of the party (while Kreisky was connected with the provincial wing, which had collaborated with the Nazis, but became leftist). He said that the West German ambassador suggested that he meet Willie Brandt, and get the Germans involved in his initiatives. He told me that he had predicted that the big economic gap in Iran would bring an explosion, which actually took place, and added that a similar explosion would take place in Egypt if the West would not invest there in a way that would lower the gap between the rich and the poor. I suggested to him to also talk with Vice President Mori Sokolovski, and he suggested that he and I should also talk to Professor Yoram Dinstein, who had been in the diplomatic service of Israel, about the political aspects of his plans. We both did not fully appreciate then the negative reactions that we would get from the two professors. Professor Dinstein, for example, asked me cynically, "What is in all this for the Peace Project?" and added scornfully, "Who is this Kreisky?" As for Willie Brandt, Dinstein had no objection. I also talked with Hannan Bar-on from our Foreign Ministry. He too was against any official dealing with Kreisky, "who was against the Camp-David Agreement, and don't forget that the University is an official body." I clearly objected to his last statement. I was glad to learn later that President Ben-Shahar, on the other hand, was in favor of Hirschfeld's ideas.

I will not elaborate on the many talks I had at that time with professors who were planning to interact with counterparts in Egypt. Usually my advice to them was to go very slowly or even wait until May 26. As for my talks with president Ben-Shahar, the only one worth mentioning is his specific advice to me not to deal with the Palestinian issue in the Peace Project[3].

3 The objection of Project Management's members Shimon Shamir and Yoram Dinstein as well as of President Ben-Shahar to any dealing of the Peace Project with the Palestinian problem is worth mentioning in the view of the huge importance today of this issue, which is now recognized by everybody. All my efforts to remind them of "the sins" of the University in failing to prepare itself and the country for the shock of peace with Egypt were of no use. They claimed that the reason for their opposition was their care for the Peace Project, by keeping it away from internal Israeli politics; but I felt that they also did not sufficiently appreciate then the importance of the issue and the rising power of the Palestinians.

Boutros Ghali. The time was between the signing of the peace agreement with Egypt and the final signing of the cultural agreement. Egypt and Israel were negotiating the autonomy (or full autonomy), which had been promised to the Palestinians in the Israeli-Egyptian peace treaty. It was clear that Israel was not very enthusiastic about giving any autonomy to the Palestinians. Prime Minister Begin appointed Joseph Burg, minister for internal affairs, to represent Israel in the negotiations, because Begin trusted Burg, and knew that he would do his best to slow down the pace of the negotiations. President Sadat appointed Boutros Ghali, minister of state for foreign affairs, to represent Egypt in the talks. It was clear that the Palestinian authority was not a priority issue for the two negotiating governments, but both of them played the same game of appearing to be negotiating seriously.

Boutros Ghali came to Israel in early May 1980 to negotiate the autonomy in Herzliya. After several unsuccessful efforts on my part, and with the help of Joseph Burg, Dan Patir, and Gomah from the Egyptian embassy, I managed to talk over the phone with Boutros Ghali. I told him about our efforts on behalf of Steve Cohen, and about keeping Ambassador Ashraf Gorbal in the picture, and he said, "You have given me two pieces of good news." He then invited me to come to talk to him in Egypt, and gave me his home phone-number. A few days later, and with the help of Gomah, I received a visa to Egypt.

Arriving in Cairo. I arrived in Cairo for a six-day visit on May 12, two weeks before the crucial Israeli-Egyptian meeting scheduled for May 26, which was expected to determine the future relations of the two countries, and which was supposed to deal mainly with the question of Palestinian authority.

I was met at the airport by Abdel Hady, who told me that the City was tensely waiting to hear President Sadat, and that I should, therefore, expect much more hesitation than before in all my meetings; and as it turned out, he was absolutely right. He said that the Egyptian public was disappointed by Israel's position on the Palestinian autonomy, on the question of Jerusalem, on the settlements in the occupied territories, as well as on other issues. He said that he had tried and failed in his efforts to arrange meetings for me with Moustapha Kamal Helmi, who was the minister of science and education in the government and had just resigned, and with Hassan Ismail, the president of the National Academy of Science. When he heard about my planned meeting with Boutros Ghali he said that this was the only way to proceed. Finally, he invited me to visit him again in his laboratory in the national Academy of Science. I then called El-Nadi in Cairo University, and he was as friendly as before. I called Tymour Kammal, who was also friendly, but advised me to wait for formal exchange of letters between our officials in our applications to the various foundations. He told me that he was hoping to become the director of the nuclear center, and was therefore careful not to make mistakes. My conclusion was that I was apparently in Cairo at the right time for understanding what was happening there, and that I was going to meet the right person (Boutros Ghali), if there was any chance at all to establish scientific collaborations soon.

Professor Edward Azar. I was invited by Ghali to come to his office at 19:30. I was worried that he might not be there because of Sadat's speech the following day, and in fact my worries were justified. I was met in the office by a man who introduced himself as Professor Edward Azar, an aid to Boutros Ghali. He told me to come the following day at the same time for a visit of 30 minutes, because, so he said, this was as much time as he, Azar, could devote to me. I was surprised by his statement, since I came to Cairo on the personal invitation of Boutros Ghali to meet him and not Edward Azar, and I wondered *who is this Ed Azar and what have I got to do with him?* Azar offered me a chair, sat near me, and started talking, and this is what he said:

He was of Lebanese origin and was a professor of political science in North Carolina. He was a good friend of Steve Cohen and his partner in research which was financed by the Ford Foundation. He had visited Israel together with Steve. and was ending his third and last week in the American University in Cairo as a distinguished visiting professor. In the previous three days he had had long talks with his friend Boutros Ghali, in which the main topic was the way to bring Steve to Cairo in order to tell the Egyptians about Israel, her people, their habits and ways of thinking.

We spent some time talking about the Al-Ahram Institute, in which he agreed that they were not the good partners for collaborations, although there were in the Institute also people, such as Professor Saad Eddin Ibrahim, who were in favor of cooperation with Israel. I then recalled what Steve had once told me, "The Al-Ahram Institute has suggested to Sadat to study Israel in order to beat her. Now the institute regrets its giving that advice, because Sadat paid attention to it, and studied Israel in order to make peace with her."

Azar returned to the presentation of his views. He said that he had learned in this visit how bad the last two meetings of Israelis and Egyptians (the meeting in Cairo of the Shiloah Institute with the Al-Ahram Institute and the meeting of psychiatrists in Washington, in which Shimon Shamir and Aharon Yariv took part) had been. The Egyptians came to the meetings with antagonistic attitudes, and saw in any word or action of the Israelis a proof of their negative perception of Egypt and her people. His conclusion was that because cooperative research projects were impossible for political reasons, the two peoples should first study each other, separately, or with the help of the Americans. He added that even businessmen, who were supposed by all the experts to be the first to be interested in collaboration, were still hesitant. It was clear to me that in spite of his negative conclusion, his own attitude was constructive and he was looking for ways to promote cooperation between Israelis and Egyptians.

At this point I interrupted his flow of talk and said that I wished to make a few comments, and he agreed I pointed out that the solution which he proposed was a sort of a compromise between two mutually contradicting elements. One element was the need of both sides to know the other, and the other element was the wish of the Egyptians not to have any contact with the Israelis. His proposed solution that each side would study the other by itself or with the help of the Americans was a strange compromise, but might hopefully suit the Egyptians at that time. I told him that his approach was wrong, since he was investigating the fields for cooperation which he should have known from the beginning that they were candidates for failure. These were the fields of the liberal arts and social sciences (the Al-Ahram conference), as well as all fields related to beliefs, to opinions, etc, including psychology and psychiatry (the Washington conference); even business is not the right field to start with.

"Wait a minute", said Edward Azar. "The choice of businessmen as the ideal candidates is the basic assumption of all people dealing with the question of cooperation. How and why are you taking issue with this universally accepted assumption?"

I started my answer by telling him briefly about our Research Project on Peace, about our thoughts and actions till then, and about our plans. I then described at length my talk with Boutros Ghali and my analysis of the reasons for the different attitudes of various groups in Egypt regarding contacts with Israelis (political, ideological, professional, and financial). I then mentioned three main groups in Egypt that differ from one another in the attitude of their members to cooperation with Israel: 1. The group which was the closest to ideology – the group of the liberal arts and social sciences; 2. The group which was the farthest from ideology – the group of the natural sciences; 3. The in-between group which included doctors, engineers, and businessmen.

For personal, ideological, professional, and financial reasons it should a priori be expected that the three groups would have different attitudes about cooperation. The Egyptian intellectual dealing with political science or with Islam was closer to the Pan-Arabian classical ideology. He was professionally tied to Arab and Muslim intellectuals, and he had additional sources of income from jobs and book royalties in the Arab countries. The physician, the engineer, or the businessman was farther from the Arab intellectual as far as ideology was concerned, and had professional and material ties mainly with the West, but had appreciable present and future financial ties with the Arab countries as well. For this reason he too was expected to hesitate burning himself by having ties with Israel.

In comparison with the people of these two groups, the Egyptian physicist, biologist, or the mathematician was professionally far away from ideology. Although he had some financial ties with the oil countries, his main present and future professional and financial ties were with the western countries. Therefore, he was less afraid than the others to be burned. Boutros Ghali agreed with me that for these reasons, ties should start between the natural scientists. I described to him all my contacts in Cairo, which led me to come up with a balanced program of three Egyptian-Israeli research projects, which would be carried out as pilots. The three were: remote sensing, nuclear physics, and the camel and goat. I added that I was guided by five principles, which were not only accepted by Ghali, but had been suggested by him. The principles were: 1. All the three were from the natural sciences; 2. Both sides were interested in them; 3. Until further agreement, the research projects would be carried out in complete discretion; 4. Each one of them had a third party (American, European, or Canadian) who could be involved if the two parties wanted his involvement; 5. The whole program was balanced in the overall scientific level of the participants; in remote sensing the Egyptians had an advantage, in nuclear physics we had the advantage, and in the camel and goat the two sides were on equal level.

I added that although I was not a social scientist, but as an experimental scientist I allowed myself to point out that apart from the scientific benefit to the participants, the acceptance of the plan and its execution could serve as a sociological experiment, where we would have direct contact between the two sides, with common interest and in full discretion. Even Boutros Ghali, who was afraid of direct contact between social scientists, would be able to use this experiment in his arguments, if the experiment would be successful. The following example would demonstrate the point: When an Egyptian physicist would work 24 hours a day with Israeli scientists and European ones, the national differences would quickly be wiped out. If they would then face technical difficulties and would solve them together, it would be very likely that the Egyptian scientist would then not look for negative behavior and perception of the Israelis (as Al-Ahram Institute's people did).

At this point Azar interrupted me with an unexpected compliment. He said that he was sorry that he had not heard about me before, but from my words he reached the conclusion that I and the Research Project on Peace had made much more progress in our thinking and actions than all the people who were dealing with this issue in the US and in Egypt and probably also in Israel. He admitted that my approach and my thesis made more sense than the hitherto commonly accepted ones. He added that the sociological experiment, which I had described, showed a great deal of understanding and sensitivity, for instance in the request for equality in scientific level. Finally he said that he liked the idea of having it as a pilot.

He then explained that he had suggested my meeting with Ghali for only 30 minutes because he thought that we were going to talk only about Steve Cohen, but after my explanations he realized that Ghali and I had other important matters to talk about. He said that Ghali wanted to bring Steve to teach elite groups such as those in Al-Ahram Institute about Israel, but Steve was known there as pro-Israeli, and there was opposition to the idea. Since Ambassador Gorbal too was apparently against bringing Steve, the Egyptian Government would not devote money for that purpose, directly or indirectly.

He told me that he and Steve had just finished preparing a manuscript on the security problems as seen by the Israelis, and they were going to give a copy to Ghali. I told him about our think tank and about the conclusion of its members from a wide spectrum of political views that we would recommend independence to the Palestinians, provided the security of Israel would be maintained. I said that the Egyptians had made a mistake in the autonomy talks when they brought it to a crisis on a security issue, in which Israel was very sensitive. Sadat understood this point well in 1977 when he offered us 100% security for 100% withdrawal. If he would come with a similar statement about the West Bank, he would gain many friends in Israel. Azar replied that both he and Steve thought this way too, and that Ghali agreed with them. He then added with a smile, "When they speak about this issue in the meeting of the Egyptian government, Ghali pretends to be looking for something in his papers so that he will not have to react". At the end of our discussion Azar went into the office to tell Ghali's secretary to leave two full hours for me to talk with Ghali, and told me that he would join us for half an hour. I thought that *if I would succeed with Ghali as I have just succeeded with Ed Azar I would be very happy.*

A talk with Boutros Ghali. The following day I came to Ghali's office, and we talked for almost two hours. Edward Azar joined us for the second hour, and his participation was very helpful.

The beginning of the meeting was devoted to politics. Ghali started by telling me that he was looking forward to the day in which he would be able to return to university teaching. He then asked me for my impressions of Egypt in this visit. I told him that I had noticed more public tension and expectation than in my previous visits. I added that in Israel there was a growing opposition to the process, mainly in the settlements in the occupied territories and their supporters, but also in the government and the general public. There was general disappointment from the normalization or the lack of it as well as anxiety about the intentions of Egypt. A growing number of Israelis felt that we had given back Sinai with its defensive depth, and were supposed to get normalization for that, but did not. I repeated my statement to Azar that creating a crisis on security issues was wrong and that I was looking forward to a statement by President Sadat understanding the security needs of Israel. I hoped that a good statement would help draw the line in Israel between the consistent hawks and those who held hawkish ideas only because of anxiety about our security.

Ghali's reaction to that was interesting. He said that the formula of 100% security for 100% withdrawal was also his opinion, and he was against breaking down the talks on security issues, but the Israeli delegation was playing a trick on them by claiming that the settlements are needed for security, so that breaking the talks on the issue of the settlements was seen by the Israelis as breaking them on the issue of security. He thought that the Israeli ministers knew his opinion, and that many of them agreed with him, but for some reason it was impossible to move forward. He said that they had tried everything: committees, sub-committees, returning to committees, discussion of agendas, etc, but no progress. I imagine that like me, he too knew that the Israeli delegation, on orders from Prime-Minister Begin, was not interested in moving forward on the issues of the autonomy and the settlements.

I repeated briefly my personal opinion that the Camp David Accord was for Begin an exchange deal, the West Bank (for Israel) in exchange for the Sinai (for the Egyptians). Ghali responded that for this reason there was not a great likelihood then for progress on the normalization and related issues. I repeated my thesis that we were not anymore two independent political systems, but one system of two coupled equations; and as in mathematics, it was impossible in such a case to solve one equation without solving the other, since in every one of them there existed a term which depends on the other. For Israel, for instance, the Egyptian insensitivity in the question of Israeli security had a negative effect on the Israeli public, while success in cooperation and normalization in general would have a positive effect. I then said the following: "We should never forget that the good will of the Israeli public is important to Egypt and that the good will of the Egyptian public is important to the Israeli public," and added, "It is commonly accepted that the control of the pace of the normalization is solely an Egyptian card, but this is only partially true. In the eyes of Begin this pace has only a secondary value, since he is mainly interested in keeping the territories and not in the normalization, so that the slowing down of the normalization pace does not affect much the Israeli government, but affects the attitude of the Israeli public towards Egypt and the trust in Egypt's intentions, and this should be important to Egypt."

At this point Ghali called Azar to come in. I told them briefly about the visit of Anabtawi and about the assistance we give to West-Bank colleges. I then described our first steps concerning Austria and Germany's involvement in future cooperation, following Ghali's suggestions, and Ghali then said emphatically, "It is important to have a third party involved." I described at length my efforts in the last couple of months in regard to possible scientific collaborations, again following the understanding between me and Ghali in our last meeting. Turning to Ghali I said, "I have been looking for the common term in the two coupled equations, trying to make it positive." I repeated the list of principles which I used in my efforts, as was agreed upon by us, and added,

"Collaboration in the natural sciences is important to the Israeli scientists, but also to the Egyptian scientists who are experiencing some kind of scientific claustrophobia, and therefore want to break out, also with us and through us, into the western scientific world. I carefully considered a large number of topics and candidates for collaboration in the following fields: Pure science (mathematics and physics); applied science (seismic studies, remote sensing, agriculture, solar energy, physical rehabilitation, and pharmacology); medicine (cancer research, urology, liver diseases, bilharzias, and eye diseases); and archeology and Egyptology. I also looked at a variety of ideas in liberal arts and social sciences, but because of our understanding, I did not consider them seriously at that stage.

I have finally decided to start with a group of three research projects, which satisfy all the agreed upon criteria. Each one of them is important by itself, and together they make a balanced program, which could also be used as a pilot and a sociological experiment. This is the proposed group of researches:

Remote Sensing. Here the Egyptian group has a scientific advantage. The laboratory, which is located in the Egyptian Academy of Science, has invited us to join them in their research. If needed, a third party can be added from the Oklahoma State University.
Nuclear Physics. The suggestion has come from Cairo University, while the scientific advantage at the moment is ours. The experiment will be carried out in a national laboratory in Switzerland.
The Desert Goat and the Camel. The proposal to improve these two animals has originated here as well as in Tel Aviv. The scientific level of the two groups is the same. The Egyptian group comes from the Atomic Energy Authority."

In response to their request, I described in detail how the idea of each collaborative research project developed and in what stage it was at that time: Abdel Hady was waiting for the approval of Hassan Ismail; Mohamed El-Nadi was waiting for the approval of Ibrahim Badran; and Tymour Kammal was waiting for the approval of Hamouda; and together, apparently along with the minister for education and science Moustapha Kamal Helmi, they were waiting for the approval of the ministry of foreign affairs. I pointed out that the success of this program, which would be carried out in parallel with the effort of Steve Cohen and Ed Azar in the social sciences, would contribute a positive term to the system of coupled equations.

Edward Azar added a few words of support, and it was clear that Ghali was positively impressed by the presentation. I told them of our efforts to arrange a meeting between the president of Tel-Aviv University (Ben-Shahar) and the president of Cairo University (Badran), and I asked Ghali if he was going to help, and specifically to tell the scientists mentioned by me to go ahead with the mentioned collaborative research projects. Finally, I asked him if he would allow me to suggest to the Ford Foundation that they consult with him after we would submit to them requests of support for the three collaborative research projects.

With regards to all my questions he asked me to first send him, through Murthada, the Egyptian ambassador in Israel, a written summary of our discussion, with a lengthy description of the three research projects which I proposed. He also wanted me to send him the list of all the research projects which the Peace Project had already approved. As for my questions, he said that he needed a green light, but did not say from whom. After that, and after receiving my account, he would get in touch with the scientific directors whom I had mentioned, and would then also let me know if the Ford Foundation and the Egyptian scientists could contact him. Talking about Badran, Ghali said that he had just sat next to him in the parliament for four hours. He told me to call Badran and tell him that Boutros Ghali recommended that he would talk to me. I then asked him if it was okay for me to tell my scientific colleagues in Cairo about our discussions, but clearly not to the press. His answer was, "Definitely. I have nothing to hide; in fact, it is important for them to know that it is in my interest that what I do is transparent, and not done under the table."

After discussing various topics, among them the Egyptian author Hussein Faouzi, Ghali said that Faouzi was very talented, but problematic, because he was anti-Arab. As for conferences, such as the one in Al-Ahram Institute and in Washington, he said that they were counter productive, and at any rate he preferred the conferences to be in places such as Harvard University because of the academic atmosphere there.

The last part of our discussion was devoted to his attempt to bring Steve Cohen to Cairo. I repeated Ben-Shahar's offer to contribute $10,000 for that, on the condition that Ambassador Gorbal would contribute $5,000. When Ghali said that it was hard for him to get funds in Egypt, I promised to try and convince President Ben-Shahar to withdraw his condition. Before parting

I promised to send him soon, via Ambassador Mortada, an account of our meeting and a summary of my personal political views. And that was the end of our friendly and informal meeting.

Professor El-Nadi. Before calling Professor Ibrahim Badran, president of Cairo University, on the advice of Boutros Ghali, I called El-Nadi to ask him if it was okay for me to mention our plans to Badran. He said that it was okay with him, and that Badran was a nice person. He also informed me that he had already talked to Moustapha Kamal Helmi, the minister of Science and education, who told him that he was familiar with my name and some of my activities in Egypt. As for the proposed collaborative research, Helmi's answer was that approval depended on the political developments following the signing of the cultural agreement a few days earlier. Nothing new in that. I called Badran's office, and was transferred from one secretary to another. I heard whispering in the background, and was asked to call again in half an hour. They promised to call me when he would come back to the office, but no call came. Having been through a similar procedure with the president of the Suez-Canal University, I was not surprised.

El-Nadi came to my hotel at 17:00 to take me to the Ghezira Sporting Club. The Club, which was located on the central island El-Zamalik, was beautiful. El-Nadi told me that in the past it used to be a club for aristocrats, but not any more, "and if it were, I would not belong to it." We started to walk around the racing court for horses, and on the way he told me about his deceased wife and about his health problems. After a while we were joined by his eldest son Adel, who was a plasma physicist in the faculty of engineering. The second son, who was an engineer and had gotten a studying award, joined us later. I learned that El-Nadi had a third son and a daughter, whose fiancé was killed in the Yom-Kippur War, six and a half years earlier. She got married again a while back.

El-Nadi informed me that he had talked with the acting head of the Atomic Energy Authority, Hamouda, and with other officials. They all had heard about me and our wishes and plans for cooperation, and they all were waiting for the decision of the politicians, i.e. of President Sadat and/or the vice president for internal affairs. El-Nadi added that Boutros Ghali, who was Badran's friend, was a key person.

We then discussed the planned experiment in Zurich, and he said that we had better wait for approval by Ghali. After we get that approval he would need travel money for his people. I said that we would be willing to help him in the first stage, and he agreed to give me a letter to the Ford Foundation. We then discussed his candidates for the various planed experiments: Professor Omar Badawi, Ahmed Ghoniem, and Tarek Hussein. He said that he had talked with Hamouda about the possibility of constructing an Egyptian-Israeli accelerator in Egypt with the financial support of the AID, and Hamouda liked the idea. When EL-Nadi suggested that it would be an accelerator for heavy ions, I said that we already had such an accelerator at the Weizmann Institute, which could be used by them too, and suggested that we should therefore look for another type of a nuclear accelerator, and he agreed.

We were quiet thinking, and then he surprised me by starting to talk about political matters. I was surprised, because I had been told that he always stayed away from politics. He said that Nasser wanted peace with Israel already in 1954, but our violent military actions in Gaza turned him to alliance with the Soviets. He then said that the oil countries were saying that because of the peace with Israel, they would fire the Egyptian teachers and would get Indian and Pakistani ones instead.[4]

Adel asked me to tell him about the political situation in Israel. I started by telling them about the work of our think tank, and then answered his request: "I will give you my simple, perhaps even oversimplified picture, which divides the Jews in Israel into three groups: 1. The first group, the hawks, is above all interested in keeping the West Bank. The security reason, which the people in this group often use, even if it has a great measure of validity, is used by them mainly to justify our staying in the West Bank. 2. On the other end of the spectrum, we find the doves who advocate giving up the West Bank for moral, political, and even security reasons. In their opinion, the security of Israel will be improved when she will stop ruling another people. 3. About half the Jews in the country belong to the third group, the center. They would agree to give up all or most of the West Bank if they could be convinced that the security of the country would be maintained. It is therefore very important to convince this group that such is the case, in order to move it from an alliance with the hawkish group, which is the situation today, to an alliance with the dovish one, and Egypt can be helpful in achieving this goal." Adel nodded to indicate that he was satisfied by my answer.

Discussing further the Palestinian issue, Adel and his father said that before

4   *The following day Ali told me that this could not happen, because the Indians and the Pakistanis did not speak Arabic.*

the peace treaty was signed, they had had a commitment to the Palestinians and to the memory of their friends who had died for the Palestinians and this commitment was still there. In the past they had tried to help the Palestinians in war, and when it became clear that this was not possible anymore, they were trying to help them by peace. "Therefore", Adel said, "it is impossible to have normalization without having at least a promise, even for the far future, that the interests of the Palestinians will be maintained." And then he added the following strong statement, "Otherwise, I will not be able to look at a mirror or to talk with scientists from other Arab countries, whom I often meet all over the world."

His sincerity was very impressive, and I told him so. I then repeated my emphasis to Boutros Ghali and Ed Azar of the importance of the Egyptians convincing the Israeli public that Israel could get 100% security as part of a reasonable solution of the conflict with the Palestinians. His strange but frank response was that my explanations seemed reasonable and rational, but he had an emotional difficulty with the normalization, which appeared to him to be shameful as long as there was no progress in the Palestinian problem. And then he added, "My friends and I will gladly join collaborations with Israeli scientists, "because we are interested in peace and in science, but we cannot do it as long as our conscience is not clean."

During the evening I explained to them my own feelings regarding the Palestinian problem as a human being and an Israeli. I told them that the Palestinian suffering concerned me as an Israeli and as a human being, even more than our relations with Egypt. I told El-Nadi that I was glad to hear the concern of his son for the Palestinians, because I had been surprised and even disappointed in my previous visits to Egypt by the apparent lack of concern of many Egyptians for the fate of their brothers, the Palestinians. I said that most Israelis were perhaps pleased by this lack of concern, but I differ from these Israelis on this issue.

At the end of the evening El-Nadi turned to me and said emotionally, "I am glad that we have become friends, and that you are not only a physicist with lots of scientific achievements, but also a sensitive human being."

At 23:00, 6 hours after he had come to my hotel, I said that we should say good bye to each other, but he suggested that we continue our conversation in a coffee house. I said that it was perhaps too late, and he suggested meeting again on Saturday. There was no doubt that this was an emotional, educational, and friendly evening, and that we became friends.

Ups and Downs. The following were my hopes, doubts, and reflections following the thought-provoking and emotional evening I had spent with the great Egyptian physicist: *I am in an interesting situation. I have good contacts; in fact, agreed research plans with three senior Egyptian scientists: Mohamed El-Nadi, Mohamed Abdel Hady, and Tymour Kammal. I still have not met the heads of their three institutions: Ibrahim Badran (Cairo University), Hassan Ismail (National Academy), and Hamouda (AEA). I have established good relations with the secretary of state for foreign affairs Boutros Ghali, who could be the one who would give the go-ahead or delay (or cancel) the okay to the three heads of institutions and perhaps also to Moustapha Kamal Helmi, the minister for science and education. Will Ghali give the go-ahead? Will he get permission to do so from President Sadat?*

Like millions of Egyptians I waited eagerly to Sadat's speech the following evening, which I watched in my room at the Sheraton Hotel together with the Israeli ambassador to Egypt Eliyahu Ben-Elissar. There was nothing in his speech about the Israeli-Egyptian relations; instead, his speech was a direct and brutal attack on the Christians (mostly Copts) in Egypt. Ben-Elisar thought that this was a focused attack with no hidden reasons. Was he right?

In the morning I went with Ali, Tabark, and their son Maged to a museum, which is located in the palaces of Muhammad Ali inside botanical gardens. I asked Ali why Sadat had attacked the Copts, and he said that Sadat had been hurt by them. However, when I asked El-Nadi the same question, he said that this was Sadat's way of applying pressure on all the religious groups, and in particular on the Islamic groups, and their political strength.

Abdel Hady came to my hotel and took me to a coffee house. In contrast with former times, I detected in him some coolness or tension, and thought that he was under pressure by the head of the Academy, but decided not to comment on that. To my surprise, he started talking politics. He told me that he had attended meetings in London of the heads of the academic institutions with Egyptian students, and the students attacked the institutions' heads on Sadat's actions. He then criticized the decisions by the Israeli government on the construction of settlements in the West Bank as well as on Jerusalem; "because by that Israel was establishing irreversible facts in the middle of the negotiations."

I gave him the same political and personal analysis which I had given Ghali as well as the details of the proposed three research projects, and he seemed a little more relaxed, and asked me if Ghali arranged for me to meet Sadat. I said that it was not up to me to ask, but I would be glad if he or Ghali could arrange such a meeting, and I would then make a special trip for that. He explained to me the difficulties of Ibrahim Badran and Hassan Ismail to meet with me or to approve, at that time, collaborations. I said that I imagined that if I had been in their place, I too would have wrestled with the problem, but I guessed that I would have decided on an unofficial and discreet meeting in order to exchange information and ideas. He then invited me to visit him the following day in his laboratory. There was no doubt that this good and courageous scientist was in a tense situation, torn between his scientific and personal conscience and the pressure from his boss. I later received a call from El-Nadi, who was friendly as before, but I detected some tension in him too. I realized that *in similarity to our two countries, I and my Egyptian friends were in one boat in a stormy sea. Will we succeed to get together to the safe coast, or is the sea stronger?*

At the National Academy of Science. At 11:00 the following day I took a cab to the National Academy, where I took the elevator to the seventh floor. The performance of the elevator and of the boy who ran it is worth describing. The elevator had a sliding door, but no buttons for floors or for stopping. The boy started the elevator moving and stopped it with a screwdriver which he was holding in his right hand. All the micro-switches for the stopping and starting were outside the elevator on its roof. When the boy wanted to move or stop the elevator, he would open the door, stretch his whole body outside, holding the door's frame by his left leg and left hand, and would touch the appropriate micro-switch with the screwdriver.

Abdel Hady was not in his room, but I met his colleague Hassan Mustapha, a charming person, who graduated from Syracuse University and used to be the dean of engineering in Ein-Shams University, and a minister of housing under Nasser. He said that Nasser had turned to the Soviets only after the American refused all his requests for help. He said that Nasser was a man of peace, but after the defeat of 1967 he could not make peace, just as Sadat made peace only after he had achieved military gains in 1973. I asked him why Nasser had not made peace between 1956 and 1967, when he could lead the whole region to peace. He hesitated for a long while and then said, "I will think about it, and I will give you an answer in another time." He then added that he had once told the American ambassador, Atherton, that the Americans should move slowly and in parallel lines with Israel and Egypt, since the situation resembled that of a young couple, whose parents were enemies; and the couple should therefore move slowly in making contact, but without touching each other in the first stage.

Abdel Hady came from a meeting with Hassan Ismail and explained to his colleague and to me why the head of the National Academy refused to see me. I reflected on the complicated situation, and only said that I understood what he had just said. What else could I say? When Abdel Hady heard about our political discussion, he told us that in his opinion Nasser had not turned to the road to peace because of his desire to be a leader of several circles: the Arab, the African, and the Islamic ones, as well as the neutral block (together with India and Yugoslavia). He had not been concerned with peace with Israel, because it could have weakened him in the worlds he wanted to lead. At this point I suggested to Abdel Hady that we had better stop talking politics, and asked if I could see his data-analysis laboratory.

A dramatic meeting with the head of the National Academy. When I came back to the office from the laboratory, I did not find Abdel Hady there, and imagined that he was again talking with his boss. I appreciated his strong interest in collaboration, and admired him for his perseverance. I felt also sorry for him and felt that I should urge him to stop his efforts. I therefore told his colleagues that I would leave a message for him and go back to my hotel, but they told me that Abdel Hady had urged them to ask me to stay, so I did; what else could I have done?. When Abdel Hady came to his office his face was pale, but he seemed pleased. With a tense smile he said, "The head of the National Academy will see you in ten minutes." So *ACT 1 of the drama came to an end, and ACT 2 started.*

I went down to Hassan Ismail's office on the third floor with lots of questions running through my mind. *How did Abdel Hady succeed in convincing his boss to see me? Did he tell him that the meeting would be private and was intended only for exchange of information? Would I find Hassan Ismail to be like El-Nadi, i.e. a great scientist, a great Egyptian, and at the same time very human?* I thought that I would soon find the answers to these questions, and I would either get an okay for Abdel Hady to collaborate with us, or at least I would get a better understanding of the difficulties in which the heads of the Egyptian Institutions found themselves at that time.

When I entered Ismail's office he offered me a chair across his desk. It was obvious that he was very tense. He asked me to start talking, and I started by telling him that I appreciated the political difficulties of Egypt in the Arab World after the signing of the peace treaty with us. I added that I was familiar and appreciative of the various sensitivities and of the need not to give publicity to many activities, possibly also to our discussion. I then told him about the Peace Project and about our efforts to advance scientific collaborations, sometimes with participation of a third party. I then related my meetings with Boutros Ghali, and ended by describing the proposed program of three research projects, as I had suggested to Ghali. Ismail listened very attentively, and I had the feeling that his coolness started to thaw. I was pleased by that, but my pleasure did not last for long. *End of ACT 2.*

In the beginning of his talk, Ismail said that Egypt had been more advanced than the other Arab or African countries, but because of Israel, her existence and the wars with her, Egypt found herself at that time wounded and retarded.[5] His dislike or even hatred of Israel became apparent as he kept talking, and my optimism quickly faded away, but I reminded him that the wars wore us down too.

He then made the following remark, "There is a variety of feelings in my country on peace with Israel. After 30 years of hostility, one should not push the Egyptians to change quickly." *Not a very encouraging comment, though it could have been expected.* But I did not expect the following: He started to talk about two kinds of people, those who were led by their hearts and those who mostly used their minds. I still entertained some hope that he meant that those who were led by their hearts were against wars and killings and supported peace and Israeli-Egyptian collaborations, but his next sentence brought me back to the cold reality. "You have to know that not all the Egyptians are like El-Nadi and Abdel Hady, who are more scientists that human beings." *What a strange statement! But in Israel too, many non-scientists talk about the scientists who dwell in their ivory towers and do not contribute to society, i.e. they are more scientists than human beings.* Then he added that Abdel Hady did not have any problems of conscience, and if he got permission, he would collaborate with us, "but we have to know and respect the emotional (human) aspects of the others in the laboratory." While he was talking another scene crossed my mind, that of

5 *Egyptian officials are repeatedly claiming now that Egypt has lost its role as the leader of the Arab World to Saudi Arabia because of Iranian political interference inside Egypt. It is curious that it is always others (Israel or Iran) who are to blame and not the Egyptians themselves.*

El-Nadi telling me that I was not only a good physicist, but a warm human being as well, obviously a different point of view on the relationship between being a scientist and being a human being. Finally, Ismail wished me luck in my efforts, and said that it would take a long time for the "human beings" to change and be like "the scientists". *The end.*

I was not 100% clear whether he classified himself as a scientist or a human being, although he would apparently say that he was closer to the latter. However, he might have thought that as a head of an institution he had to take that stand; and I still remembered that he, as a scientist, was getting ready to collaborate with Yochai Bin-Nun. I had not talked to Ibrahim Badran or Hamouda, but I could guess that their official position would be similar at that time, but from what I had heard, their personal position might be more positive.

I returned to Abdel Hady's office and reported to him about my meeting with his boss. The deputy head of the Academy came in and shook my hand, but did not look at me. *Is he one of the anti-collaboration human beings?* Hassan Mustapha, on the other hand, offered to drive me to the hotel and was again very friendly.

Tymour Kammal called me and told me that all the people in his laboratory were excited about the possibility of collaboration, but Hamouda told him to wait for the political developments following the very recent signing of the cultural agreement "and then we will be able to do many things at a fast pace and turn the desert color to green." He added that we should wait with the submission of the application to the Ford Foundation, and I recalled that Abdel Hady had made a similar request. On the other hand, El-Nadi permitted me to talk to the Foundation in his name too, but did not bring his letter to my office, as promised. Flying back home, I felt sorry for these open minded and open hearted great scientists and great human beings, whom political considerations put in an almost impossible situation.

CHAPTER 9.
CORRESPONDENCE WITH DR. BOUTROS GHALI

The Israeli-Egyptian cultural agreement was signed on May 8, 1980. The political tension got heated, and Defense Minister Ezer Weizmann, one of the architects of the Israeli-Egyptian peace treaty, resigned on May 25. The autonomy talks kept lingering.

On June 22 1980, I wrote a long letter, which included summaries, to Dr. Boutros Ghali, the Egyptian secretary of state for foreign affairs, as requested by him. Because of the importance of this letter and the correspondence which followed, and their influence on the continuation of my activity and that of the Peace Project, the entire correspondence will be presented in the book in full. I attached to my letter the following three documents:
- I. POLITICAL OBSERVATIONS;
- II. STARTING UP SCIENTIFIC COOPERATIONS;
- III. PROMOTING ACADEMIC REGIONAL COOPERATION.

The third document had also been sent to other addresses, including the Ford Foundation. The documents will appear as appendices. This is the text of my letter to Dr. Ghali:

> Dear Dr. Ghali,
> I would like to thank you again for your invitation and for the opportunity to have had two talks with you. As suggested, I have prepared[1] a summary of the ideas that were raised in our discussion on May 14, as well as in our previous discussion on March 12. I have taken the liberty of also including[2] a second summary, which also contains some thoughts that were raised in the course of my talk with Professor Azar on May 13.

1   *See Appendix XI*
2   *See Appendix XII*

The first summary deals with political matters, and the opinions there, are mine and not necessarily those of the Research Project on Peace. As I did not take notes during our discussions, I may have, unintentionally, made some mistakes, or may have erred in emphasis. For this I apologize in advance.

I have not given publicity to our discussions or to my many talks with Egyptian scientists. However, as you suggested, I have told several Egyptian Colleagues of our discussions.

You will also find a third manuscript, dated December 1979, and entitled "Promoting Academic Regional Cooperation".[3] This manuscript, may give you some ideas of our activity and thinking in 1978-1979.

I am sending you this letter, which includes the three above-mentioned manuscripts, by means of my colleague, Professor Shimon Shamir, who is leaving for Cairo very shortly. Professor Shamir has been a board member of the Project since its inception, and I trust that his presence in Cairo will advance and deepen our dialogue.

****

On June 6, two weeks after sending my long letter to Boutros Ghali, I had some good news to report to him, so I sent him the following letter:

Dear Dr. Ghali,

The Ford Foundation has recently informed me that the Foundation has approved, in principle, a grant of $35,000.00 to the Research Project on Peace of Tel Aviv University, to further scientific co-operation between scientists from Egyptian institutions and from Tel Aviv University. In their letter the Foundation requested budgeting along these broad lines: "a third of the amount on your own travel costs and administrative expenses, a third on the most likely one collaborative project, and the final third on fostering the other project ideas".

3 See Appendix IX.

I wish to re-emphasize my conviction that the cause will be best served by a maximum discretion, and I have attempted to convey this in my response to the Ford Foundation. Again, please accept my thanks for your interest and assistance and my expression of hope that our efforts will meet with success.

Until I left, a few weeks later, for my Sabbatical leave in Saclay, the French National Laboratory, I had not heard from Boutros Ghali. Professor David Horn, who had been the chair of the research committee of the Peace Project, was appointed as the director of the Project, at least until my return from the sabbatical leave, but continued in this post after my return with my recommendation. On September 6 1980, the following letter arrived at the Peace Project from Dr. Gomah of the Egyptian Embassy:

Dear Sir,
I have the pleasure of enclosing herewith a letter from Dr. Boutros Ghali, Minister of State for Foreign Affairs, to Professor Avivi Yavin. It will be greatly appreciated if the said letter can be delivered to him as a project director.

The enclosed letter was written on August 7, and was addressed to the Project Director. It was sent to me from Tel Aviv to Saclay, and was a response to my long letter of June 22, but did not mention my July 6 letter about the Ford Foundation. And this is what was written in this letter of Dr. Boutros Ghali:

Dear Professor Yavin,

I have the pleasure to acknowledge receipt of your letter dated June 22, 1980.
I would like to inform you that the summary of your thoughts as well as the manuscript on 'Promoting academic regional cooperation' have been forwarded to my colleague Dr. Moustapha Kamal Helmi[4], Minister of State for Education and Scientific Research, with the hope that such exchange of views would pave the way for a fruitful academic cooperation.

---

4 *The situation in the last thirty years has not improved, and if at all, it has worsened. It has been reported in the Israeli press that Farouk Hosni, the Egyptian minister of culture has recently said that he will burn any Israeli book that he will find in Egypt, and that the Jews lack culture, and steal other peoples' culture. What a shame!*

The tone of the letter is positive, even encouraging, but I have, unfortunately, never heard from Dr. Helmi (or Dr. Ghali following this letter), and to the best of my knowledge neither have Mohamed El-Nadi, Mohamed Abdel Hady, or Tymour Kammal. At any rate, neither of them received a green light for cooperation with us, most likely for political reasons. This unfortunate event, or the lack of it, means that the scientific needs and good will of scientists in Egypt and Israel, who spent many months trying to advance science in the Middle East, went down the drain. What a pity!

Some friends tried to console me by saying that the little small-scale scientific collaboration that took place in the following years may have benefitted from our experience; may be. My own hope is that people in the Middle East and elsewhere, who will try to start collaborations between enemies, will benefit from our experience. As the reader will learn in the rest of the book, I myself was not that fortunate.

****

Upon returning from Cairo, I reported to the University president, to the Steering committee, and the Project management what I had done in Cairo in my short visit, and informed the Project Management that I was leaving for Saclay for a year. The Management meeting was devoted to the discussion of past, present, and future of the Project. I was moved by members of the Management who said that it would be difficult to find a replacement for me, even for a year, because – as Aharon Yariv said - "Avivi Yavin is crazy for peace". Management member Yoram Dinstein spoke about the practically frozen relations with Egypt at that time, and added that once the relations would warm up again, the Management should call me back from my Sabbatical leave. It was finally decided that David Horn would be the acting Director and Yonatan Shapira would replace him as the chair of the research committee.

As I have already said, there were various opinions in the Management about the role of the Peace Project, with some people who supported my actions almost 100% of the time, and some who, in fact, were actually opposing many of my ideas and actions. One of the constructive members was Professor Zeev Hirsch. It is for this reason that I was surprised when he approached me after the meeting and told me that he opposed the direction in which I had been leading the Project. His explanation was that rather than attempting to establish cooperation with Egyptian scientists, the Project should concentrate on internal academic research on the question of moving from war to peace. He also said that there were too many physicists in the Management. I was sad to hear that, especially from Zeev Hirsch, and I told him that I was sorry to hear that this was his opinion. I added, "You are clearly entitled to have that opinion, but we are in total disagreement." In retrospect I realize that we actually differed about the role of the Project from the outset. He most likely saw it as developing into a peace institute, similar to the ones that exist in several places in the world, while I put the greatest emphasis on scientific collaborations.

****

My position as the director and leader of the Research Project on Peace came to an end. I left for the French national laboratory Saclay near Paris, and Professor David Horn became the new Project director. The University wanted to give Dr. Boutros Ghali an honorary doctorate, and he wanted to get it in Paris, and not in Israel. President Ben-Shahar knew about my close relations with Ghali and our mutual respect; in fact, when Ben-Shahar had wanted to visit Egypt and meet Ghali a few weeks earlier, I advised him not to do so at that time because of the atmosphere that existed in Egypt soon after May 26. This is why the President asked me to help in the arrangements for the ceremony, and to pay attention to all the delicate aspects, and I did so. For unexplained reasons, and as they had done before in the Toronto campaign, the Public Relations Department of the University did not invite me to the ceremony in Paris, but sent one from their office to go along with President Ben-Shahar. The event turned out to be a total disaster. Boutros Ghali stood up, and attacked Israel for its support of racist South Africa. President Ben-Shahar was not aware of Egypt's criticism of us on this issue, and did not know what to say; Boutros Ghali then left the ceremony. When Ben-Shahar told me about this unfortunate incident the following day, I felt that he wanted to say, "Where were you last night when I needed you?" but he kept quiet. It is a pity that this event somewhat spoiled the good relation with Dr. Ghali, which I had so carefully tried to build. In spite of this incident, Boutros Ghali agreed, as promised, to appear on December 12 1980, in an academic symposium at Tel-Aviv University, as the guest of the Peace Project, along with Dr. Moustapha Khalil, Egypt's foreign minister. He also appeared at a second symposium on June 1 1982. These two symposia were published by the Peace Project as Peace Papers, but unlike Abba Eban's talk, they appeared only in English.

When I returned from my Sabbatical leave in the summer of 1981, I was asked by President Ben-Shahar to return to the position of director of the Peace Project, because, so he said, he needed me. I refused, mainly for the following two reasons: 1. My three Egyptian colleagues had not received a green light for co-operation with us, so that my program, which had received financial support from the Ford Foundation, still could not be carried out; 2. The opposition to the Project on campus was increasing steadily, mainly for internal political reasons[5]. I stayed as a Management member, and was watching painfully at the slow decline of the beautiful Project. As for the grant from the Ford Foundation, I decided that since it was earmarked for collaborations which were not possible, we had to return the $35,000 to the Foundation. I wrote a letter to that effect to the Foundation, but the then rector, Professor Ben-Shaul, who was formally in charge of all outside grants, refused to send the letter or to return the money to the Foundation. He corresponded with them for several years until they agreed that the money be given to Professor Shimon Shamir to help him open in Cairo the Academic Center, the Israeli branch of our National Academy of Science. I felt ashamed by this behavior of my University, and never again contacted the Ford Foundation for new projects, which I later initiated, which will be described later.

After many years the University received a donation of two million dollars from the Steinmetz family for the establishment of a center for peace research, named after their late daughter Tami. The rector was then Professor Yoram Dinstein (law) and the director Professor Shimon Shamir (history). President Dinstein, along with the Steinmetz family, decided that the center would support the faculties of liberal arts, social sciences, and law. They were thus making sure that no money or influence would go to east-campus faculties (the faculties of natural sciences), and that the money would be spent in-campus on research on peace and not for collaboration in research with Egyptians or other Arab scientists.

---

5 *Whereas the conceptual disagreement with the direction that I had taken was expressed openly by my friend Zeev Hirsch, staff members in the west-campus faculties, especially in liberal arts, social sciences, business, and law, went so far as asking secretly candidates for the forthcoming election for a rector for their opinion on the Peace Project, saying that they would not vote for a candidate who supported the Peace Project. Although I had attempted to convince the west-campus faculty members that the Project was there in order to help them, and never compete with them, they were not convinced, and possibly were even somewhat jealous of some of our achievements.*

Had I been naïve in going against political forces in Egypt as well as in my University? Judging from the results, the answer must be "yes".

My last visit to Egypt. Four years passed since my last visit to Egypt in May 1980, after which I quit my post as the director of the Peace Project with the feeling that nothing important or constructive would happen in the near future. In October 1981 President Anwar Sadat was murdered, and Hosni Mubarak replaced him. His policy was similar to that of Sadat. In June 1982 Israel invaded Lebanon and stayed in South Lebanon for 18 years. This invasion and occupation increased the tension with Egypt.

In the three years that followed my return from Saclay, I decided, not to re-visit Egypt until conditions there would change, although I still had most of the grant from the Ford Foundation. The main reason for my decision was that I had actually made all the necessary agreements with El-Nadi, Abdel Hady, Kammal, and Badr, and we all were still waiting for the decision of the Egyptian government. In spite the warm words in Ghali's letter to me of August 1980, nothing actually moved as far as our proposed collaborations were concerned. My other reason for not wanting to visit Egypt was not to cause discomfort to my friends there, since I knew that their hands were tied, and a visit on my part would look like I was trying to apply pressure on them. I explained my reasons to William Carmichael and Ann Lesch from the Ford Foundation, and they sympathized with them.

In April 1984, after much hesitation, I made a decision to visit Egypt in order to find out if I was right in my assessment of the situation and in order to make my personal decision concerning the grant from the Ford Foundation. In order to soften the pressure which the Egyptian scientists might feel, I decided to come as a tourist. For the same reason I did not notify most of them about my coming, but did call El-Nadi with whom I had established special friendship. I took with me my family as well as Mira Offer, the widow of my physicist friend Shimon Offer, and their children. We decided to tour Luxor and Alexandria as well as Cairo.

I found in Cairo what I would call "a cold peace", which was getting colder every day. I had heard rumors about all kinds of internal pressure on the government to annul the peace treaty with Israel, while the government was still holding, but people were not sure for how long. Naturally, my expectation from Egypt was that two years after the breaking of the war in Lebanon, they would be ideologically against a warm peace with Israel, but I was hoping that because of the elapsed time since the signing of the peace treaty, they would slowly get used to living in peace with us.

The scientific relations, or whatever there was of them, were embarrassing to me and to my Egyptian colleagues. I had been corresponding with them, mainly with El-Nadi, but did it from Europe or the US, never from Israel. I had also called them by phone, but never from Israel, since I knew that receiving letters or phone calls from Israel might cause them some difficulties with their colleagues, or students, and possibly also with their security services. *Would this leprosy syndrome ever come to an end?*

We arrived in Cairo on April 12 at 19:00 by bus, and stayed in Egypt ten days. Already in the taxi to the hotel I noticed a great change in the city. I saw only few pictures of the murdered Anwar Sadat, but many pictures of President Hosni Mubarak, of the late Abdel Nasser, as well as of the two of them together. The attitude towards us in the taxi, the street or the hotel was correct, but cool, unlike the treatment we had gotten in our first visit. In particular, we noticed that when they learned that we were Israelis, they did not say "welcome" as they did 4-5 years earlier.

In that evening I made only two calls. I called Tabark, my student from the University of Illinois, who became my friend in our first visit to Cairo five years earlier. Her daughter Sonya told me that her parents were abroad, but she expressed interest in meeting my children Talma and David as well as the Offer children. I also called my friend Professor Mohamed El-Nadi, who sounded very excited and said that he would come to the hotel right away, and that he planned to see me several times during the ten days.

El-Nadi arrived in our hotel soon afterwards, and we invited him for dinner at the Sheraton, where we spent several pleasant hours together. When I told him about the coolness we felt upon arrival, he said that the reason for the coolness was the war in Lebanon. He then described at length the treatment that the Egyptians were receiving in the oil countries, where his son, the medical doctor, was working. He went there because the salaries in the oil countries were 15 times higher than in Egypt. However, the people there were trying not to hire Egyptians for fear that they would bring with them revolutionary ideas, and preferred Indians, Philippines and others wherever Arabic is not crucial.

The language at the university courses depended on the teacher. I asked him if the Egyptian people as a whole hated President Sadat. "Yes" he said, "but not because of the peace but because of the corruption which made his family rich. Sadat made peace because of popular demand, as the Egyptian people got sick of wars."

We then shifted to talk about physics. He told me that Professor Omar Badawi had to come back from doing research in Berkeley, because the Egyptians did not have sufficient funds for staying abroad for long periods. I told him of my intention to give my grant back to the Ford Foundation because it had been given to me to carry out collaborative research. He asked me to wait another year; "perhaps something could be arranged in the meantime." He suggested to me to find a scientist with international recognition who would ask Mubarak to approve cooperation in science, "because neither Ghali nor Helmi had the authority to do so." I later said to my wife that there was no dent in our friendship with El-Nadi, but his attitude toward Israel had definitely worsened.

I called Tymour Kammal and left a message with his wife, but he did not call back. Also, the children of Tabark and Ali as well as the grandchildren of El-Nadi did not come to our hotel to play with our kids, as promised. *Was it all the result of the coolness of the political relations? Was this the end of the story, or a temporary decline, after which there would be another warming of relations?* I still had not heard from Abdel Hady, whom I had telephoned earlier. I hesitated calling Badr; since I had heard rumors that he was also getting cooler toward Israel, perhaps because he became more orthodox as a Muslim.

****

We toured Cairo and then we flew to Luxor and toured the Valley of the Kings, Karnack with the palaces and famous polls, and the Luxor Shrine. Back in Cairo we had an interesting conversation with our taxi driver, who had graduated from Cairo University, and was a high-school teacher of chemistry. He was also working 16 hours a week as a taxi driver, but his income from the two jobs did not enable him to get married. When I told him that I knew Professor El-Nadi he got excited, and said that he admired this great scientist. He praised Sadat for the way in which he got his people out of the circle of wars. "Nasser was a sentimentalist rather than a realistic politician, and the Egyptian people, who were also sentimentalist, followed him. Mubarak had not yet proven himself as a leader. The Arabs got Egypt involved in wars, and enjoyed seeing her get entangled." In his opinion Israel was a wise country, and the Jews were wise people who had taught the Egyptians many important things.

Soon after arriving at the hotel I had an unexpected visit from Badr, who turned out to be very friendly, contrary to the rumors I had heard. He spoke again about the peace and about his own contributions to it. He repeated his thesis that Judaism was a religion and that Zionism was nationalism, an opinion shared by many Arabs. He was angry with our actions in Lebanon, but was very friendly toward me. He told me that in 1982 they held a conference on urology, half of it in Tel Aviv and half in Cairo. He added that he was then freer than before and could come to visit Israel. While we were talking there was a knock on the door, and in came El-Nadi. I said to both of them that I was unhappy that the relations between our two countries were still not normal, and that there was no scientific collaboration, which could help us get to normal relations. I also complained that practically no Egyptian had visited Israel and that included both scientists and tourists. They said somewhat reluctantly that the Egyptians were not used to travel abroad.

After Badr had departed, I spoke with El-Nadi, mainly about physics. I told him about my experiments with low-energy antiprotons at the LEAR facility in CERN, Switzerland. He expressed interest, but said that he was working on plasma of quarks and gluons, and was therefore interested in very high-energy antiprotons. I offered him my assistance if he would decide to visit CERN. We ended our discussion without speaking about scientific collaborations or even mentioning the Ford Foundation. I did not raise these topics in order not to make him feel uncomfortable, because it was apparent to me that the political constrains still made all hopes on these issues futile. Too bad!

I could not make contact with Abdel Hady; he may have been out of town. A day before leaving Egypt we visited Alexandria. In the evening Tymour Kammal called me and was very friendly over the phone. He said that the political situation was tough, and that when it would improve, we would be able to cooperate. His advice was to pray to God that the situation would improve. He also told me that in various conferences he had reported on the research studies of Amiram Shkolnik on the goat, the camel, and on the use of brackish water. About an hour later, El-Nadi came to our hotel and took us to his club. He repeated his contention that all depended on the actions of Israel. He expressed hope that the Labor alliance would win the national elections in Israel, and then, he was sure, King Hussein would be happy to negotiate peace. He added that the Saudis were waiting for such an opportunity, and the Egyptian people in their entirety were ready for a true peace and for the commercial advantages that such peace would bring with it. He stressed that the war in Lebanon was then the reason for the worsening of the Egyptian-Israel relations. He blamed Sharon's bombing of the Palestinian refugee camps of Sabra and Shatila; and I told him that in my opinion Sharon's actions were very bad, but the Israeli army did not bomb Sabra and Shatila. He then said that he would mail me a copy of his talk for the conference in Heidelberg. When I told him that I had talked a few days earlier with Ann Lesch the representative of the Ford Foundation in Cairo, he contributed no comment. My summary was as follows: *there is no doubt that El-Nadi is as friendly as before on a personal level, but was definitely less eager to even talk about scientific collaboration than 4-5 years earlier. Perhaps, if the Labor Alliance would win the elections (which it did not), and if the democrats would win the 1984 elections (which they did not), something might move again. It is clear to me that I have to return the grant to the Ford Foundation (which did not happen because of the rector's objection), or to ask them to let us freeze it until the conditions would change.*

In my office in Tel Aviv I reflected on my forth visit to Cairo and concluded that I had been right in the previous four years. A visit by me, even as a tourist, created unnecessary pressure on my colleagues as long as the political situation had not changed. The Egyptian behavior became less emotional and more businesslike. I could say that there had been an emotional retreat. On the positive side I concluded that the two peoples had started to get used to each other. To a large extent, we were not any more *past enemies*, and were beginning to be *neighbors with neighborly problems*. As for scientific cooperation, to a large extent we had started from *never*, we had gone to *not yet*, and ended in May 1984 with *who knows if, when, and how?*

In retrospect I can say today, that my dreams of large-scale scientific collaborations turned out to be just dreams, and the main fault, if there is any, is my own. There were two main forces acting against my efforts: the Egyptian government's refusal to normalize relations and forces at Tel Aviv

University; the first being the stronger factor. Can I blame them? I don't believe so; after all they made peace with us and lost the leadership in the Arab World for a long time. Also, the Israeli government did not help much; in fact, the invasion of Lebanon made the normalization of relations all but impossible. The elements at Tel Aviv University have a variety of reasons to put obstacles on my way, mainly ideological or personal, that in one way or another stemmed from internal campus politics and jealousy. I do not blame them; but I am sorry that they won.

CHAPTER 10.
INVOLVING THE AMERICAN PHYSICAL SOCIETY

In the years that followed the decline and end of the Peace Project I kept asking myself for the reasons that I failed with the constructive goals of the Project, or rather what I should have done differently. It was obvious that although we put in a great deal of thinking, time, and efforts, the obstacles, the external as well as the internal ones, were stronger.

At the end of 1986, when I spent a Sabbatical leave from my University, this time in Vancouver BC, I was appointed by the American Physical Society (APS) a member of its Subcommittee for International Scientific Affairs (SISA). As in many other events that had happened to me, I asked myself how I could advance my hopes and dreams of peace and cooperation, especially among scientists, by my membership in SISA. The following idea then crossed my mind: The APS was a big and strong body, with a tremendous prestige and influence in the whole world, including Israel and Egypt. Therefore, so I thought, if I succeeded in involving the APS in a worthwhile Israeli-Egyptian scientific project, their participation might overcome the many obstacles that I had encountered in our region.

For the first meeting of SISA that I was about to attend, I sent the secretary of the APS, Professor W. W. Havens, the following manuscript, to be distributed to SISA's members, with a request that it be included in the agenda of the meeting:

COLLABORATION AMONG PHYSICISTS IN COUNTRIES WHERE POLITICAL CONDITIONS HAVE STARTED TO RIPEN

It is an honor for me, a new committee member, to speak to you on this occasion. New committee members should always listen first, but since I will be in North America for only one

206

year, I have decided to present my idea in my first meeting. This idea may sound strange to you, but I hope that you would consider it seriously. The idea is for a new, perhaps revolutionary program, which could add a new dimension to APS activities, and will require much preparation and planning. I am talking about the encouragement of contacts between scientists of different countries, with a certain political curtain or barrier between them. I believe that this program, if successful, could make a non-trivial contribution to physics.

Introduction. The full title could have been: Should the APS become involved in encouraging collaborations among physicists in countries where political conditions have started to ripen, and what, where, when, and how should it be done?

The goal of such a far-reaching program was to lend a helping hand to physicists, both mature and young, who, up until recently, have found it difficult to develop their talents adequately because of political constraints in their region.

Two conditions should be satisfied for this program: 1. There should be both a genuine need and an interest in the program among the physicists in the region (where by "region" I mean a geographic region such as South America, or the Middle East; or several countries such as the US and the USSR, or Israel, Egypt and Jordan). 2. Political conditions have hitherto hindered any collaboration, but these conditions have started to change. A legitimate question then comes to mind:

Why should the APS be involved? Before I even outline the proposed program, I will start with a critical point of view. A "purist" may argue: The APS is an American society, and should keep its activities in the USA; and the proposed program has political implications, and the APS should therefore not get involved. The past history of the Society and the existence of SISA indicate that the APS has rejected this point of view. International activities, which advance our understanding of the physical world, should be pursued by the APS with courage and caution.

Although the Society cannot and should not be involved in regional politics, it should be recognized that the success (or failure) of any program might have indirect political consequences. However, it should be emphasized that political goals, noble as they may appear to some Society members, cannot and should not be the goals of the program.

The Israeli-Egyptian Example. Before the Israeli-Egyptian peace treaty in 1979, there was practically no collaboration between Egyptian and Israeli physicists (perhaps with very few exceptions). The peace treaty has brought hope to some, fear and unhappiness to others; but the main obstacle to full-fledged collaboration was, and still is governmental, as I will later discuss.

Following President Sadat's visit to Jerusalem, I worked full time for three years, trying to organize scientific collaborations between Israeli and Egyptian scientists in all academic fields, both in research and in teaching. I traveled to Egypt several times, visited a few universities as well as the Egyptian National Academy of Science, gave informal lectures, and even examined candidates for collaboration with our scientists. Students and young faculty members were crowding my hotel door, urging me to include them in the proposed collaborative activities. Three heads of laboratories agreed with my ideas on collaborative research to the last detail. I also met twice with an Egyptian minister, who seemed to be encouraging. I could go on and on, but the picture should be clear by now; there was a definite interest on both sides, and the question is: why?

It was clear from the outset that science in both Egypt and Israel would benefit from the proposed collaboration. Let me select nuclear physics as an example. Egypt educates a large number of experimental nuclear physicists, but they have little equipment, and insufficient number of books and travel grants. They are isolated, from the world of physics to a large extent, although in these circumstances they still do well. On the other hand, Israel has a great need for experimental nuclear physicists, who could use the accelerator at the Weizmann Institute in Rehovot, or collaborate with groups from Tel-Aviv University and other universities in doing research in the various meson factories in the world.

But although the needs and interests in scientific collaboration were there in both countries, and even grants were available from various foundations, the politicians weighed the *pros* and *cons,* and decided, perhaps temporarily, to say "niet!" (In the applied disciplines the situation today is somewhat better; in at least three large projects – marine biology, agriculture, and medicine – there is some collaboration, apparently with the help of US funds.) In what follows, I will try to benefit from the experience gained in the example above, recognizing the difference between the nuclear physics example that was described above and the program being proposed here to the American Physical Society.

The Proposal. The first question now is whether the Society should accept the idea that it should lend a strong helping hand in situations, where there is a great need, but conditions are not yet fully ripe for collaboration between neighbors, and assistance by the Society may make the necessary difference in overcoming the difficulties.

Finding the first candidate will then be the next step in the proposed program. It can be a geographic region or a group of countries. I suggest that the Middle East presents an adequate test case. The needs and obvious benefits are there, as well as the apparently slow but steady improvement of the political atmosphere. A less attractive, but perhaps easier alternative is just Israel and Egypt. We note that in this proposal the US will not be a collaborator, as in the US-USSR case or the US-China cooperative program, but only an initiator and helper.

With the help of the many APS members from the Middle East, some of whom are always present in the US, our Society might approach the national physical societies as well as the national academies of science in the region. If a number of them agree on the desirability of such a program, even if they express some reservations, an organization could be formed to define the goals and to carry out the program. On the other hand, and knowing the region as I do, I suggest that a formal inquiry could result in many *formal* negative answers, or no answers at all. My feeling is that if such is the case, a determined, largely unilateral action by the APS could result in quiet acceptance followed by broad collaboration. Obviously, this is a very delicate point.

What can we do? Although the goals of the proposed program can be far-reaching, the selection of activities to pursue should follow the rule that progress in this case can be achieved only in small steps. "Nothing succeeds like success", but we should also remember that "nothing fails like failure". The following is a list of possible activities, not necessarily in any order of priority:

A general meeting of the APS, to be held in a "neutral" East-Mediterranean country, to which Middle East physicists will be invited to participate actively. Financial support will be provided, especially to young physicists and students. Possible locations: Greece, Turkey, Cyprus, or even Italy. The sponsors will be the APS and the host country.
The same as above, but the meeting to be held in an Arab country or in Israel. Locations that come to mind: Santa Katarina, Eilat-Aqaba, or Morocco.
Workshops on topical subjects to be held either in a "neutral" country, in Israel, or in an Arab country.
Grants for scientific collaborations. The research can be carried out either in the Middle East or in another country (such as the US).
Grants for students of one Middle East country to study in another Middle East country.
A "Triestino" in the region, in applied fields such as water desalination and/or solar energy, or in the field of astronomy, perhaps in the Sinai (if Egypt agrees).

The main criterion for any activity, such as a meeting or a workshop, is that it be open to all physicists from the region. Grants for research or for study will be allocated according to two criteria: Scientific merits and degree of collaboration between countries, where collaboration was previously impossible.

Possible sources of funds: US government (AID etc), Middle East governments, the APS, Middle East physical societies, and foundations.

I wish to reiterate that having a broad program is important, but it is crucial to start with the selection of one activity, and to carry it out successfully.

Conclusions. We have already posed the question of *why should the APS be involved.* We will now add another question: *Why should we expect the APS to succeed where others have largely failed?* I believe that I have already answered these questions briefly, and I will now elaborate by giving three reasons:

The US as a country (and the US physicists, as individuals within the APS) has a long history of involvement. Perhaps the right word is "care". US physicists care.
The APS has a lot of experience in international scientific collaboration. American physicists advocated scientific collaboration and actually collaborated with Soviet physicists a long time before the formal political détente. Other examples of such collaborations are US-China, US-South America, etc.
The prestige and weight of the APS, along with the expected benefits to the countries of the Middle East from active APS involvement, may very well tip the balance to *success* where others have failed. And I re-emphasize that the potential for contribution to physics from such a success is not negligible.

For today's meeting I suggest that

We discuss the general idea, i.e. the advisability for the APS to get involved in international situations, which were described above (See the title).
If our Subcommittee accepts the idea, we can discuss the choice of first candidate (such as the Middle East).

A detailed plan can then be prepared and discussed in the next meeting.

Before ending I wish to add one observation related to the question of academic initiatives in the political world. You must have noticed that I refrained from referring to specific political problems, although such problems could present major obstacles. Let me point out three such examples:

The traditional refusal of Arab countries to collaborate with Israel.
Egypt's reluctance to collaborate with Israel, lest such actions would hamper her attempts to return fully to the Arab World.
The status of Arab universities in the West Bank, and Israel's possible objection to full-fledged Palestinian participation in the program.

In commenting on these political obstacles, I adopt a "purist's" point of view: We should do what we believe that we have to do as scientists, and we base our actions on the accepted principles of science and of our Society. Such principles are: 1. Science is international, and does not recognize borders. 2. Scientists who want to do physics have the right to expect help from their colleagues. 3. Scientific meetings should always be open to everyone. 4. Scientists should have the right to travel and collaborate according to their choice. I believe that adherence to such principles, along with the weight of the APS, could eventually overcome the above-mentioned political difficulties.

****

The meeting of SISA took place in Washington DC on January 8, 1987. The chair asked me to present my proposal. The committee members seemed very interested, and toward the end of the meeting I received a note from one of the secretaries saying that I had to be very influential if I succeeded in causing the old Society secretary to stay awake during the whole long discussion. Many members took part in the discussion that followed, mostly supporting the idea. It was finally decided to focus our attention on either a conference or a workshop on a specific topic, which was basically the activity suggestion No. 3 in my manuscript. Finally, the chair asked me to prepare a detailed plan for action for the next SISA meeting.

After the meeting I talked at length with Harry Lustig, the treasurer of the APS. We decided that our first step should be the appointment of a committee that would prepare the whole plan. We thought that it would be very important to select as the committee chair a senior physicist with no connection to the Middle East. Lustig suggested Robert Wilson from Cornell University, who had been an assistant to J. Robert Oppenheimer, as well as a president of the APS. We hoped to get his agreement, though we knew that he was very sick. Wilson agreed to meet us in the following conference of the APS at San Francisco. In San Francisco he agreed to chair the conference committee, and that pleased us very much. He then suggested selecting for the proposed conference a subject from the forefront of physics, and added that the conference should not be political. We gladly agreed with his suggestions. We then discussed the membership of the conference committee and agreed to add Louis Rosen, the director of the LAMPF accelerator in Los Alamos, as well as a member of the APS of a Lebanese decent, so that together the committee would consist of three Americans (Wilson, Lustig, and Rosen), a Lebanese , and an Israeli (A.I.Y.) All five agreed. Later we added the Nobel Laureate Leon Lederman, who had initiated the APS program for aiding physicists in South-America through the Fermi Lab, of which Lederman was the director. We brought our suggestions to the next meeting of SISA, and the suggestions were approved.

At the first meeting of the conference committee that took place in New York we decided that the proposed conference would be on quarks and nuclei. We decided that the speakers would be physicists from the front line in the world, and we assumed that the selected candidates would largely accept our invitation to be speakers because of the special nature of the conference. As for the participants, we decided that we preferred young faculty members and students from the Arab countries and Israel. We accepted the suggestion of the Lebanese member that we should also invite Greek and Turkish young physicists, "so that the Israelis and the Arabs would see that there are other political conflicts in the world." His suggestion was accepted and broadened to include all the Mediterranean countries. However, we decided that financial help would be given only to participants from the East-Mediterranean countries. Wilson and Lustig volunteered to try and get financial help from the various foundations (Ford, Rockefeller, etc) and I volunteered to prepare a list of speakers. As for the venue, the suggestions were: an island in the East-Mediterranean, obviously in agreement of and cooperation with the local physical society. One of the important decisions at that meeting was not to have in the conference any political activity or political lecture.

The decisions of the conference committee were approved by SISA, thus giving us a green light. Almost all the very many people I spoke to, among them candidates to be speakers at the conference or past presidents of the APS such as Ernest Henley and Eric Adelberger, and directors of national laboratories such as Erich Vogt from Vancouver, expressed support for the idea, and some were even enthusiastic. I felt good, and thought that I was finally on the right track.

The chair of SISA brought the subject for discussion to the various APS bodies, and with the help of Wilson, Lustig and Haven it was approved by all the relevant Society bodies, including the APS council. The council, on its part, set only one condition; namely, that everything would be done in coordination and participation of the European Physical Society (EPS). The reason for this condition was that the EPS was closer to the Mediterranean than the APS, and the smaller EPS might be offended if it were not brought in as an equal partner. On the surface, the condition seems fair and reasonable, but it ended as a major detriment to the whole plan, and eventually caused its demise.

Europe is different from the USA in many respects, but for our case here she was not only closer to the Mediterranean geographically, but also politically and economically. In addition, Europe was split and not as united as was the US. The first reaction we received from the EPS was basically encouraging, but they added several conditions, which our committee thought were acceptable. The trouble was that each time we accepted a condition they added another one, until we suspected that they might be doing it purposely. The EPS representative was Roberto Salmeron, a French physicist of Brazilian decent. At a certain stage Louis Rosen, the new committee chair, and I traveled to an EPS conference in Yugoslavia, mainly in order to prepare our proposed conference. We met Salmeron and other EPS officials and agreed with them on all the details of the proposed conference; so we left Yugoslavia very content, but instead of moving forward, the EPS put in new obstacles, the reasons for which were not clear. Most of us suspected that the EPS was afraid of expected negative reactions from some Arab states. We were surprised to learn that the European physicists did not possess enough courage to withstand such Arab pressures.[1] Whatever the reason, the condition that the APS council put on us, namely to cooperate with the EPS, turned out to be extremely detrimental; and after several more years of foot dragging the idea died, just as did my previous efforts on the Research Project on Peace. The only thing left for me was to say again *too bad!*

---

1 *An Israeli member of EPS, who participated in a discussion on the proposed conference in one of the EPS committees, reported to me that he had even detected some comments there with anti-Semitic flavor, such as, "I understand why the APS supports the idea; after all, 50% of its members are Jews."*

CHAPTER 11.
A POSSIBLE NEW CONTRIBUTION TO THE PEACE PROCESS

On my second Sabbatical leave in Vancouver a few years later I was again think-ing about the Research Project on Peace, on its many pioneering achievements and final failure. I was also thinking about all the ideas that had never material-ized, and then I recalled an idea I had had then, and for some reason, perhaps because of the many pressures, I had never tried it out. I therefore developed the idea further, and in 9.12.1989 wrote it down.

A NEW MEANINGFUL CONTRIBUTION TO THE PEACE PROCESS IN THE MIDDLE EAST

Abstract

Arabs and Jews in the Middle East mistrust and fear each other for good reasons. Hard liners on both sides reinforce each other, indirectly but persistently, while peace is largely conceived to be unworthy of the risks it entails. The absence of attraction toward peace is an essential miss-ing term in the peace equation in the Middle East. To a large extent, the coolness of the peace between Egypt and Israel can, therefore, be blamed on the lack of interest in the fruits of peace. It is hereby pro-posed to fill the gap and supply the missing term by presenting the people of the Middle East a picture of a possible attractive peacetime life in future Middle East. A book written by a first-rate author, who is considered politically neutral and hitherto uninvolved in the conflict, could achieve the goal; while a movie or a TV series based upon such a book, would help reach a larger Middle East audience. It is proposed that the background of the story would be the future region as a whole, facing challenges in its competition with other regions of the world. The characters should come from many parts of the region, and present-day political difficulties would be mentioned only indirectly, because they would have been solved. The book should leave the impression that only when present difficulties are solved, can the region face new future challenges successfully. The actual story is clearly left to the author. I are looking for a foundation or a person, who will appreciate the importance of adding attraction toward peace to the peace equation, and who will undertake to finance the execution of the proposed program.

The Middle-East Peace Equation. Both Arabs and Jews believe separately, and for good reasons, that the whole country of Palestine (or Eretz Israel) belongs to them and only to them. The symmetry of the situation is demonstrated further by the strong mutual suspicion that exists between Arabs and Jews. The Jews see any Arab move as a trick designed to cut the area of the State of Israel piece by piece, as one cuts a salami sausage, until the Jews will be pushed into the sea. The Arabs too have a salami theory of their own, treating any Israeli action or plan as designed to slowly incorporate more and more Arab territory into Israel. Therefore, the atmosphere after a century of bloodshed is that of mutual mistrust, suspicion and fear. Such an atmosphere puts security considerations on top of the national priority lists on both sides. As is the case in all conflicts, the increase of military might in one side always causes a similar increase in the other side, and vice versa. While this process of *positive feedback* and escalation is constantly taking place in the security or "war side" of the equation, there is almost no reinforcement in the "search-for-peace side". It is widely believed in the region that peace will come (for better or for worse) only as a result of outside pressure.

In the Middle East, wars may be repulsive for some people, but attractive for others, who want to achieve some national goals through them; however peace rarely attracts anybody. We often hear statements from regional leaders that nothing is dearer to their hearts than peace, but such statements are greeted by everybody on both sides with cynicism, and seen as nothing but empty PR statements, aimed at the outside world. In no part of the Middle East is peace really conceived as being attractive, as a possible beginning of a better, brighter future for the peoples and nations of the region. *The absence of attraction towards peace is the missing element, the missing term in the peace equation.* And this is where the proposed program wishes to make a meaningful contribution.

The peace between Egypt and Israel. I will use the Egyptian-Israeli peace as an example. Before the peace treaty was signed, most analysts had assumed that Israelis would flood Egypt soon after the signing. They would come in person, and bring with them plans for direct cooperation in business, science, art, etc. These "experts" had assumed that the Israeli public, long under siege and isolation from all their neighbors, would use the opportunity of peace to break into the outside world. What actually happened was a slow and careful increase in business, trade, and even tourism, and definitely with no enthusiasm. Even the Research Project on Peace of Tel Aviv University, which started big, and was supposed to coordinate and encourage collaborations in academic activities, was eventually grounded, somewhat because of lack of enthusiasm and even opposition to its goal. The traditional reasons for the absence of enthusiasm or *cold peace* between Egypt and Israel, given by all observers, are mutual mistrust as well as Arab pressure on Egypt.

But there is another important reason for the coolness of the peace. For the preceding thirty years, Israelis and Egyptians had gotten used to the no-war no-peace situation. The prospect of an unfamiliar peace had been subconsciously frightening, as it represented an uncertainty or even a threat to jobs, business, personal safety, etc. This attitude can be called *the fear of the unknown.* No picture had existed, even a vague one, of a better future, with new opportunities that could come with peace, not even a fiction like Herzl's Altneuland that has had such a large influence on the Jewish world for a hundred years. I re-emphasize: One of the major reasons for the coolness of the peace between Israel and Egypt is the fact that the attraction towards peace is missing in the minds and hearts of most Israelis and Egyptians.

Making peace look more attractive. I want to fill the gap, to supply the missing element, to make the picture of life in peacetime Middle East look attractive rather than frightening, familiar rather than totally unknown. I believe that most Jews and Arabs, except for the relatively few ideologically extremists, could be attracted to a vivid picture of a peaceful future, and that their apparent coolness and fear are the result of never having been given the opportunity to relate to such a picture, since it has never really been in their national agendas. Obviously, the wars as well as the disagreement on the solution of the Middle-East political dilemmas have made all thinking about peace appear utopian.

It is perhaps expected of us at this point to present our own solution for the political problems, or a practical path to follow in order to remedy the situation.[1] Instead, I will now leap forward and paint a picture of a *possible optimistic future* with the hope that such a picture will help most Arabs and Jews to overcome their hate, suspicion, and fear. In doing so, I will mention present-day political difficulties only casually and indirectly. The attractive future in our picture should have its own challenges, common to the Middle East as a whole. These new challenges should put in proper perspective, play down and diminish the importance of present political difficulties, thus making people more open-minded and receptive to serious solutions of present-day problems. I maintain that if people on both sides are shown a possible picture of a future, in which their children as well as their nations can be prosperous and safe, the present strong hate and fear could lose their choking grip.

This is the goal of the program. The undertaking is big, yet the goal is clear and focused. I do not pretend to have, nor do I intend to suggest here solutions to present-day political problems, but rather to give them a more balanced perspective, so needed for good solutions. I believe that if succeeded, I will have added the missing attractive term, thus contributing significantly to a constructive solution of the peace equation.

The proposed method. Our goal is to make a constructive and meaningful contribution to the peace process by supplying an important missing element, that of attraction toward peace. The first tool that comes to mind is a novel or a play, written by a world-renowned author, in which the story takes place in a peaceful future Middle East. Making a movie out of it could achieve even a stronger impact. Examples of modern-time impact of a book are Herzl's Altneuland, with its vivid picture of a Jewish state that influenced many Jews to accept Zionism, and Orwell's 1984, that painted a frightening picture of what life could be in a future totalitarian state. The script of the proposed book is clearly left to the author, provided it is judged effective in painting an attractive picture of a peaceful future Middle East. If needed, assistance in the form of technological forecasting should be provided to the author. I expect that the movie (or play) will first be shown in the West, and hope that it will then attract favorable attention in all parts of the Middle

1 *The manuscript was clearly written before the Palestinian-Israeli Oslo Agreement or the four-partite Road Map*

East. I wish to stress three additional points: 1. The audiences that I am mainly addressing are the Israeli Jews (as well as other Jews) and Arabs (in the region as well as around the world). The program will fail if it reaches only audiences outside the Middle East, as recent history has often taught us the futility of relying solely on international public opinion. 2. The picture of the attractive future should appeal to doves and hawks on both sides alike (perhaps not to the extreme hawks). The picture should, therefore, not contradict the minimal fundamental desires of most Arabs and Jews. A necessary condition then is that the painting will be of a distant future. 3. The author should be politically neutral, preferably a non-Jew and a non-Arab. The best origin for candidates should be people from hitherto uninvolved countries in Middle-East conflicts, such as Japan or Australia.

A specific example. Let us take a TV series as an example. The story could take place in the year 2020 in the twin-city of Aqaba-Eilat, the commercial capital of the Middle East Community (M.E.C.). Freeways connect the city with Istanbul via Tel Aviv and Beirut or Sodom and Damascus, with Baghdad via Amman, and with the Persian Gulf to the east and Cairo and Tripoli to the west. Modern railroads run parallel to the freeways. There are borders or rather demarcation lines, similar to the borders, which exist now between countries in Western Europe. The Aqaba-Eilat city is also the site of the new Middle-East University, the pride of the region, which is considered, around the world, as an excellent center for the study of oceanography, arid lands, and solar energy. Its convenient location, close to Israel, Egypt, Jordan, and Saudi Arabia, as well as Eastern Africa, gives it an added attraction. Tourists fly regularly to Lod in Israel or Amman in Jordan, visit Jerusalem and historical sights in Israel and Jordan, and end up in one of the hotels along the coast of the Red Sea. High-tech industries have branches in many Mid-Eastern countries, with Israel serving as the center, while the center of the Mid-Eastern chemical industries is in Kuwait. As Iraq specializes in space technology, the main space plant is in Baghdad, while Ramallah (or Gaza) serves as the financial capital of the M.E.C., having gained the status of a free city. Jerusalem is the medical capital of the region, and caters to the needs of the region, while also treating patients from around the world. Arab medicines, which hitherto have been unknown in the rest of the world, find their modern use in the complex of laboratories and pharmaceutical factories in Jerusalem, while the east and west shores of the Dead Sea become the world centers for treatment of skin diseases.

There is, within the region, unofficial but noticed competition between the Israeli Jews and the Palestinian Arabs as to who contributes most to the prosperity of the Middle East. The Israelis point out proudly to their previous achievements in the State of Israel and to their international connections, while the Palestinians emphasize their importance to the region because of their renowned high motivation.

There is an economic crisis hovering over the Middle East because of a dramatic technological breakthrough in China, which threatens the economy of the M.E.C., and people throughout the entire region are busy looking for a way to beat the new challenge. Political difficulties of the past are rarely mentioned, and people are satisfied that a general peace treaty between Israel and the Arab countries was signed before the end of the twentieth century, enabling all the people of the region to prepare fully for the new economic threat from the Far East.

Conclusions. In the previous section I described briefly a possible background for the story. It is essential that the characters in the story come from the entire region, and that they and their families interact strongly with one another. The characters will hopefully become household items (ala those of Dallas, Dynasty, or the Bill Cosby Show). It is important that the book be read and the TV series be watched in both Israel and the Arab countries in order to provide continuously positive feedback to the developing peaceful relations in the region.

The plot could evolve around competition of the Middle East *as a region* with other regions of the world, while the interdependence and mutual assistance of the various countries in the Middle East would be recognized as a necessary ingredient for success. The characters and the readers should be so involved with the new regional challenges that the readers practically forget the political difficulties of the twentieth century. In fact, full success will be achieved if the readers (or screen watchers) would wish that these difficulties found their peaceful solution quickly, so that the countries of the Middle East will be able to unite in time to be ready to meet the challenges of the year 2020.

I believe that the program outlined above can have a strong impact on the atmosphere in the Middle East, thus contributing significantly and constructively to the peace process. The execution of the program is challenging. The selection of the author and approval of the book/script are very important but difficult, and should be supervised by first-rate media people for the program to achieve the desired strong impact. It will also require a large amount of money from a person or a foundation, which share my belief in the program, and wish to support it. It is clearly possible that the book, movie, or TV series will turn out to be financially profitable, but support is requested even before the financial prospects are fully known.

****

After reading the manuscript, Edith Lando, a Vancouver woman interested in peace, invited to her Vancouver home twelve local people connected with art, advertisement, and movie making in order to get advice on how to proceed. Their main advice was to focus on finding a person or a grant, which will undertake to finance the project. We turned first to the Bronfman Foundation, but they notified us that the subject though interesting, did not satisfy their criteria for support. We then tried to find contributors in Hollywood, among them Richard Dreyfuss, but failed, possibly because we did not try harder; and that most likely because of my physics research in Vancouver, and because I got tired. I was therefore left only with the written manuscript, which like its "elder brother" – the Peace Project - failed in its attempt to create an attractive picture of life in a peaceful Middle East.[2] And again I have to say: *Too bad!*

2   *My attempt preceded that of Shimon Peres, who was talking about the creation of "A New Middle East". Up till now he too has failed in his attempts.*

CHAPTER 12.
A MIDDLE-EAST UNIVERSITY

After a few years of secret talks in Oslo, an agreement was signed in March 1993 between the Israeli government and the Palestinian Liberation Organization on the lawn of the White House. The Israeli Prime Minister Yitzhak Rabin, somewhat reluctantly, shook hands with Yasser Arafat, the president of the P.L.O. A new era of optimism spread through the entire Middle East, and enabled, soon afterwards, the signing of a peace treaty between The Israeli prime-minister Yitzhak Rabin and King Hussein of Jordan. In spite of political resistance in Israel to the peace agreement, which would mean giving up captured lands, the labor government tried hard to cooperate with the newly formed Palestinian Authority, but did little to control the Jewish settlers in the West Bank and Gaza. The Palestinian population in the occupied territories, on the other hand, was divided, and part of it kept up their bloody attacks on Israelis, mainly in the West Bank. The weak Palestinian Authority tried to control these attacks, but did a poor job at it, partly because it was weak and had little infrastructure of security forces, but perhaps also because Yasser Arafat did not completely give up the old hope of one day getting the whole country. On this background there were official and unofficial groups of Israelis and Palestinians, who kept working together on the advancement of the economy of the country west of the Jordan River, and achieved great success, as the economy started to flourish both in Israel and in the West Bank and Gaza.

My proposal with Reyad Sawafta. In the summer of 1994, while I was again in Vancouver doing research, I talked at length with Reyad Sawafta, a Palestinian physicist who had studied both in the US and Canada, and was in Vancouver working on his Ph. D. When we met at the TRIUMF Laboratory in Vancouver we quickly became friends, because like me he too thought that it was futile to argue the question of who was historically and judicially right in the Arab-Israeli conflict, in particular the Palestinian-Israeli one, but rather look at peaceful solutions to the conflict which would benefit both sides. We talked about what we two could do to advance the Arab-Israeli budding peace; and the idea of a Middle-East University somehow popped up. We both felt that it was a good idea, and Reyad asked me to write a first draft. Although I was still reflecting about the failed ideas of the Middle-East conference run by the APS and of the proposed competition on writing a book about the peaceful future Middle East (see previous chapters), I got excited about the new idea. Since my work in the Research Project on Peace 15 years earlier, I had not been so excited. The reason is that I could again work on the two topics that were so close to my heart and mind, namely peace and academia. I therefore wrote down the first draft of a proposal and showed it to Sawafta. He made a few comments, and added a few items. I then consulted with my friend Judah Eisenberg, who had helped me so much on my previous endeavors. The following is the proposal, which was written by Reyad Sawafta and me on 1.9.1994:

THE RED SEA ACADEMIC INSTITUTE
A PROPOSAL

With the agreements signed recently between Israel and the Palestinian Liberation Organization and with Jordan[1], and with the advent of a hopefully imminent comprehensive peace in the entire Middle East, new and exciting opportunities in the academic field present themselves. Young people of the region have been suffering at least two disadvantages in comparison with their colleagues in other countries: they have fewer adequate universities and research institutes, and there is very little scientific collaboration in their region, so necessary for progress in our time. This situation has now lasted for many decades and graduates of high-schools as well as college graduates have to travel to distant countries, which could provide them with adequate academic opportunities; and they often remain abroad, thus depriving their own society and the whole region of the use of their talents and expertise.

The various countries of the region might have different needs and level of education, but they all suffer from the same unfortunate situation, and will all benefit greatly from its early amelioration. This proposal is aimed at this goal. While political considerations make

---

1 *The actual peace agreement between Israel and Jordan was signed a few weeks later.*

it possible to present such a proposal at this time, and while the establishment of the Red Sea Academic Institute that we propose here could have political ramifications, the main goal of this proposal is to promote higher education and research in the Middle East, and should be pursued entirely on this basis.

Where does one start? There are in existence various small, mostly bilateral scientific collaborations in the region, involving both Israelis and Arabs, but there is no large-scale regional academic collaborative activity, and no plan exists for such an activity. Whereas a full-scale university, with undergraduate as well as graduate studies and rich research activity, seems very attractive, it may be too big a project to start with. In fact, even just an undergraduate college, or alternatively a research institute, might be too far-reaching in the beginning, unless the program is extremely attractive, and addresses immediate needs. Another possibility is to hold a regional summer or winter school, or courses in selected disciplines, every few months. Clearly, whatever the choice, it should leave the door open for expansion in the future towards a full-fledged academic institute or a university, with the rate of growth depending on the interests of the various peoples and availability of funds, as well as on the success of the ongoing plans at that stage.

There is one potential advantage to the proposed program over similar such regional activities in the world. This has to do with the fact that the Middle East has been at war for a very long time, and is therefore one of the few places in the world where new and strong cohesive forces have just started to be active. Academic people and politicians see the Middle East today as perhaps the only region where international efforts might bear immediate fruits.[2] This could provide strong motivation for philanthropists and politicians to support the proposed effort. In fact, it is expected that world organizations such as the UN and UNESCO, as well as some rich countries, would be interested in lending a helping hand. With a responsible academic program, it is also expected that first-rate scientists and educators, who usually frequent almost only front-line institutes, could be attracted to lead and carry out teaching and research activity in the new institute.

2 *These statements about the situation 15 tears ago are still true, but destructive forces on all sides of the Middle East all but destroyed the hopes which existed 15 years ago.*

One can think of the proposed institute as the regional center of knowledge and training, with emphasis on high-tech and advanced research, solving important regional problems such as the development of new energy and water sources, the advancement of agricultural techniques, the cure of regional diseases, etc. The necessary budget clearly depends on the choice and scope of the activity. Whereas a series of courses (in fields such as physics, energy, desert studies, oceanography, Middle-East economy, languages, Middle-East cultures, and archeology) or a summer institute may require several hundred thousands dollars a year, a college or a research institute will require at least one order of magnitude more, while a full-fledged university is again 10-100 times more expensive than a college.

Irrespective of the question of which program to begin with, the question of location is of great importance. There is one spot where several countries meet, the Aqaba-Eilat-Taba region, involving Jordan, Israel and Egypt, with the West Bank and Saudi Arabia close by. Actually, other countries in the region, such as Syria, Lebanon, Iraq, and Sudan, as well as the Gulf and North Africa countries are not far away. It is for this reason that we suggest this location as the home for the proposed institute.

A Founders Committee is required in order to explore the ideas presented above. Members from all countries of the region will be welcomed to join that Committee, since all these countries are expected to benefit from the proposed activity. However, taking into account the current political climate, it is expected that the starting core will be formed from the ranks of respected Egyptian, Israeli, Jordanian, Palestinian, and possibly Saudi academic and research leaders. The Founders Committee can also include first-rate scientists from other countries as well as public figures with interest in the project. The Committee should hold its first meeting soon in a convenient place such as Taba. The main items on the agenda should be:

A long-range multi-stage program, such as a summer school and bimonthly courses, followed by a college and a research institute, with a university as the final stage.

Details of the first stage (the summer school and bi-monthly courses): topics, students, teachers, budget, etc.

Affiliation with existing institutions (universities in the region,
UNESCO, the UN University, etc).

Organizational structure to handle future activities and the selection
of a director or a president.

The Founders Committee should produce a document setting forth
its concrete plans, and this document would be presented to individuals, organizations, foundations, and governments, whose involvement and assistance is sought. The Committee will need a budget
(seed money) for its activity, about $30,000-$50,000. The formation
of a wide-base committee, the agreement on the plan, culminating
with a written proposal, and the required seed money are crucial
pre-requisites for the launching of efforts to establish The Red Sea
Academic Institute.

****

Sawafta sent the proposal to several of his Palestinian friends, and they liked it
very much. I too sent it to various friends, and I received encouraging reactions
as well as suggestions of how to proceed. I also received a strange reaction from
Professor Shimon Shamir, who used to be on the Management of the Research
Project on Peace. In his letter to me he said that the subject was problematic,
and that there were other proposals. I later discovered what was behind this
strange comment and I will discuss later what he unfortunately meant.

Unlike my situation with the Peace Project, this time I had no staff and no
budget; however, I had a lot of experience. As for a personal budget for travel;
office equipment, etc, I decided to finance it from my own pocket. I defined
the first goals and the first requirements needed for starting the activity: 1. the
support of distinguished scientists; 2. the support of scientific institutions; 3.
a meaningful participation of Arab scientists and scientific administrators (I
assumed that I would have no difficulty in finding Israeli ones for that); and 4.
financial support for the first activities.

While I was on my first steps I was approached by Professor Galileo Violini,
an Italian physicist, who told me that he and Professor James Vary from Iowa
State University were inviting me to a scientific conference in San-Salvador.

Just as in previous conferences organized by Violini in Colombia, to which Violini had invited me, this one too was about the future of physics in Central and South America. But they had another reason for their invitation; they had heard about my plans for a Middle East academic institution, and wanted to coordinate activities with me. Vary was then in the midst of an attempt to establish a scientific center in his university, and was therefore interested in the ideas of Sawafta and me. Vary also introduced me to Professor Seif Romahi, who was a president of a Jordanian college, and who was trying to found a new Jordanian university, specializing in applied science. Romahi was also in good relations with the royal family in Jordan. I then corresponded with Romahi about possible collaboration, but unfortunately nothing came out of this correspondence.

On the advice of friends I traveled to the offices of UNESCO in Paris in order to meet Siegber Raither, a UNESCO employee, who was a physicist with a Ph.D. degree from Harvard, and was very interested in the idea of setting up a Middle-East university. Raither told me about the many activities that he knew to be connected with the subject in one way or another, and helped me a great deal in UNESCO. He told me about a group, including the physicists Guido Fubini from Italy, Maurice Jacob from CERN, and Eliezer Rabinovice from Jerusalem, which had already organized a conference in Dahab in the Sinai, and about peace symposia organized in Jerusalem by Professor Jehiel Becker. This information was encouraging, and indicated that other academicians in Israel and Europe were getting involved in activities related to academia and peace. I was impressed by the plan of Fubini et al, which was called Middle East Scientific Collaboration (MESC), and dealt with subjects that interested me.

At a certain stage Vary and Violini decided to visit the Middle East in order to investigate the possibilities of cooperation, and got a UNESCO grant to finance their trip. They asked for my help in organizing visits for them in Israel, and I gladly agreed, and even went along with them to some of those visits. I used the opportunity of the visits to describe my own plan to heads of the academic institutions in Israel that we visited, and most of them seemed very interested and encouraging. Violini and Vary also visited Jordan as well as the West Bank. At the end of their visit they recommended to UNESCO to establish a Middle-East university along the lines that they had heard from me.

****

228

A talk in the Jerusalem conference. One day, while I was in the US, I received an invitation from Jehiel Becker to a symposium in Jerusalem, the subject being The Contribution of Science to Peace. In the symposium I met Reyad Sawafta as well as Violini and Vary. The conference was also attended by faculty and students from Israel, the West Bank, and Gaza. I was glad to see the many people interested in cooperation in the Middle East, but was unhappy to learn about unpleasant competition among the various groups, who were competing for financial assistance, publicity, and honor. The following is the talk I gave in that conference on 21.1.1997, more than two years after Reyad Sawafta and I had written our proposal:

IS THE MIDDLE EAST READY FOR A REGIONAL UNIVERSITY?

Introduction. I wish to start my presentation by thanking Professor Yehiel Becker (Hebrew University) as well as Joseph Shinar and James Vary (Iowa State University) for organizing this important and timely symposium on the subject of the contribution of science to peace. I also thank them for inviting me to present my ideas concerning the establishment of a Middle East University in steps.

In 1994, a Palestinian physicist, Reyad Sawafta, and I wrote a proposal, which we called "The Red Sea Academic Institute", and distributed it among friends and other interested parties. Although some of them were skeptical, by and large, the proposal was met with warm reaction, and we thus were encouraged to pursue it vigorously[3*]. I will now summarize the main points of that proposal, with the hope that the presentation will encourage discussions, and will interest people here to join our effort.

There are several reasons for the great need for an open regional university in the Middle East:

Distance and isolation. In comparison with scientists in places such as Milan, Zurich, and Bonn, or Ames and Chicago, scientists in the various countries of the Middle East are hours away from the big scientific centers of the world. Moreover, because of the political situ-

3

ation, they have largely been isolated from colleagues in neighboring countries.

Absence of critical masses. Few countries in the region have sufficient manpower to sustain frontline efforts in research, and often have insufficient number of university teachers of high standard or large enough student body for such teachers.

Imbalance. While one country might lack a critical mass in one field, it might have a surplus in another field, but due to the political situation, it cannot pull forces with neighboring countries.

Brain drain. The above-mentioned difficulties, along with economic hardship and the absence of internationally competitive industry, are among the major reasons, which cause a severe brain drain (or brain overflow) that the Middle East is experiencing. Hundreds or even thousands of well-qualified young scientists go to the developed world to study, and often stay there, depriving their own society and the entire

Impossibility of meaningful research. It is all but impossible to carry out meaningful research in some fields, where the borders to neighboring countries are closed. For instance, how can medical researchers protect the population of their country from an epidemic disease if the source of the disease is in a neighboring country, with whose scientists they cannot collaborate in research or even exchange data? Researchers in bird migration, agriculture, fish culture, etc. are faced with the same difficulty.

The greatest advantage of being in a university that is open to everybody is the opportunity to study, teach, and carry out research together with scientists from the entire region. Also, facing the challenges that were mentioned above *together* is also an excellent way to understand one another, a pre-requisite for living in peace.

My previous efforts. I have to admit to you that I have made several efforts to achieve scientific collaboration in the middle-East region, and have failed.

1. A letter to Cairo. My attempts to start scientific collaborations between Arab and Israeli scientists began a long time ago. In 1975, as the dean of the Faculty of Exact Sciences at Tel Aviv University, I wrote a letter to the dean of science in Cairo University, proposing to start scientific collaborations between our faculties, even though our politicians were not yet on "talking terms", just as Russian-American scientific collaborations started years ahead of the political detente between the two countries. Neither my government nor the Egyptian government was happy with my letter, and I received no answer from Egypt.

2. *The Research Project on Peace.* In early 1978, soon after the historic visit of President Sadat to Jerusalem, we started a big all-departmental project at Tel Aviv University, which we called The Research Project on Peace. As the Project's first director, I traveled several times to Egypt, attempting to establish a multi-project program of scientific cooperation. Although I met with some warm support in the scientific community in Egypt, and gained the personal interest and support of Dr. Boutros Boutros Ghali, the then Egyptian Minister of State for Foreign Affairs, the government of Egypt did not give its official blessing, which at that time was necessary.

3. *The APS-EPS Mediterranean Conference.* My third attempt to start scientific cooperation was the submission of a proposal, in 1986, to the American Physical Society to use its influence and organize a conference on quarks and nuclei on an island in the eastern Mediterranean region. I proposed further that mostly Arab and Israeli students would attend the conference, and that the lecturers would be first-rate scientists. Although the APS approved the proposed program, it could not reach an agreement with the European Physical Society, and without such an agreement the program came to a halt.

4. *Recent successful attempts.* As we all know, several Arab-Israeli groups have recently had some measure of success in collaboration, mostly in small projects, often with the help of a group from a "neutral" country. The conference in Dahab organized by the Middle East scientific Collaboration, about a year ago, is such an example. There have also been cooperative programs in medicine, agriculture, and some other fields. Although small and uncoordinated, these examples show that there is a growing interest to cooperate freely in the sciences, and harvest the fruits of such a long overdue activity. The present symposium, which is organized with the blessed help of UNESCO, is a good indication that we might finally be on the right track toward full and free scientific cooperation in the Middle East.

5. *The Working Group.* Following my talk at a meeting in San Salvador, in which I presented the proposal of Reyad Sawafta and myself

to establish a Middle East institute, I was approached by Professor James Vary, who asked me simply, "How can I help?" This was a pleasant and welcome indication that the idea of a Middle East University has a strong appeal. UNESCO then sent a mission to the Middle East, composed of Professor James Vary, Dr. Hildegard Vary, and Professor Galileo Violini. They met with various scientific leaders in the region, and recommended to establish a major academic institute in the region, similar to the one Sawafta and I had proposed. I myself have been in contact with such regional scientific leaders in an attempt to form a high-level Working Group for the planning and development of the proposed Middle East University.

A University in steps. Planning the whole program, which will lead to the establishment of a full-scale university, is clearly up to the Working Group, which should be composed of university presidents, deans, and institution heads (or former ones) as well as senior scientists, mainly but not exclusively, from the Middle East. We will not attempt to pre-empt here the working of this group, but only to point out a few major topics, which they will have to deal with, starting with the steps of the program.

Courses, summer schools, and conferences. The first and relatively simple step is to put as many of the small existing and new such cooperative programs as possible under the same roof, by establishing the needed infrastructure: simple housing, administration, etc.

Colleges. The next major step will be the establishment of a new (junior) college. There are today in existence several plans for colleges in the region that will be open to Arabs and Jews, and it is recommended that they be coordinated and supported by the proposed program if they agree to become part of the major program that we propose here.

A research institute. The establishment of a research institute or several such institutes is the natural next step. Such institutes in physics, astronomy, oceanography, microbiology, and other disciplines have recently been proposed, some of them on a very high scientific level. Coordination and the use of the same physical and administrative infrastructure can be highly cost effective.

A University. A full-fledge university, with an undergraduate as well as graduate school, and with research institute(s) is clearly the major and final goal of the program. The courses, summer schools, and periodic conferences could then take place on the university campus.

Students. Students are expected to come primarily from countries that are taking part in the peace process. At present, this means Egypt, Israel, Jordan, and the Palestinian Authority. They will hopefully also come from other Middle East or East- Mediterranean countries, such as Saudi Arabia, Sudan, Syria, Lebanon, Greece, Turkey, and Cyprus. The so-called Diaspora is a promising source of Arab as well as Israeli students, many of whom are eager to come back to the region and contribute to its development. This process could then be labeled "reverse brain drain". However, the University will clearly be open to students from all over the world.

Faculty. It is expected that in the first stages of the plan, professors who work full time in the new college/university as well as professors from existing universities in the region, who will be on part-time appointments, will do most of the teaching. The percentage of full-time professors will increase with time. The Diaspora is expected to be the major source of teachers and researchers. Since the university will be an open institution, academicians with no Middle-East background will be invited to take part in its activities from the beginning. In fact, due to the unique character of this university, we expect scientists of high caliber, who usually prefer established universities, to join this pioneering endeavor.

Topics It is advisable to start with science and technology for two reasons: 1. the region needs science and technology to meet modern-day challenges, and catch up with lost time. 2. Science and technology are universal, and do not involve politics to a large extent. Topics such as basic science, computer science, agriculture, medicine, water, energy, and desert studies will be among the first ones to be emphasized, depending on the availability of personnel and funding. For instance, if an interest develops to emphasize microbiology, and funds become available for this purpose, this topic should get priority in development. Semitic languages as well as Mid-Eastern cultures and history will be introduced as early as possible, but this should be done very carefully, so as to avoid getting involved in ideologies in an immature state in the University development. Teaching will be in English.

Location. An ideal location is a meeting point of several countries, which is also attractive to live in. Such a venue is the Aqaba-Eilat-Taba region, the meeting place of Jordan, Israel and Egypt, and with a great deal of attraction due to the Red Sea. It is also close to Saudi Arabia, Sudan, etc. The northern tip of the Dead Sea, near city of Jericho, is another possibility, as it is the meeting point of Jordan, Israel, and the Palestinian Authority. It is also located a small distance from existing Jordanian, Israeli, and Palestinian academic institutions, which can provide teachers and laboratory space, especially in the beginning. After one of the two locations is chosen, a second campus in the other location can be built at a later stage, as part of the same university.

Supervision. UNESCO seems to be the best organization to launch the program and supervise it, because it is the recognized international cultural organization. Other candidates are internationally known universities in the region (such as the University of Rome) or out of the region (such as Harvard or MIT). A third possibility is a joint sponsorship of the universities of Cairo, Jerusalem (or Tel Aviv), and Amman. The Working Group will make the decision on the supervisor(s).

Budgetary Matters. It is difficult to give even a rough estimate of the budgetary needs for each step of the program, as it depends on so many unknown factors. Yet we can say that some seed money, about $100,000, will be needed for the activity of the Working Group, which should last about one year. A similar amount will be required for the design of the first and second stages of the program. The exact amount will greatly depend on whether existing or new plans for the college will be used. The design of the institute and of the university, at a later stage, will clearly require a great deal more. Whereas carrying out a modest program (first stage) of courses, summer schools, and conferences will require between $300,000 and $500,000 annually. Millions of dollars will be require annually for the construction as well as operation of the college or the institute, and tens of millions dollars, or more, will be required annually for the full-fledge university. The most critical amount, which will decide the fate of the program, is the amount of $100,000, which is needed right away to activate the Working Group and start the planning. We know that UNESCO cannot contribute appreciable amount of money, but we expect UNESCO to be a major factor in a campaign to raise the necessary funds. We also expect UNESCO to contribute significantly, directly or indirectly, to the activity of the Working Group. There are three sources of funding that should be approached: 1. participating countries (governments or existing universities), 2. international organizations, and 3. philanthropists who would be interested in supporting such an important and pioneering program. Personally, I wish to see a consortium of Gulf countries and world Jewish organizations taking the lead together in supporting the program.

Is the region ready? This is definitely an important question. My experience with the Research Project on Peace in the early eighties and the APS-EPS attempt ten years later, to organize a Mediterranean conference has taught me that such endeavors should be attempted when the conditions are right, and should then proceed with a great deal of vigor and tact. We should also bear in mind that although the peace process is moving forward, there are always ups and downs. It is therefore important for the program not to be dependent on fluctuations in the political arena, and to proceed, as much as possible, independently of such fluctuations. It is for this reason that at this moment I propose to form only the Working Group, and to put it under the auspices of UNESCO. With the success of the activity of the Working Group, and after the political situation clears up, we will be able to go on to the next step of the program.

A recent encouraging development. A very important development took place on my way to the symposium. On the invitation of UNESCO, I stopped over in Paris and talked with their personnel. I then had a long meeting with the Assistant Director General for Science, Professor Maurizio Iaccarino, as well as with some other high-level officials in the science sector. Professor Iaccarino was very interested in the proposed program; in fact, he said that he was enthusiastic about it, and promised the help of UNESCO as well as of himself, personally. Specifically, he offered assistance in the formation of the Working Group, in enlisting the support of Nobel laureates, in mustering the funds needed for the Working Group, and in supplying the needed UNESCO umbrella. As I said, this is very encouraging, and indicates strongly that we are on the right track. (The details of the meetings at the UNESCO office will be discussed later I the book).

****

A while later I heard from Raither in UNESCO that my name got somehow involved in the rivalry between groups with plans for cooperation in the Middle East. This saddened me, because I did not belong to any of those groups, but was willing to assist any of them who asked for my assistance (like the organizational help I gave to Violini and Vary). Since I was afraid that involving me in such rivalries might hurt my plans for building the Middle East Academic Institute, I notified Raither and the various groups about my readiness to help any of them, without competing with any other group, or belonging to any of them. As an example, I present now a section from the letter I wrote to Maurice Jacob from CERN:

> Like you, I am aware of other groups that are thinking of programs along similar lines. I believe that any thinking here can be helpful. However, I have also heard that my name is linked to such groups, and wish to stress that I am not committed, nor am I a member of any of these groups. I wish to help any one or any group, which is doing constructive work (and thinking), and will welcome any support that I can get for my ideas. From my past and present activity, and from my acquaintance with people such as yourself and Eliezer Rabinovice, it should be clear that I would strongly welcome coordination and collaboration with MESC.

In his responding letter Jacob told me that my letter as well as my talk in the conference in Jerusalem had been read to the participants of the management meeting of MESC. He further analyzed my ideas and plans, agreeing with most of them, but said that his group's order of actions was different than mine. The most interesting part of his letter is the revealing information of what had transpired in the European Physical Society when the American Physical Society had turned to them suggesting my idea for a Middle-East conference. He added that at that time he had been the president of the EPS. The following is the relevant section from Jacob's letter to me:

> A word about EPS since I had to deal with the matter there in 89-90.

The APS approved the idea but they agreed with the EPS dropping the project when it was not considered as workable, and rightly so, since the time proposed would have fallen during the Gulf War. As you know, the Middle East contacts, which we had through EPS, as well as the interested divisions, were not encouraging at all. Things were not easy. Yet you and Bob Wilson were good visionaries since something like Dahab could work a few years later.

I was glad that the misunderstanding between me and one of the groups was ironed out; and although I was not sure that Jacob's explanation about frustrating the APS initiative included all the reasons for it, he at least recognized that we had originated the ideas of Middle-East conferences (although, in his opinion, our idea had been tried out too early).

****

The APS continued to support my old and new ideas. The new director for international affairs, Irving Lerch, liked the idea of Sawafta and me for a Middle-East University as did the APS treasurer Harry Lustig. They both informed me that past and present presidents of the Society also liked the idea of building the University in steps, as did almost every American scientist I talked to. As an example, I will bring the Nobel Laureate Norman Ramsey, who not only supported the idea, but was also willing to sign a letter to all the laureates to support it.

When I was in Boston I met the founders of a Jewish-Arab organization, whose president was the sister-in-law of Yasser Arafat. The organization was collecting donations for a Middle-East University, but their idea was totally different than that of Sawafta and me. While Sawafta and I talked about a university open to Arabs and Jews on the border between states, the Boston group talked about building new campuses only in Arab countries, which would be under a roof of one University like New-York-State University or the University of California. In my discussion with them I said that their idea was barely connected with peace in the Middle East, at least not between Israel and the Arab countries. Nevertheless, I wished them good luck.

In Boston, I also met Jawad Anani, an important Jordanian political and business personality of Palestinian decent, who later became the deputy prime minister of Jordan. He seemed very interested in the idea of a university on the border of our countries. He described to me at length the structure of higher education in

Jordan as well as the presidents of the various universities and colleges. Finally, he suggested getting in touch with his younger brother, a chemist, who could be my contact in Jordan.

****

One of my most important meetings at that time was in Israel. I read in a newspaper about Israel Goralnik, the general manager of ORT–Israel, with close to one hundred thousand students in its vocational schools, who had been the general manager of the ministry of labor. He had notified the press that he was about to get a donation of 30 million dollars from an anonymous philanthropist in order to build a new college in Israel for both Jews and Arabs. I called Goralnik who had been a close friend of mine since we had been together in the boy-scouts. Goralnik had been a highly respected public servant and education leader, who had lost his right arm in 1948, in Israel's War of Independence (which the Arabs call the Nakba –the disaster), when he caught a hand grenade and threw it back to save his colleagues. I asked Goralnik to tell me about the planned college, and he did. I then told him about the proposal of Sawafta and me, and asked him if he would agree to build his college as part of our plan in Aqaba-Eilat-Taba or in the north of the Dead Sea. He got excited about the idea, and said that he liked the idea of building his college together with me. Goralnik and I visited the ORT College in Carmiel in the Galilee, and studied the plans for the new college, including the drawings, administration and budget. I reported the information to Reyad Sawafta, and he was very pleased.

One day I was told by Goralnik that Shimon Peres, the person who was supposed to get the big donation for the new college, invited him and Professor Shimon Shamir, who was then the Israeli ambassador to Jordan, to travel with him to Jordan. The purpose of the trip was to meet some Jordanian dignitaries, possibly also King Hussein's brother Hassan, in order to discuss the building of the new college. Goralnik asked Peres to add me to the trip, but Peres refused. Goralnik came back and reported to me about the talks in Jordan, and surprised me by adding that he trusted me and relied on me personally and professionally, and would not act on this matter without me. From our friendship of close to sixty years I knew that unlike some other so-called friends, I could rely on his friendship one hundred percents.

After several more trips of the three people to Jordan it became apparent to Goralnik that the main plan was not to build a college on the Israel-Jordanian border, rather to build a most advanced laboratory for genetic studies, apparently north of the Dead Sea, The director would be Professor Daniel Cohen, a French professor, and one of the world's greatest scientists in the field. Only then I understood why Shimon Shamir, the former member of the Management of the Peace Project, with whom I had collaborated many times in the past, had been cool to my idea of a Middle-East Academic Institute. I told Goralnik that in my opinion there was little chance for success in their plan, because a most advanced laboratory on genetics could not be on the priority list of Jordan or any other Arab state. I added that Jordan lacked the infrastructure in men and material for such an advanced laboratory, and that such a plan should rather be part of our grand plan, but at a much later stage. I then added that in spite of my doubts I wished them good luck. Goralnik then said that he trusted my expertise and intentions, and added that he had no intention to go into that project without me. A real friend! Unfortunately, the laboratory was not built, and it was not clear who got cold feet, the philanthropist, the prince or the scientist; or perhaps the political situation killed this project as it had done to so many of my own plans.

****

The auspices of UNESCO to a Middle-East University. In spite of the many disappointments, I did not give up, and continued my frequent correspondence with Siegbert Raither from UNESCO, who was very supportive. One day he invited me to come to the offices of UNESCO in Paris and present my ideas to the assistant director general for science.[4] I stopped in Paris on my way from the US to the conference in Jerusalem, which was organized by Professor Yehiel Becker. I was looking forward to also meeting the staff members of UNESCO, whom I had met in 1972 and 1974, when I represented Israel in the science committee in the bi-annual congresses of UNESCO. My talks with them were very helpful as was the discussion with Avi Shocket, Israel's representative to UNESCO, who liked my ideas and offered his help. I was then invited to the office of Professor Mauricio Iaccarino, the organization's assistant director general for science, for a long discussion. Several heads of departments also took part at the meeting. Iaccarino had read the proposal of Sawafta and me, and said that he was excited about the idea and the role that UNESCO could play in it. Just as Boutros Ghali had done after my meeting with him almost twenty years earlier, he too asked me to write down a detailed account of our discussion, which I did after the conference in Jerusalem; and this is what I wrote on 3.2.1997:

4   In my presentation at the Jerusalem conference I talked briefly about my visit to UNESCO, as described earlier.

It was a great honor and pleasure for me to meet you, two weeks ago, and discuss our plan to build a Middle-East university, where Arabs and Israelis can study, teach, and carry out research together. As you know, when Professor Sawafta and I wrote our proposal for such a university several years ago, we thought of UNESCO as an ideal organization for sponsoring such a daring, yet worthwhile project. I was very encouraged to learn that you too share our thoughts. It was also gratifying to realize that you considered favorably the possibility that UNESCO, with its international standing and influence, would take a major role in the execution of this challenging endeavor.

I presented the proposal in Jerusalem in the Conference on Science and Peace, which was organized by Professor Yehiel Becker. Many of the participants, and in particular those from UNESCO, supported the idea warmly, as did the participants at our meeting in your office. An Arab student from Gaza, who was able to study in the Hebrew University in Jerusalem only because he could show the authorities, on both sides of the border, that he had a UNESCO grant, emphasized UNESCO's essential role at the Conference.

If I am allowed yet another personal note, I would add that I was touched by your expression of personal interest in our project, and welcome it full-heartedly. You also expressed a request that I would be strongly connected with the project, and I can assure you that such will be the case. I trust that your suggestion of a proper UNESCO consulting position for me and perhaps for some other major participants from the Middle East will help overcome some possible political difficulties.

The following is a report[5], which summarizes the main ideas that were discussed at our meeting in your office, with suggested steps to follow. Clearly, the first and imminent step should be the establishment by UNESCO of a Working Group for planning and development of the University.

****

Since Iaccarino seemed interested in the University project, and all but said that he wished he himself had come up with it, I was full of hopes. After all,

5 *See Appendix XIII.*

UNESCO is the main international culture organization, and although they could not promise me full financial assistance, Iaccarino promised some seed money and help in getting front-line scientists to help me. However, instead of a response from Iaccarino, I received information from several sources in UNESCO; the most worrying one told me that there was competition in UNESCO on the question of which section would have the attractive project. Some officials even claimed that the University project fitted exactly with their approved plans. I kept corresponding with Raither and Shocket, who continued their enthusiastic support, but nothing from Iaccarino, who might have lost the battle inside UNESCO. Whatever the reason, this specific avenue was finally closed.

****

The political situation too got worse. Prime Minister Yitzhak Rabin was murdered on 4.11.95 by a Jew. This was a big blow to all peace seekers, but we all hoped that Shimon Peres, who took over the premiership, would continue to advance the reconciliation with the Palestinians, and indeed Sawafta and his Arab friends stayed with me, working on the University project. However, the traditional enemies of peace, including the Hamas and other extreme Palestinian organizations in the occupied territories, joined by the Hezbollah in Lebanon, increased their attacks on Israelis. Shimon Peres, who had decided to have national elections in Israel in a relatively short while, was afraid to be seen as weak on security, all but forsook the budding peace track, and concentrated on showing a strong hand inside the territories. He also launched a big attack across the Lebanese border. The Israeli army, by mistake, bombed a UN camp and killed more than one hundred civilian refugees. Rather than apologizing for the terrible mistake, as Deputy Prime Minister Yigal Alon had done years earlier when an Israeli plane dropped a bomb on a peaceful Arab village by mistake, Peres did not apologize; rather he showed his toughness by only accusing the other side for causing the war. Having left the peace track, and attempting unsuccessfully to imitate the extreme Israeli militant right, Peres lost the national elections to Benjamin Netanyahu, the extreme rightist, on 29.5.1996. In the beginning, Netanyahu declared that he was accepting the Oslo Agreement as an existing fact (though an unhappy one), but he did his best to frustrate it, thus pleasing the peace enemies on both sided. After several months of the Netanyahu regime, the spirit of Oslo died out, and the efforts of reconciliation came to an end. The terror acts against Israelis increased their pace and cruelty as did the Israeli reaction to them. These unfortunate developments hurt very much the efforts of Sawafta and me. On 9.4.1997 I described our situation to Raither in the following way:

We are now at a "low", and we do not know how long this low will last. Some think that a project such as ours may be a good thing, especially at this time, since it introduces some positive elements into the equation. Others think that it is crazy to talk about regional cooperation at a time like this. Unfortunately, irrespective of the question of who is right; it is very difficult now to get Arab scientists to join the effort.

In spite of all these difficulties, Sawafta and I still did not lose all hopes that our idea would keep running, or rather would start. In his letter to me on 4.5.1997, Sawafta told me about the hesitation of some of his Palestinian friends in staying involved in an Israeli-Palestinian project, but added:

James Vary and I visited the Palestinian universities right after the meeting in Jerusalem, and found that there was a lot of interest in our idea. The only problem was that the political climate did not help in taking any serious steps toward making it a reality. Most people with whom we discussed the idea preferred the Jericho option for the location. There were other ideas, for example, for industrial and research parks to be somehow connected with the university, which was already part of our thinking.

I was somewhat surprised that his Palestinian friends were hesitating to act because of the worsening of the political situation, because I had thought that unlike the situation before the Oslo Agreement, the Palestinians after the Agreement were the most interested party in Israeli Palestinian cooperation. Unfortunately, Sawafta was not the only one that reported to me on the Palestinian change of attitude.

****

Before giving up completely on the Middle-East University, I told my wife Rivka that if I had the budget that Goralnik had talked about ($30,000,000), I might still be able to move the University idea in spite of the political difficulties. Rivka's response was, "Why don't you try the richest man in the world? If you find a way to get to Bill Gates from Microsoft, you might be able to convince him to build the University. I urge you to fly to Seattle and suggest to Bill Gates that the University on the northern tip of the Red Sea will carry his name, and will be mostly devoted to science and technology, with special emphasis on computer studies. He might like the idea if you also suggest to him that on the University main tower, and facing the Red Sea, will be written:

THE BILL GATES UNIVERSITY
A GATE TO PEACE
THROUGH SCIENCE AND TECHNOLOGY

What can you lose?" I liked the idea[6], and although I was very tired, and practically with no funds or help, I flew to Seattle. My first talk was with Professor Ernst Henley, an old physics teacher of mine at the University of Washington, and a former president of the APS. Like many others, he said that he was excited about the idea of a Middle-East University, and suggested talking with Nobel Laureates such as T. D. Lee. As for Bill Gates, Henley said that he knew him personally, and Gates had just contributed ten million dollars to the department of physics at U. of W. for a hall carrying his mother's name. He suggested writing a letter to Bill Gates with a copy to him, and he would help me with Gates. However, he added that I should do that only after I form the Working Group with the distinguished scientists and Arab scientists and administrators in it.

I then realized that I was in a vicious circle, some sort of a CATCH 22 situation; in order to move forward, I needed Arab scientists and administrators; for them to agree to work with me in spite of the tough political situation I needed funds; but to get the funds, I needed the Arabs. I therefore decided to wait for the improvement of the political situation, but it got worse and worse. I also turned to some rich Israeli philanthropists, but they were skeptical and turned me down. Regretfully, I finally had to give up.

A UNESCO chair for scientific cooperation. In the mid nineteen nineties all the Israeli universities received a request from the education minister to suggest candidates for a UNESCO Chair for Scientific Cooperation. The information supplied by the minister's office said that UNESCO was interested in a person who had experience in international cooperation between North and South. The dean of the Faculty of Exact Sciences at that time was Profes-

---

6   It is unfortunate that Rivka had not thought about it a few weeks earlier, because we were then in Seattle having a pizza and into the almost empty pizzeria walked Bill Gates and his family, and took the table next to us. I could have then apologized for the intrusion and could have just said a few words about the idea. Who knows? Perhaps it would have worked.

sor David Horn. Being familiar with my record, he decided to nominate me as the University candidate for the Chair. He therefore asked me to describe my ideas and plans if I got the UNESCO chair, and then sent the plan to the University president at that time, Professor Yoram Dinstein, suggesting my candidacy. These ideas and plans are presented below.

SCIENCE AND TECHNOLOGY AS A BRIDGE BETWEEN NORTH AND SOUTH

Introduction. It is hereby proposed to establish a UNESCO Chair for International Scientific Collaboration at Tel Aviv University. The proposed UNESCO Chair will utilize the vast experience gathered at Tel Aviv University in science and technology as well as in university teaching and international collaboration. The Chair will concentrate its efforts on promoting transfer of knowledge between North and South, and strengthening scientific research and higher education in the developing countries.

The State of Israel is geographically located between north and south as well as between east and west. In many ways it is both a developing and a developed country, with a great deal of experience in the transition between the two phases. It has also had a rich experience in the initiation of a variety of research projects in science and technology, as well as in building new universities. Recently, Israel has absorbed a large number of well-trained scientists from the former Soviet Union, who are eager to share their knowledge with those who are willing to learn. The country has had much experience in international scientific collaboration, by hosting a variety of projects, some specifically aimed at the developing world, and by participating in programs organized by other countries.

Tel Aviv University, which was established about thirty years ago, has played a significant role in the international effort of the State of Israel. The Faculties of Exact Sciences and of Engineering are noted for the organization of conferences, workshops, visit exchanges, and post graduate teaching, many of which aimed at the developing countries of the world. The School of Physics, in particular, has had official and unofficial collaboration programs with schools and institutes in the developing world. One example of such collaborations is the agreement, which the School of Physics has recently signed with the Centro Internacional de Fisica in Bogota in Colombia that is coordinating the future physics plans of the Andean countries.

A pioneering program of building new scientific cooperation was launched at Tel Aviv University in 1978, soon after the historic visit to Jerusalem of the late Egyptian president, Anwar Sadat. It was aimed at establishing scientific collaboration between Israeli and Egyptian as well as other Arab scientists, and was called the Research Project on Peace.

Goals of the program. The proposed UNESCO Chair has five basic goals

Advancement of university teaching and research in science and technology in developing countries.

Training post-graduate students in basic and applied sciences.

Promoting scientific collaboration between scientists from North and South.

Transfer of scientific information and knowledge from developed to developing countries.

Assisting regional and sub-regional efforts in the developing world in building new universities and research institutions as well as in launching new scientific projects.

A great deal of emphasis will be given to physics programs, both basic and applied. One of the main efforts will be in post-graduate education. Qualified students from the developing countries, notably from Africa, the Middle East, and South America, will be invited to get their post-graduate education at Tel Aviv University. Assistance in supervision of such students in their native countries will also be offered. A very efficient way to foster these programs will clearly be to invite the professors from these countries to visit Tel Aviv University. Professors and students will be invited to take part in ongoing research, and to join their colleagues from Tel Aviv University with the specific research to be performed inside or out of the country (in international laboratories, particle accelerators, etc). On special occasions, and budget permitting, universities in developing countries will be visited, mainly in order to assist in the establishment of new laboratories or in the choice of new projects to embark on. Lectures

245

and seminars containing up-to-date information will then be conducted in the universities of the visited country. Assistance will be given to the organization of topical conferences and workshops, to be preferably held in a developing country.

The above-mentioned program is clearly very ambitious, requiring a great deal of time and money, as well as setting up priorities. Whereas countries in the Andean Region, with which we have already established a tradition of cooperation, are in need of assistance, they are located far away from Tel Aviv University. Africa is clearly closer, but not much scientific collaboration in physics exists there today. The Arab World, and in particular Egypt, is a neighbor who can be considered partly developed and partly developing. Cooperation with Egyptian and other Arab scientists will be one of the major goals of the proposed program. Collaboration with universities in the West Bank and Gaza is a goal of utmost importance in spite of present political difficulties. Although the universities and colleges there are young and operate under difficult conditions, they have managed to attract young faculty, and some of their professors have already given seminar talks at Tel Aviv University. We will offer these universities a great deal of help in accepting their qualified post-graduate students, in providing full or part-time positions to their professors, in helping them build their laboratories, and in collaborating with them in research. One cannot overstate the importance of such a collaboration offered by qualified people in a suitable university.

I had a strong feeling that with the Chair, I could contribute to the scientific ties of Israel and of Tel-Aviv University with the whole world. Dean Horn assumed that my candidacy was strong because of my vast experience in scientific collaboration and because of my ties with UNESCO. I too believed that the Israeli minister of education would approve my candidacy, and I was sure that UNESCO too would be pleased to approve it. I did not get the Chair, but not because of a decision by the minister of education or by UNESCO. I did not get it because, as Dean Horn told me, President Dinstein decided not to submit my candidacy to the ministry of education. What is the reason of this action or inaction of my old colleague and member of the Management of the Research Project on Peace, who had said that if the political relations with Egypt would improve, the Peace Project should call me back from my Sabbatical leave in Saclay? Could it be on an advice he had gotten from Big

Brother (See Appendix III), or because of the emphasis that Horn's letter put on collaboration with universities in the West Bank, an idea Dinstein always disliked, or from other reasons known only to him? What was left for me to say again was only *too bad!*

UNESCO made another attempt to harness me to the subject of scientific collaboration in the Middle East, when the organization asked me to help in transferring an electron synchrotron from Germany to Israel for the use of scientists of the whole region. The synchrotron could accelerate electrons up to 500 million electron-volts, therefore producing x-rays of up to 500 million electron-volts. It would mainly be used for material and biological research, and for teaching. The Germans had built a more advanced accelerator, and were ready to donate the old one with no cost, and perhaps also to set it up and start it running here, but requested that the countries in the region would carry the cost of running the synchrotron along with the experimental equipment around it. I looked into the matter and learned that the Israeli scientists working in this field were not very interested in an old accelerator, and in spending the little research money they had on running it, while they were using the front-line accelerators in the world. Unfortunately, our scientists did not appreciate the advantage of having a regional accelerator in our country. Such an accelerator could encourage scientific collaborations and teach regional students. [7]

7   I have recently learned that the accelerator was eventually give to Jordan, and was placed in northern Jordan inside a complex of laboratories. It will be used by scientists from the whole region, including Iran and Israel. Professor Eliezer Rabinovice from the Hebrew University is associated with this project.

CHAPTER 13.
CONCLUDING PERSONAL REMARKS

How does one summarize decades of activity, sometimes only as part of the daily activity, and often throughout the whole day? It took me more than two years to put together in writing all my thoughts and plans as well as my actual activity, full of struggles, on the question of peace and scientific collaboration in the Middle East. I then translated the whole book into English with the hope that not only Israelis, but also people abroad, and in particular in Arab countries, would one day put into use my thoughts and plans, even those that failed. What is left for me now is to look at the entirety, to summarize it, and to provide answers to some of the questions which are called for.

The reader who is browsing through the many pages, like me at this moment, might be somewhat impressed by the number of different subjects related to peace which occupied me in tens of years. In the beginning I tried to be involved in politics, by coordinating the activities of the many groups and parties in Israel devoted to peace. When this failed I left politics completely, and represented Israel in two UNESCO conferences. The coming of President Sadat to Israel and the shame I felt as an academician for not preparing ourselves for the opportunities that peace could bring us caused me to propose the formation of the Research Project on Peace and to be its director. I failed in my attempt to make it a project for all the universities in Israel, but succeeded in uniting in the Project all the efforts in my university related to peace. The project also undertook on itself national goals, and organized a workshop, together with public experts, on a national authority and a national center dealing with all the issues of peace and regional cooperation. The Project also agreed to be responsible for the talks with Egypt about the activity in the field school in Santa Katharina. We then formed a think tank that worked alongside with public experts, trying to foresee the advantages and dangers to the country from the advent of peace with Egypt. The think tank also studied the Palestinian problem which was expected to affect our budding peace relations with Egypt. We selected a Management for the Peace Project, whose members were senior professors at the University, as well as a public Steering Board. The Management appointed a research committee which looked at submitted research proposals, and when approved, granted them financial help. The Management also established a program called "Peace Papers", which invited Israeli and Egyptian speakers, and their lectures were published in English, while the first lecture, that of Abba Eban, was published in Hebrew, English, and Arabic, and was sent to various Arab universities and libraries. We organized an international conference, the subject of which was "Toward Peace in the Middle East and Beyond." The University President Ben-Shahar got from the Knesset a grant of $50,000 as well as other grants, and I got a grant from the Ford foundation of $35,000 to finance the first collaborative researches with Egyptian scientists.

As the Project director and representing the University president I traveled twice to Washington to meet with scientists, senators, and philanthropists. In those travels and in other events I formed strong ties with senior Arab scientists. When it became possible, I traveled several times to Egypt and visited three universities there as well as the Egyptian National Academy of Science. I gave an informal lecture at Cairo University, where I also examined candidates for collaborations with us. In these visits I formed close friendship with Egyptian scientists, physicians, and authors, and a special close friendship with the most senior physicist there, Professor Mohamed El-Nadi. In my talks with the Egyptians we discussed several possibilities of scientific collaboration, and finally reached an agreement with three senior Egyptian scientists on collaboration on three topics: nuclear physics, remote sensing, and the desert goat. I talked twice at length with Dr. Boutros Ghali, the Egyptian Secretary of State for Foreign Affairs, with the second discussion being initiated by him. He welcomed my plan for the three collaborations, which was a balanced plan, and was based on the equality between the two sides. Unfortunately, the plan did not get the green light from the Egyptian government. The coolness of relations between the two peoples because of what was going on in the occupied territories and because of the war in Lebanon slowed down the activity of the Peace Project, and finally brought it to an end in the mid nineteen eighties.

Several years after the collapse of the Peace Project, I decided to learn from my experience and to use the power and prestige of the American Physical Society to help me get regional cooperation. The idea was to have a workshop on quarks and nuclei in an East Mediterranean Island. The APS supported the idea enthusiastically, but the European Physical Society failed it.

After several efforts on smaller projects, I turned enthusiastically to a new pioneering project, to build a Middle East University in steps. I wrote a proposal together with Reyad Sawafta, a Palestinian physicist. The idea gained support in the Middle East region and in many parts of the world and UNESCO too supported it. However, the political developments in Israel following the assassination of Prime Minister Rabin, the murderous attacks by Arab terrorists, and the hatred toward the Oslo agreement of the Israeli right, slowed the project down and finally killed it. In all these projects I tried to advance peace and scientific collaboration, the two ideals which were dear to my heart since my graduation from high school. In what follows I will assess these activities and draw some conclusions, with the hope that they might help others trying to do similar things, in the Middle East or elsewhere; and I will do it by attempting to answer some questions such as: What was my degree of success in achieving the goals I had set in the beginning? What were the reasons for the successes or the failures? How much benefit or damage did I cause? Was I a prophet ahead of his time? And what caused me to spend so much time and efforts on all the subjects described in this book?

There is no doubt that one of the main criteria for judging a certain endeavor is the result. In looking at the results I have to conclude that I had very little success if any, in spite of all my efforts in so many years. For each subject separately, I can point out the main responsible factors for its frustration. For instance, the indecision of the Egyptian government as well as the resistance inside my university were the main causes of the failure of the Peace Project; the objection of the European Physical Society caused the failure of the East-Mediterranean work shop; and the political and military conflict in the Middle East caused the failure of the plan to build a Middle-East University. I imagine that apart from all these causes, I too must have contributed to the many failures.

I do not believe that I have caused any damage to the relations between us and our Arab neighbors, to the State of Israel, or to Tel Aviv University. On the contrary, I believe that the ties I created with senior Egyptian academicians and scientists helped change their minds and those of some of their students about Israel and her scientists, and opened the door for future scientific ties. In the discussion of these issues with my wife Rivka she said that good ideas were sometimes expressed and tried out before their time, and this was the reason why people did not pay attention to them. She pointed out two examples from my own experience, not related to peace: 1. in the early nineteen seventies, I suggested to the senate of Tel-Aviv University to establish appropriate tools for the absorption of massive immigration of academic people from the Soviet bloc, lest a dream became a nightmare. The recommendations of a committee, which I headed, were put in the rector's drawer and stayed there, while the massive immigration of academicians from the former Soviet Union took place about twenty years later. 2. Also, in the early nineteen seventies, I wrote a proposal for getting ready for a wide social use of home computers, a subject which became popular several years later. "It is possible," Rivka said, "that in the peace issue you were also ahead of our time." Was she right? It could be. The Dahab conference, which took place a few years after the failure of my proposal to the APS of an East-Mediterranean workshop, could be an example supporting Rivka's idea.

Finally, I will try to answer a question which may have bothered many readers; namely, why does an established physicist decide to burden his life and that of his family in dealing with peace and collaboration issues instead of staying in the laboratory and do undisturbed research? One often hears a general of an army, any army, say, "as a general I know the death and suffering of war, therefore I am fighting for peace", but there is almost no general who admits that he fights for war. The same thing is true about people in general; they often go to wars, but they claim that they fight for peace.

In my first novel On Love and War I describe Ehud who was agonizing over the question whether to join the so-called Israel War of Independence and kill or maim people he did not even know. When he was convinced that not joining the weak defense forces, which were also defending him, was immoral, he joined them and postponed his moral-philosophical doubts for after the war, but promised himself that after the war he would pay humanity back his debts by trying to prevent further wars. I used to recite to my little daughter, "I promise you, my little girl, that this will be the last war", but in my heart I knew that the only thing I had the right to promise was that I would do my best to prevent further wars.

I saw the war-disabled, the orphans and the widows of the Sinai War and the Six-Day War crying to us and to anybody who had a sensitive heart, "Why? Why did it happen to me?" Afterwards, when I was the dean of the Faculty of Exact Sciences during the Yom-Kippur War, I saw what the War had done to my students. There were some who did not come back, and others who came back wounded in their arms or legs, or with burnt faces or hurt in their souls. I then remembered my Egyptian student Tabark crying for her brothers who were fighting the Israeli Army in the Sinai in the Six-Day War. And the doubting questions broke into my mind in all their severity: Do I have the right to continue sitting in the academic ivory tower without trying to stop the killing around me of people, Jews and Arabs alike? Don't I have a duty, especially as a professor, to use all the knowledge that have accumulated in order to prevent further terrible damage of wars from my students and other students in the region, Jews and Arabs alike? With these questions came back to me the promises I had made to my self after the War of Independence and to my little daughter. Along with this I remembered the beautiful pictures which I used to draw in my mind, of a future which is not only without wars, but also good and more beautiful, in which students and scientists from the whole region study and do research together. These two forces, that of the desire to prevent future wars, and that of the struggle for a better future for the children of the region, were the forces which pushed me to act tirelessly as I did, and this is what apparently brought the member of the Management of the Peace Project, Retired General Aharon Yariv, to say, "We have to admit that Avivi Yavin is crazy for peace."

PHOTOGRAPHS

With Dr. George Assousa in the Sinai

With Dr. Tabark Noweir

Dr. Ali El-Saidi

A view of the Nile from the Shepherd Hotel

Tahrir, the main square of Cairo

The Cairo Tower

A suk in Cairo

The Hussein Mosque

The empty building of the Arab League

The Israeli Embassy

The museum of captured Israeli weapons

Rivka with the teachers of the Children Village

Rivka with the tour guide

Mona, a receptionist in the Hilton Hotel

With Professor Mahmoud Badr

With Hussein Faouzi and Professor Itzhak Kelson in Tel Aviv

With Israel Goralnik

The Political Role of Arab and Israeli Intellectuals –
Hopes and Disappointments
(Dixon, Illinois, 1969)

As the title suggests, the talk addresses both Arab and Israeli intellectuals. The reason that I have agreed to participate in this conference, and have decided to talk about this specific topic, is my deep conviction that not only is there a role for intellectuals in this complex and highly emotional conflict, but there is also a duty, which is very little tended to.

Following a bloody war in 1948, in which I took part as a young soldier, Israel achieved independence - the fulfillment of Jewish dreams of 2,000 years. It also brought about the establishment of a shelter for all persecuted Jews. How painful is the thought that had the State of Israel been established ten years earlier, millions of European Jews could have been saved from Nazi execution. But as is always the case, this war resulted in the death and injury of many young people on both sides. It also brought misery to many displaced Palestinian Arabs. I now have a direct interest in doing my best to see to it that my son will grow up free from the need to kill or be killed, and that my daughter, who often recites Bob Dylan's songs, will be "free from the worst fear, the fear of bringing children into the world". I want my children to grow up as proud and free Israelis, in a safe and secure Israel, free from foreign domination, and dominating nobody.

****

It is usually argued by most Arabs that the main reason for the wars and continuing tension in the Middle East is the fate of the Palestinians. In my talk I will fully adopt this Arab point of view, and I will address my talk to the fate of the Palestinians and the question of coexistence of Palestinians and Israelis.

One reason for the complexity of the Palestinian-Israeli conflict is the simple fact that there is indeed a genuine conflict of interests between the national aspirations of the Jews and the Palestinians, at least in their extremes. This is often demonstrated when an Arab or an Israeli talks about his people's rights in Palestine, be they legal, political, or moral. The weakness in each position and argument usually appears when each talks about the lack of rights of the other. My rights to my country go back to the Bible, to 2,000 years of Jewish yearnings, to three generations of pioneers in Israel, and to the losses and sacrifices of so many of my friends; and these rights do not depend on others, be they Arabs, British, Russians, Americans, or even the United Nations. At the same time, and in all fairness, I fully admit that the personal as well as national rights of the Palestinian Arabs in the country (if and when they decide that there is a separate Palestinian nation) do not need Israeli approval, or that of the French, the Jordanians, or even the United Nations.

The main problem, which we are therefore facing, is the following: In the small country west of the Jordan River there exist not one but two national groups with rights of various degrees, who have not yet found, nor have they seriously sought a possible coexistence formula. This formula should be based on the recognition that both sides have national rights, and the solution should answer the most fundamental needs of both sides.

The existence of a theoretical solution to the national conflict is only a necessary condition for its resolution. It still does not tackle the *how*, the *when*, and the *by whom* (or *against whom*), practical questions, which are of utmost importance. Furthermore, although the theoretical and practical questions are indeed difficult, burying our heads in sands of emotions, bias, and ignorance will not help. *Is it then too much to expect intellectuals on both sides to address themselves to these problems?*

The situation is further confused by the inclusion of outside elements, such as the big powers, the Arab states, and world Jewry. For us the ties with the Jews around the world are one of our fundamental rights, a right that no other nation should question. In all fairness, and even if we do not understand or like it, the Palestinians have ties with the Arab world. However, the problem takes a turn for the worse when the Arab states move in with their armies, and in doing so bring over their own separate political, economic, and military interests, which are often in conflict with those of both Israeli Jews and Palestinian Arabs. Then, and only then, they stop being just an ally of one side, and

266

become an outside belligerent intruder. Worse than that, the Arab countries have often been outside exploiters, who use the conflict in order to further their own internal and external interests.

Sooner or later, the Palestinian Arabs will have to ask themselves: Why weren't the Palestinian refugees in the Gaza Strip allowed to settle in Egypt between 1948 and 1967? Why were they treated there as second-class citizens? Why have Palestinian refugees been discouraged from settling the Jordan Valley? Were all the Palestinian refugees in the Arab states persuaded to stay in camps for decades only to further the eventual destruction of Israel, or because they were a threat to the stability of the host states? Moreover, did President Nasser arm himself to the teeth, tie his country to the Soviet Union, and bring about the disastrous 1967 war, which resulted in hundreds of thousands more refugees, only to help the Palestinians? And why are the Palestinians the ones who always end up the main losers? *Is it not time for the Palestinian intellectuals to ask themselves what should come first, President Nasser's interests or the life and future of the refugees, the details of the borders between Egypt and Israel or their own national independence?*

The involvement of the big powers increases the complexity of the situation by bringing in strong and dangerous outside interests. Until 1948, the British often played the Jews and Arabs against each other in order to further their own interests. The interests in the region of the United States and of the Soviet Union, as well as those of France are well known. A child could see the dangers, which these powerful self-interests are bringing to the area. Take 1956 for example. Did the British and the French invade the Suez Canal in order to separate the Israeli and Egyptian armies, as they claimed, or in order to promote French and British interests? In the long run, is it not in the best interests of both Arabs and Israelis to prevent their countries from becoming an Orwellian playground for the big powers, from becoming another Korea, or another Vietnam? Have these examples not demonstrated clearly that it is much easier to convince a big power to move in than it is to have the big power leave? And again, *who else if not the intellectuals should be expected to see the danger and warn their societies?*

We now come to another problem, which is of a different nature, and which makes the solution even more difficult to achieve. I am referring to the asymmetry between the Israelis and the Palestinians in both status and state of national development. On the one hand, we have the Israeli Jews, who have seen one third of the world Jewish population killed in the Holocaust. They started immigrating to the area one hundred years ago, dried many swamps, built roads, and established a new form of social life – the kibbutz, as well as new universities of world fame. And even more impressive is the Israeli intellectual community, which is active, soul searching, and often highly critical of its political leadership. On the other hand, there are the Palestinian Arabs, both in Palestine and in the Diaspora. They are the most advanced Arab people, and yet they have basically been asleep, while the British, the Russians, the UN, the Arab states, and Israel have continuously made decisions that affect their lives. They do not have political institutions and leadership, and what is worse, they do not have an independent, soul-searching intellectual community, which can criticize their political leaders and help them lead their society[1].

In June 1967, the Palestinians awoke from their dreams, and found the Humpty-Dumpty promises of Arab leaders broken to pieces. They still did not look for the real causes of their misery, and for a possibility of an honorable solution, but blamed the Israelis, and embarked on a kill campaign. So Al-Fatah was reinforced, and Yasser Arafat was alleged to be the Middle-East Che Guevara, who would defeat the *new Crusaders* – the Zionists. Clearly, this is not a complete state of awakening, because just as they have already learned that Nasser is not Saladin and Dayan is not Richard Lion-Hearted, so they will soon realize that Yasser Arafat is not George Washington and Golda Meir is not King George. And I ask: *Is it not the duty of intellectuals in the twentieth century to awaken their society from dreams of knights and Crusades to the reality of co-existence?*

Let us focus our attention now on the absence of real critical political thinking in the Palestinian society. I do not mean that the Arab students and intellectuals do not know Israel's faults. They study at length all the injustices inflicted on them by Israel and Zionism. Some of them give brilliant anti-Israel talks, full of quotations from UN resolutions and from various Israeli leaders and newspapers. But do they also address themselves to the real issues of their society? Do they steer their society away from its course, which has proven to be disastrous so many times in recent years? Just as many Israeli intellectuals recognize that whether they like it or not, Palestinian Arabs do have national rights, is it too much to expect Palestinian intellectuals to appreciate Israel's

---

1 *Today, 40 years later, the situation has greatly changed; the Israeli intellectual community is less critical of their government, while the Palestinian intellectuals are much more soul searching.*

national rights? Is it too much to expect a student to doubt what his political leaders tell him? Isn't the doubt a prerequisite for intellectualism, at least since Descartes? It is perhaps not surprising to hear their politicians say that "we will never negotiate or make peace with Israel; however, if Israel obeys the UN resolutions, there will be peace". This self-contradictory position may be a good shelter for politicians, but can it satisfy open-minded and forward-looking intellectuals? Why do Palestinian intellectuals join their politicians in blaming only King Farouk's corruption for the 1948 defeat, the British and the French for the 1956 defeat, and the Americans for the 1967 defeat? Aren't Palestinian intellectuals the one element in their society, which does not need scapegoats, and which should analyze past mistakes for the sake of the future? Is it not a legitimate intellectual question to ask whether there is a peaceful solution, which will prevent future disastrous wars and new imaginary scapegoats? *Is it not the real duty of the intellectual in his society to provide answers to questions like these, rather than just echo the politicians?*

One of the contributions of the American academic community to the relaxation of tension between the US and the Soviet Union was its successful struggle with the State Department on the question of academic exchange programs. Unfortunately, most Arab students, the future intellectual elite of the Arab world, which is being trained in the democratic United States, refuses to sit, think, and talk together with Israeli students. Can we imagine a Czech student losing an opportunity to talk to a Russian student, or a Viet Cong refusing to talk to an American student? Why don't Arab students confront Israeli students, in American and European campuses, in order to talk and argue about grievances and solutions? In exploring peaceful solutions they might even find allies among the Israelis. Some Arab leaders say that they are willing to sacrifice millions of Arab lives for the sake of destroying Israel. Is it not legitimate to save these lives, and doubt whether war is the only worthwhile solution?

Hopes for a peaceful settlement between the Palestinians and the Israelis depend, first of all, on the awakening of Palestinian intellectuals from looking up to Arab politicians with outside interests and selfish motives. The Palestinian Arab society was under foreign domination before June 1967, and still is under foreign Arab and Israeli domination. They have a legitimate right for national independence. Israelis too have a political interest not to dominate the Palestinians for the good of the Israeli society itself. This common interest may be a ray of hope and should induce intellectuals on both sides to seek together a peaceful solution, which will include independence for the two peoples. *Middle-East politicians have not done so well at war, is it not time for intellectuals to try together for peace? As future intellectual, scientific, and political leaders we owe it to our societies. I think that we owe it to ourselves as well.*

APPENDIX II.
Yigal Alon's Letter

In response to my letter about the Rabat resolutions Deputy Prime Minister and Foreign Minister Yigal Alon wrote to me the following letter on 17.2.1975:

Honorable Professor Yavin,

I read with great interest – although with some delay because of work load – your manuscript which you composed "How to turn the Rabat Resolution from a gain for the PLO to political advantage for us". There is no doubt that your analysis is deep and that the policy that you propose is daring and imaginative. The question is if not too daring and too imaginative.

My opinions and ideas concerning the Palestinian issue are known publicly, and I am sure that you would not suspect me that I belong to those who delude themselves that if we ignore this central problem it will somehow be solved by itself. On the contrary, already years ago I expressed my opinion publicly more than once or twice that the Arab-Israeli conflict had started with the Palestinian problem, and that this conflict will not reach its full solution without settling the Palestinian problem.

But because of my assessment of the reality of the situation I do not think that the policy which you suggest is the best alternative for the constructive solution of the Palestinian problem. I agree with you that if we had taken a forward looking initiative concerning this problem in the interval of six years between the two wars, our situation would have been much more comfortable today. But also in our situation today your suggestion seems to me to be too drastic; i.e. it relies on several weak assumptions, and takes too many risks, which could turn our intentions up-side-down.

In the scope of this letter I will obviously not be able to broaden the field and get into a comprehensive discussion which your manuscript definitely deserves. I will therefore only make one generalizing comment: in order to put the PLO to test and fail it, or at least to bring it back to its real size, there is no need to take the heavy risk of unilateral evacuation, and without an adequate preparation of the main part of the territories. After all, if we evacuate these territories and the aggressive and terrorist acts against our towns and people will emanate from them again, it will not be so easy for us, from the political point of view, to renew our control over them, while just because of the weakness of the regime there, the effectiveness of our retaliatory actions, which we have effectively used against Jordan, will be hampered. Moreover, even if the United States would want it, there is no guarantee that it would effectively be able to prevent completely a Soviet penetration into these territories

In order to achieve this goal against the PLO, there is another political alternative which is less risky. And in fact, in the few weeks that have passed since the peak of the PLO in the Rabat conference, there has been a non un-meaningful decline in its status, and it is in fact continuing to decline.

And again, thank you for sending me the manuscript, which although I disagree with its conclusion and its recommendation, I found it to be very interesting and thought provoking

With my blessings

Yigal Alon

APPENDIX III.
The Big-Brother Syndrome

Having sent the letter to the Egyptian dean on September 21 1975, several years before peace talks between Israeli and Egyptian representatives started, I felt good that I had followed my conscience and had done it in the open. Also, I was told in the military-security office that nothing would happen to me, though this was said as a private opinion. So, did anything really happen to me? Officially, the answer is no, but after sending that letter I encountered a new phenomenon. Up until then, whenever I flew abroad for research, being on military reserve, I would get a permit to go abroad from the military-security office right away. After sending the letter to the Egyptian dean I encountered difficulties in getting the permit. I went to Professor Yuval Neeman, who was then a special advisor to the defense minister, showed him a copy of the letter I had sent the Egyptian dean, and asked him if he thought like me that scientists should have maximum freedom in trying to build scientific collaborations. He promised to look into it, and although he never said a thing to me afterwards, I never encountered any difficulty in getting permits in my subsequent trips abroad.

This was not the first time that I felt the strange ways in which "Big Brother" operates. In 1971, at the home of a local reform rabbi, I gave a political analysis to a large group from the neighborhood, and was told afterwards that one of the women in the audience whispered to the people sitting next to her, "Don't listen to Avivi Yavin; he is from the Matzpen (Compass) Group." I did not think much of this since I did not know exactly what the Matzpen Group stood for. Several months later I was told by Shlomo Lahat, Tel Aviv's mayor and a friend of mine, that when my name was mentioned at a party in his home, somebody said that I was from Matzpen. Lahat told him that as a friend of mine he could tell him that this was nonsense. The subject started to worry me, and I decided to find out what the Matzpen Group stood for. I learned that they were anti-Zionists, very extreme revolutionaries, possibly close to being Trotskyites. I then wondered how anybody could associate these ideas with mine for the following simple reasons: I am a liberal and believe strongly in individual freedom; I believe in peace and non violence; I always saw in Zionism a movement for national liberation, and I believe that all peoples have the right to a state of their own; I do not believe in socialism and in international revolution, which is supposed to get everyone (left alive following the revolution) free. Moreover, in talks with American friends I used to say that I considered myself lucky to have been born in my country at a period similar to that of the Americans at the time of George Washington. It therefore is beyond me how anybody in his right mind could associate a person with such opinions with the revolutionary anti-Zionist Matzpen Group.

Am I paranoid? The following story will prove that my suspicions of Big Brother are justified. A few years later, I was told by a friend that one of our old boy-scout friends had peeked in "my file" (where is such a file?) and saw that I was a member of Matzpen. He therefore warned her not to be in contact with me anymore. In other words, I was leprous. What turns the son of a high commander in the Haganah, who was in the Palmach, and fought in Jerusalem in 1948 into a dangerous person in the eyes of the state? The organization which possesses "my file" must have the answer, or perhaps George Orwell, if he were alive, could provide the answer. My only guess is that my commitment to peace and my desire to prevent unnecessary wars and bloodshed of young people made me dangerous in the eyes of somebody. How and to whom can one prove that his sister is not a prostitute when he does not have a sister? In my case, I believe that the vicious untrue rumors behind my back hurt me and my actions for peace. I am also afraid that I am not the only one who has suffered from a "secret file" without any reason, and without knowing that such a file exists. With my full appreciation for the security needs of my country Israel, a free country which strives to be normal cannot allow such a situation to exist.

APPENDIX IV.
Suggested Research Projects to the Faculty

The following is a list of the 27 research project's which the Yariv Committee suggested to the faculty in the beginning of 1978:

1. A collaboration between Israel and Egypt in development projects in Africa.
2. Providing information on the Arab countries to the various research projects.
3. The various characteristics (the state, the society, the political structure) of Egypt and the rest of the Arab states.
4. The possibilities of forming a common market in the Middle East.
5. Israel's place as a provider of financial services in the Middle East.
6. Trade relations between Israel and the Arab countries (Egypt first).
7. Tourist relations between Israel and the Arab countries.
8. Cooperation between Israel and the Arab countries in transportation and communication projects.
9. The Israeli experience in getting rid of total illiteracy and the possibility of its application in the Arab countries.
10. What can be done in the public educational systems of Israel and the Arab countries in order to eliminate the mutual hatred?
11. The Israeli experience in public health and the possibility of applying it to the Arab countries.
12. The identification of specific diseases in the Arab countries and the ways to treat them.
13. Cooperation between Israel and the Arab countries in energy and water.
14. The exchange of scientific and technological knowhow between Israel and the Arab countries.
15. Cooperation between Israel and the Arab countries in industrial production.

16. The possibility of strengthening the ties between the intellectual and professional elites of Israel and Egypt.
17. Potential dangers to Israel after the peace treaty.
18. Control mechanism and control systems for Arab-Israeli cooperation.
19. The Arab minority in Israel after the peace treaty.
20. The problem of the working force in the Israeli economy.
21. The influence of peace on the Jewish national values in Israel and on the relations between Israel and the Diaspora.
22. The influence of the peace treaty on the political structure in Israel.
23. Cooperation between Israeli and Arab universities.
24. Israeli-Arab cooperation in agriculture.
25. The application of Israeli experience in Arab countries in welfare issues.
26. Cooperation between the blood institutes in Israel and Egypt.
27. A safe and cooperative market in the Middle East.

APPENDIX V.
The Peace-Project Document
(After one year of activity)

THE TEL AVIV UNIVERSITY RESEARCH PROJECT ON PEACE

Developments since the dramatic visits of President Sadat to Jerusalem and of Prime Minister Begin to Ismailia have demonstrated the unfortunate fact that, in all the long years of war, serious planning for peace has been sadly neglected. Believing that such planning is essential for the ultimate attainment and maintaining of peace, and wishing to contribute to the peace-making process, Tel Aviv University has decided to initiate a new academic project, the objective of which is to investigate the various aspects of peace. It is expected that the Research Project on Peace (or in short, the Peace Project) will continue for several years. The University possesses the human resources, academic traditions and organizational talents necessary for tackling this task, which it considers to be both a great challenge and an unusual opportunity. More specifically, the goals of the Peace Project are to analyze present problems relating to the prospects for peace in the Middle East, to improve our understanding of the political, social and economic aspects of the transition from war to peace, and to explore the prospects of securing and stabilizing peace through political, economic and cultural cooperation. These activities will be carried out according to the accepted practices of the scholarly world, including, of course, complete academic freedom for participating researchers.

Tel Aviv University decided to undertake this Peace Project upon the recommendation of a university committee headed by Maj. Gen. (Res.) Aharon Yariv. Professor Avivi I. Yavin, former dean of the Faculty of Exact Sciences, was appointed director of the Project. To ensure that the Peace Project would be in close contact with the institutions concerned with policy making and implementation, a Steering Board composed of senior scientists, civil servants, business, and political leaders was established.

Members of the academic staff have been asked to submit proposals for research projects connected with peace (its advancement, stabilization, implications, etc) and cooperation between Israel and Egypt (or Israel and the Arab world). This approach has already produced results and numerous proposals have already been submitted. Scholars from Tel Aviv University are already at work on some of these projects. In addition, suggestions for research projects from various economic circles and other groups in the country have already been received.

One of the major activities in the first year will be an international conference TOWARDS PEACE IN THE MIDDLE EAST AND BEYOND, to be held in the spring of 1979. The conference will deal with political, economic, scientific, cultural, social, and legal aspects of the peace process, and with various programs for regional cooperation. Plans are also being prepared for a series of conferences on specific problems connected with the peace process and with regional cooperation. The Peace Project intends to publish a series of reports on the research projects under the heading of "The Tel Aviv University Peace Reports", which will also include the proceedings of the conferences. The Peace Project is also planning a series of monthly lectures on some aspects of peace and the peace process. These lectures will be published in Hebrew, Arabic and English, and distributed in Israel, the Arab countries, and the Western World.

Following the Camp David summit meeting, the Research Project on Peace decided to exploit the organizational and research base that has been achieved to expand its own activities, and to make it more available to the state and the region as a whole. A number of specific projects for cooperation between Tel Aviv University and academic institutions in Egypt were considered. A workshop with the participation of senior scholars from various faculties of the University, public figures and government representatives examined the coordination of national efforts in investigating the implications of peace and possible regional cooperation. Towards this end, the Peace Project envisages establishing an Institute for the Study of Peace and Regional Cooperation. A proposal based on the conclusions of the workshop was submitted to the Ministry of Finance and has received preliminary approval and a promise of financial support.

The several activities being undertaken by the Tel Aviv University Research Project on Peace are open to participation by faculty members of all institutions of higher learning and research in Israel, as well as to members of the public from all sectors. Efforts are being made to include Arab scholars in the various activities, in the hope that major Arab universities will eventually become partners in the Peace Project.

APPENDIX VI.
A Letter to the faculty

The following is a letter that was sent by me to all the faculty members at the University on 3.7.1978:

In a letter which was sent to you a week ago whose title was "Academic activity at the University for the advancement and strengthening of the peace" I described the Research Project on Peace, its structures and plans. I also explained there that the Project is the University "roof structure" whose aim is the coordination of the activities of the various units (staff members, departments, and institutes), to assist their activities, and to initiate new activities of the various units in research, which aims at the advancement and strengthening of peace. Any University research activity, whether it already exists or planned for the future, whether in one discipline or interdisciplinary, falls within our attention, if it deals with an aspect which is connected to peace. For instance, research on the economy of the Middle East could be important both to our country and to the whole region, but falls exactly within our jurisdiction if it deals meaningfully in collaboration between Israel and its neighbors.

The Research Project on Peace is happy with every existing activity and is suggesting to all the staff members to consider diverting part of their research to deal with a subject connected with peace. Every staff member will obviously select the subject by himself/herself; however, if asked, we will be willing to help in that too. We have already in the Project's office about 40 topics for research projects, part of them suggested by the Yariv Committee, part were submitted to us by the Department of the Treasury, and part suggested by other sources. We will be happy to offer these topics and others reaching our office in the future, and to get new ideas from the staff.

A staff member selecting a topic will be able to carry out the research by himself, with his students, or with other staff members within the University or from the outside. Cooperation with Arab scientists is obviously one of our main goals, and an initiative in this direction will be welcome and will get help and priority from us. It is possible that some of the topics will be determined to be fit to serve for a M.Sc. or a Ph.D. thesis, and if a topic has been suggested by the government or another public source, it is possible that a contact be created between the researcher and that source.

The Research Project on Peace is also ready to supply financial help in the administration and execution the researches by giving them financial grants. At this stage we will consider grants between 10,000 and 100,000 Israeli liras a year.

APPENDIX VII.
A List of Participants in the Workshop[2]

Prof. J. Eisenberg (physics), Prof. S. Abarbanel (mathematics), Prof. Z. Hadar (management), Prof. Y. Orgler (management), Y. Alsheich (First International Bank), Prof. A. Arian (political science), y. Ish-Shalom (ministry of welfare), Prof. H. Ben-Shahar (economics), D. Beit-Or (Project secretary), D. Brodet (Treasury), H. Ben-Sheffer (academic secretary), Y. Ben-Zvi. Prof. E. Berglas (Treasury), Prof. A. Barnea (management), A. Golan, Prof. Y. Gross (law), Prof. Y. Dinstein (law), Prof. Z. Hirsch (management), R. Harel (ministry of transportation), N. Wolf, Prof. A. Zandback (medicine), A. Tieberg (Manufacturers Association), Prof. A. Yavin (physics), Ret. Gen. A, Yariv (strategic studies), Y. Jacobson (economist), D. Cochav (Leumibank), Prof. D. Levhary (economics, H.U.), Prof. B. Lev (management), A. Levin, Prof. B. Modan (medicine), Prof. M. Sokolovski (biology), R. Siebel (foreign ministry), Y. Farag (police), A. Zipori (defense), Prof. A. Kleinman (political science), Dr. E. Reches (Shiloah), A. Rimon (General Headquarters), B. Rabinovitz (Labor Society), Prof. A. Razin (economics), Avi Shlush, Prof. A. shapira (law), Prof. S. Shamir (history), Dr. a. Schwartz (economy), B. Thorn (ministry of trade and industry), P. Tamir (Manufacturers Association), A. Tamari (Treasury).

---

2   *Most of the participants were members of the boards of the mentioned organizations or in their research-and-development departments.*

APPENDIX VIII.
The Program of the Peace Conference

The following is the complete program, lectures and speakers, of the conference on 11-14.6.1979:

TOWARD PEACE IN THE MIDDLE EAST

PLENARY SESSIONS

Monday evening: OPENNING CEREMONY:
The TAU Orchestra, conductor – S. Ronly Riklis.
Opening Address: A. Yavin (Research Project on Peace).
Welcoming address: (H. Ben-Shahar, President TAU).

TRANSITION FROM WAR TO PEACE
"The Modern Experience" – H. Bull (Oxford).

Tuesday morning: TRANSITION FROM WAR TO PEACE– continued
"Franco-German Reconciliation – A Case Study" – A. Grosser (Paris).
"The Israeli Economy in Transition from War to Peace" – M. Michaeli   (H. U.)

Afternoon Session
"Legal Aspects of Transition from War to Peace" – Y. Dinstein (TAU).
"The Psychology of Transition from War to Peace" – H. Kelman (Harvard).
"Israeli Society in Transition from War to Peace" – Sh. N. Eisenstadt. (HU).

Wednesday morning:
COOPERATION IN THE MIDDLE EAST
"The Middle East in the World Economy" – L. Klein (Pennsylvania).
"Interdependencies – Promises and Pitfalls" – E. Morse (US State Department).

283

PARALLEL SESSIONS

INTERNATIONAL RELATIONS AND POLITICAL SCIENCE
"Theories of Negotiation" – I. W. Zartman (NYU).

"Mediation in the Arab-Israeli Conflict: The Past and the Future" – S. Touval (TAU).

"Statesmen and Scholars" – N. Oren (HU).

"Intragroup Dissension and Conflict Resolution: A Laboratory Experiment with Arab and Jewish Students" – D. Jacobson (TAU).

A round-table discussion: "The Contribution of Different Schools of Thought and Theories in International Relations to the Analysis of Conditions Leading to a Stable Peace in the Middle East".

LEGAL ASPECTS
"Political Aspects of Cooperation in the Middle East" – P. Eliav (Ministry of Foreign Affairs, Jerusalem).

"Human Rights in the Territories in the Period of Transitions" – T. Meron (NYU).

"Legal Aspects of the Peace Treaty" – R. Sable (Ministry of Foreign Affairs, Jerusalem).

"A Framework for Cooperation with Regard to International Waterways in the Middle east" – R. Lapidoth (HU).

ECONOMICS
"Egypt's Economy: The Challenge of Peace" – G. G. Gilbar (Haifa U.).

"The Economic Consequences of Peace in the Middle East" – E. L. Feige (Wisconsin).

"The Effects of Peace on the Egyptian Economy: Some Methodological Comments and a Few Quantitative Implications" – E. Sagi (Pennsylvania).

"Conflict Management in Multinational Companies and the Middle East Peace" – I. Walter (NYU).

"Business Cooperation in the Middle East: Attitudes of Businessmen in Israel, Egypt, and Jordan" – S. Cohen (CUNY).

SCIENCE AND TECHNOLOGY
"Israeli Technology Transfer in the Agricultural Sector: Implication for International Cooperation" – Y. Abt (Cent. for Int. Coop. in Agr. (Rehovot).

"A Wrap-up of the Experience in Technology Transfer in Agriculture to the Arab Sector in Israel" – I. Arnon (Agricultural Bank, Tel Aviv).

"The Linkage Between Technological and Social Innovation" – T. Herman and A. Wiener (TAHAL).

"The Role of the R&D Institute in Technology Transfer" – J. Schechter (Ben Gurion U.).

RELATIONS BETWEEN JEWS AND ARABS

"Relations Between Jews and Arabs: The Interpersonal Level" – Y. Amir (Bar Ilan U.).

"Jews and Arabs: A Socio-Psychological Aspect" – Y. Peres (TAU).

"Relations Between Jews and Arabs in the Context of Israel's Reality" – M. Sharon (HU).

PUBLIC HEALTH

"Cooperation in the Area of Public Health" – a general discussion – B. Modan (TAU), M. Davies (Hadassah Med. Sch., HU), H. Doron (Kupat Cholim and TAU), L. Epstein (Technion, Haifa), M.A. Klingberg (TAU).

TRANSPORTATION

"A Transportation System for the Middle East" – G. Hashimshoni (The Israel Inst. for Transp.).

"Physical Communication Lines Between Israel and Her Neighbors Towards Peace" – E. Efrat (Ministry of Interior).

"Towards Land-Based Passenger Transportation System Between Israel and Egypt" – K. Blum ("EGGED").

"The Concept of Transshipment Center" – M. Rom (TAU).

STABILIZING PEACE IN THE MIDDLE EAST

PLENARY SESSIONS

"Nationalism, Religion, and Politics in the Middle East: Arab and Moslem Perspectives" – E. Sivan (HU).

"Nationalism, Religion, and Politics in the Middle East: Israeli and Jewish Perspectives" – U. Tal (TAU).

"Internal Political and Social Consequences of Peace: Israel" – Y. Shapira (TAU).

"Internal Political and Social Consequences of Peace: Egypt" – S. Shamir (TAU).

"Israel, the Palestinians, and the Arab Countries" – G. Ben-Dor (Haifa Univ).

"Inter-Arab Relations" – E. Kedourie (London Sch of Ec. & Pol. Sci.).

"The Middle East and the World Powers" – Y. Rabin (Knesset).

SYMPOSIUM
"Peace in the Middle East: Beginning of a New Era?" – A. Yariv (TAU), H. Fish (Bar Ilan), Y. Leibovitch (HU), Anwar Nuseiba-Advocate, R. Yaron (Israel Broadcasting Authority).

APPENDIX IX.
Promoting Academic Regional Cooperation
(A summary of activity, December 1977-December 1979)

In December 1977, following the historic visit of President Sadat to Jerusalem, Tel Aviv University decided to meet the new challenge by setting up a new project, the Research Project on Peace. The goals as well as the first steps of the Project are described in a separate manuscript APPENDIX V. Academic regional cooperation has been one of the main goals of the Project from its beginning, as stated in that manuscript, "Efforts are being made to include Arab scholars in the various activities, in the hope that major Arab universities will eventually become partners in the Project". Since actual cooperation between Israeli and Egyptian scholars was practically impossible until the signing of the peace treaty, and will continue to be very difficult at least until normalization's beginning, hopefully in February 1980, our efforts have been concentrated in two directions:

1. Coordinating existing academic activities in the University in the areas of planning peace and regional cooperation, as well as promoting new activities in these areas.
2. Establishing ties with academic and political organizations in Israel, Egypt and the United States, which will enable us to embark on a large-scale program of cooperation with Egyptian scholars and academic institutions, once normalization takes place.

Internal Academic Activities. We have already approved and granted financial support to a variety of research projects, which are now in progress. Professors of Tel Aviv University carry out most of these projects. However, as a result of visits to Egypt by members of our faculty, new research programs are to be undertaken, mostly in collaboration with Egyptian scholars. Some of them will be trilateral, with American, Canadian, or European universities acting as hosts.

A conference entitled "Towards Peace in the Middle East" was held in Tel Aviv in June of this year (1979). Internationally known experts presented papers on the human experience in settling armed disputes, as well as on specific aspects of peace, reconciliation, and regional development of the Middle East. Scholars from Tel Aviv University and other Israeli institutions of higher learning also presented papers, both in plenary and parallel sessions, which were open to the public. An average number of 250 people attended the sessions. The conference received publicity both in Israel and abroad, including Egypt, and Egyptian scientists requested and received copies of papers presented at the conference.

Mr. Abba Eban M.K. delivered a first lecture in a series entitled "The Tel Aviv University Peace Papers" in May of this year to an audience of more than 500 people, consisting of Israeli government officials and senior academics, Arab leaders and intellectuals, and members of the diplomatic corps. The title of Mr. Eban's lecture was "Israel's International Relations in an Era of Peace". The lecture is being published as a book in three languages, Hebrew, Arabic and English, for worldwide distribution. The next speaker in the series will be a prominent Egyptian scholar.

Ties with Other Organizations. Under the auspices of Mr. David Rockefeller, the President of the University, Professor Haim Ben-Shahar, held several meetings with the Egyptian Ambassador to the United States, Mr. Ashraf Ghorbal, and agreed with him on the principles and guidelines for future academic cooperation. Several Scholars from Tel Aviv University have recently visited Egypt. Professors G. Cohen, A Rubinstein, and S. Shamir participated in May in a political seminar at the Al-Ahram Institute in Cairo. Professor G. Givon, an Egyptologist, visited Cairo in August, and was invited to carry out research in Egypt in collaboration with Egyptian Egyptologists. In September, the Project director, Professor A.I. Yavin, visited three universities as well as the Academy of Scientific Research in Cairo, and laid the foundations for several future collaborative research programs in the natural sciences. Professor S. Shamir of the Shiloah Institute was in Egypt again in October, and held discussions with scholars and government officials. Professor M. Gil of the Jewish History Department was in Egypt in October to study old Jewish manuscripts. Professor S. Somekh, the head of the Arabic Department, has been invited to Cairo, and plans to be there in the very near future. Professor H. Neufeld has been invited to lecture on cardiology in Cairo University in

January 1980. Professor Rainey of the Archaeology Department is going to Egypt in January 1980, in order to carry out research in the Cairo Museum.

Due to the sensitivity of the subject, the Research Project on Peace has maintained low profile and has tried to avoid public exposure as much as possible, especially on matters that concern contacts with Arab scholars and organizations; and those working in the area are aware of these efforts.

In his report to the US Agency of International Development, Professor Herman Pollack devoted several pages to the Research Project on Peace. In the final report to the A.I.D. in February 1979, in discussing Israel, Mr. Joseph C. Wheeler said, "Israel embraces the idea of cooperation with enthusiasm.... Each of the major universities set up some kind of committees or ad hoc working groups to explore possibilities and develop proposals. The most advanced is the Research Project on Peace at Tel Aviv University".

Programs of Cooperation. Phase I, in which there is only unilateral activity and planning, will come to an end with normalization of relations between Israel and Egypt. This will mark the beginning of Phase II, that of actual normal relations between Egyptian and Israeli scholars and academic institutions. In the present transition period from Phase I to Phase II, we have embarked on several cooperative programs at a pace and form set by the possibilities and constraints of the political arena. The following examples, which at this stage should be considered as confidential, will serve as illustrations:

1. Following a discussion in Cairo between the director of the Remote Sensing Laboratory of the Academy of Scientific Research and the director of the Research Project on Peace, plans are being made to hold soon conference in Tel Aviv, Cairo, or Stillwater Oklahoma, to discuss cooperation and training of scientific personnel in the area or remote sensing.
2. The details of a trilateral conference on Cultural Contacts in Islamic and Jewish History are being discussed in Cairo, Tel Aviv, and Cambridge USA. The conference will, most likely, be organized by the American University, and will be held in Egypt.
3. Prior to the transfer of the field station near Santa Katarina, our scholars agreed with scholars of the new university in Ismailia, which is in charge of the station, that cooperative research will go on in that station.
4. Three groups from the Physics Department of Tel Aviv University have reached agreements with physicists from Cairo University, through direct

and indirect discussions, to cooperate in research. The cooperation will start in France, Germany, and the United States, and will later continue in the Middle East as well.

5. A senior professor of urology from Cairo University has recently visited Tel Aviv University, and plans are in progress for holding conferences on urology both in Tel Aviv and in Cairo, soon after normalization starts.

6. A seismic study of the Red Sea will begin early in 1980. Scientists from the Institute of Geophysics in Hamburg, the Helwan Seismological Observatory, and the Department of Geophysics of Tel Aviv University will conduct the study.

These examples demonstrate the extent of interaction that has already been achieved, as well as the existing constraints. In most of them we still have to postpone actual cooperation, or at least its public announcement, until formal normalization takes place. In some cases we plan to start outside the region and continue later in Egypt and Israel. In other cases we have resorted to trilateral cooperation, at least in the first stage. Still, we feel that these cases, which are only examples, will serve as pilots for future cooperation. Since the political future is always uncertain, especially in the Middle East, it is essential to start academic cooperation in carefully selected and well prepared cases, as soon as possible. Successful cooperative research or academic conferences could have favorable and irreversible effects on the relations between Egypt and Israel. It will also demonstrate to the other nations in the region that cooperation can be beneficial to all the parties involved.

Beyond Cooperation with Egyptian Academics. Although Phase II, that of establishing academic cooperation with Egyptian scholars and institutions, has not yet officially begun, the Research Project on Peace is already preparing itself for the next phase, that of cooperation with other Arab academics. In the last year we have established some contacts with professors and administrators of the three major colleges in the West Bank. Due to the sensitivity of the parties involved and the political inequality between them, conditions that are not conducive to the establishment of normal academic relations, we have been cautious in pursuing these contacts. Yet, the heads of the West Bank universities are aware of our interest in developing normal academic relations with their institutions, and we expect that progress in establishing such relations will continue. Relations with academics in other Arab countries are more problematic than relations with Egyptian academics, and will, most likely, have to await progress in the political arena. Unfortunately, the scholars of the region have not learned from the American-Russian experience, which demonstrated that academic détente can, and perhaps should precede the political détente. Still, the Research Project on Peace is preparing itself for wider academic regional cooperation, utilizing the experience acquired from the Israeli-Egyptian case.

APPENDIX X.
The Papers Presented at the Think Tank

I. Possible Reasons for Sadat's Peace Moves – Moshe Keren[3]

1. The destruction of Israel as a state is the first reason that comes to mind. The whole move is then nothing but a grand hoax, possibly an Egyptian hoax, or an Egyptian-Soviet hoax, or even an Arab one, involving several Arab countries. It is also possible that Sadat wanted to improve Egypt's political and military positions, and then to return to an all-out war in an appropriate time. Also, there is a group among the Arab intellectuals who think that Israel would disintegrate at a time of peace.

2. There could also be global reasons for Sadat's moves. Sadat realized that after 1973 the Americans adopted a new plan to establish peace in the region under their auspices, a Pax Americana, and decided that Egypt should strive to be involved in it. The Americans are interested in pushing the Soviets out of the region, and oil is a major reason for that. This should fit well with Egypt's attempts to get out of its dependence on the Soviet Union. It is possible that Egypt would like to attack and conquer oil-rich Libya with the help of the Americans, with no hostile interference from Israel. Other reasons of global nature could be the peaceful development of the Suez Channel, the disenchantment from the Soviet capabilities to apply pressure on Israel, in particular to give up the lands conquered from other Arab countries. All these reasons have very little to do with Israel, and the peace with her is a means to get closer to the West and away from the hug of the Soviet Bloc. The emphasis is not on *peace* but on *no more war*. Sadat's jumps and changes of mind come from his unique personality, which is a mixture of a person who is a deep thinker and a primitive one. He felt a need to be continuously in the headlines because of his personality as well as his wish to keep his leadership position.

---

3   *Most of the participants were members of the boards of the mentioned organizations or in their research-and-development departments.*

Internal reasons could have convinced Sadat to forsake the war path. He may have wanted to strengthen his status in Egypt by honestly wanting to make peace with Israel and to cooperate with her. He may have been tired of the wars in which Egypt always sacrificed more than the other Arab states, and he also got tired of the Arab partners, especially the extreme ones such as Libya and the PLO. With peace, he was hoping to regain his territorial losses in the only possible way. He was clearly interested in getting massive economic and military aid. He could have been afraid of an Islamic revolution and wanted to establish a strong force in the region which could stand in their way. It is also possible that he wanted to erect a monument to himself, just as the Pharaohs or the Indian kings of Mexico did.

In summary, The list of motives or possible reasons has been presented as a background for discussion. There is always a possibility that the truth is a mixture of reasons, and that, in the future, Sadat may adapt different options. It is therefore important to identify signs of change.

II. A Pessimistic Scenario – Yakir Aharonov

The underlining assumption of this scenario is that Sadat's initiative is a long-term hoax, whose aims are: Improving the image of Egypt; while at the same time isolating and weakening Israel and presenting her as opposing a true peace by her rejection of reasonable conditions for the solution of the problem of the Palestinian refugees. It will also enable the immediate weakening of Israel as a result of the return to Egypt of the Sinai with its rich oil fields. Egypt will then be in an improved position to start a new war with Israel. The rest of the Arab countries will again accept Egypt as their leader, and will recognize the genius of Sadat's strategy. At the same time, the relations with the US continually improve. However, there are also some risks to Sadat in these actions, because the Egyptian public may feel ill-at-ease with the continuous changing from peace to war, to peace, and war again.

Let us consider the following possible scenario: The process moves forward, but at a slow pace, with the Egyptians continually applying pressure on Israel for further concessions. Their moving in the direction of peace is only formal, without the participation of the people, so that going back will be possible. If necessary, Sadat can resign, proving further that his actions were intended to destroy Israel, and that he was right.

The most important challenges for us vis-à-vis this pessimistic scenario are the following: To look for early signs that this indeed is Sadat's intention; to identify in full his intentions; and to make sure, by holding secret talks with the United States, that Israel will be strong enough if and when it becomes apparent that Sadat's moves were a big hoax?

There are more questions which should be considered: 1. how is the Soviet Union involved in Sadat's strategy? 2. Are the anti-peace Arab countries involved? 3. How will the US and the European countries react if Egypt will return to the war path after she gets back the Sinai? 4. Is it possible that this pessimistic scenario is one of several scenarios, and Israel is capable of convincing Sadat to accept a different one, for instance, by cooperating with him on the autonomy to the Palestinians? 5. Is it the right time to apply pressure on the Americans?

III. Optimistic Scenarios – Avivi Yavin

Introduction. The optimistic view was dominant in the first generations of Zionism. It is missing today in our whole political spectrum. The optimistic scenario is the opposite of the pessimistic-Holocaustic one, whose characteristic phrases are "There is no other choice" or "The whole world is against us". The Pessimistic view sees only one part of the peace agreement – the concessions, and not our gains. The optimistic scenario claims that there is another choice or possibility and that peoples act in accordance with their interests. Therefore, in our actions we should attempt to build common interests with the Egyptians. The most important part for us in the peace treaty is not our concessions, but the big step forward that peace enables us to make. Such a step may require concessions, but their importance is diminishing in relation to the gains which the treaty makes possible. The main goal of the optimistic attitude is to show that there is (or can be) an optimistic scenario, which, by its nature, will show how the situation can get better if we think, plan, and do certain things.

There are two alternative or complementary optimistic scenarios: the continuous scenario and the visionary one. The continuous or straight-forward scenario starts by looking at the present and pointing out the reasons why we believe that the future will be better, as well as what we should do to get a better future. On the other hand, the visionary scenario starts by looking into a picture of a possible better future, which could be accepted by all major elements in the region, and intentionally ignores all the present obstacles. It claims that these obstacles would lose their apparent importance in view of the optimistic future. Let us look at Zionism as an example for the visionary scenario. The anti-Semitism in Europe, so claimed Theodor Herzl, would not be solved by improving the life of the Jews there or by lobbying in the courts of European kings, rather by the vision of a future Jewish state.

1. *The continuous optimistic scenario.* In the next two-to-three years, Israel will withdraw from the Sinai, and full normal relations will develop with Egypt, while the autonomy will have started to work, with passive agreement of the Palestinian leaders in the West Bank and in the Gaza Strip. Many Israelis and Egyptians are developing common interests, and they are interested in developing further the personal and national ties. The cooperative industrial and agricultural production as well as tourism is aimed at a third party, which is the rest of the world. The government of Israel understands that self determination for the Palestinians is unavoidable, while the Palestinians in the West Bank and Gaza find themselves in a fast economic, political, and personal process of improvement, although they still might not admit it publicly.

The Arab world, as well as the Palestinians themselves, starts internal debates whether or not it should join the peace process. There are loud voices there which say that it is possible to live with the Israelis and point out that Israel withdrew from the occupied Sinai with no real external pressure; therefore, there is a reasonable chance that the Israelis will allow the Palestinians to have full independence. The development of the West Bank with the help of Arab and western money, as well as Israeli, Egyptian, and local knowhow, creates common interests to a growing number of the people and governments of the region. Countries of the Third World start recognizing Israel and trading with her and with the Egyptian-Israeli firms, as well as with the cooperative projects, which include firms from the West Bank and Gaza.

Jordan joins the process, and a new political and economic union (perhaps a confederation) of Israel, Jordan, and the Palestinian entity is formed. Egypt, Saudi Arabia, and the Gulf countries later tie themselves to the union. The new economic-political agreements turn the rich Middle-East region into a new superpower next to the United States, the Soviet Union, and Western Europe. This superpower undergoes a fast process of development, which benefits all the peoples of the region.

The problem of the Palestinian refugees, who are dispersed all over the world, finds its solution by their absorption in the blossoming economy of the Middle East, while politically they can become citizens of the Palestinian entity (or of a future Middle-East confederation). The new absorption capability of Israel attracts large aliya (Jewish immigration) from the western countries, from South America, and from the Soviet Union.

The continuous optimistic scenario, which has just been outlined, with possible changes and exchanges of the order of steps, has made several optimistic assumptions. These assumptions, like the whole scenario, definitely need investigation. The following are some of these assumptions: 1. There is a desire by the important countries of the region to solve the Arab-Israeli conflict; more specifically, the dominant political factors in the region will prefer a constructive solution which benefits all, including Israel, over the present situation in which Israel is isolated and under pressure, while Arab groups, such as the Palestinians, suffer as well. 2. The superpowers will help the process, or at least will not hamper it significantly, provided that this optimistic scenario is consistent with, or at least does not work against the interests of a superpower. 3. There will not be any new dramatic developments in the world and in the region, which will fail this scenario. Such developments could be a regional war on oil, a use of nuclear weapons, the expansion of the Khomeinism, etc.

2. The optimistic vision as a guide to the present. Many of today's political difficulties seem insoluble at present. However, the underlying assumption of this scenario is that there are a sufficient number of positive elements in the region (natural resources and geographic conditions), which in principle enable a positive or constructive solution for all the peoples of the region in the future. In other words, let us assume that the vision could indeed become a reality in the future. The basic national and economic requirements of all the people here could then be fulfilled. (If there is no truth in this assumption, there is no hope for a full constructive solution of the major difficulties, although partial solutions might be possible).

A vision, and especially an optimistic one, can often catalyze and can even spur the solution of problems. For instance, the vision of Theodor Herzl guided all stages of the establishment of the State of Israel. Even the pessimistic vision in George Orwell's 1984 book had great effects; it has warned and guided the actions of many people who object to totalitarianism. With the help of a clear optimistic picture of a possible future, if and when it is accepted by the relevant political factors in the region, many present problems will lose their appearance of being insoluble, because they will be viewed in a new perspective. Problems which today seem not to have any solution in a direct approach, such as Israel's borders with the surrounding Arab countries, independence to the Palestinians that will not endanger Israel, the problem of the Palestinian refugees, and the right of Jews to settle everywhere in Eretz Israel (Palestine), will be naturally solved as a consequence of the optimistic vision that is being realized.

Let me now draw an outline of such an optimistic situation that can in principle exist in a couple of decades. The Middle-East region is a union of states like Western Europe or even like the United States. Roads, railroads, water channels, oil pipes, and air routes join the Gulf countries with the Mediterranean Sea, traversing through many countries in the region. Regional tourism is flourishing. Agriculture and industry, including water and energy, are planned by regional experts, and various components are produced in different locations, which are dictated only by economic considerations. Items produced in the region get preferred treatment (custom, tax, etc) throughout the region. The whole region becomes an absorptive one, benefitting the Jewish and Palestinian Diasporas. The political-security borders lose their meaning, similar to the situation between Holland and Belgium or between Ohio and Indiana. Jerusalem becomes the pride of the region and a symbol of coexistence in peace. It becomes the capital of Israel, in which (like in Geneva) the governing institutions of the whole region as well as of the Palestinian entity are located. Jerusalem also becomes a major cultural and religious center for the peoples of the region and of the whole world.

This optimistic vision poses some great challenges: How to convince the peoples and governments in the region to accept it? If accepted, how to make sure that while moving forward, the political, economic, and military balance will be maintained? How to move the peoples from the present state which is full of hatred and suspicion to the future which is described above?

I wish to suggest to the serious people with doubts as well as to the cynics: there is no doubt that the optimistic scenarios sound utopian. They might very well be so, but shouldn't these optimistic scenarios be considered seriously by the public and the governments, who always consider only the dangers and destructions that we all are facing? Being continuously occupied only with the dangers freezes the imagination and leads to political and economic impotence.

IV The Black 26ᵗʰ-of-May Scenario – David Horn

This paper will deal with the question of what could happen if the critical and final meeting of the Israeli-Egyptian negotiating teams next month (in May 26, 1980), which will mainly deal with the question of the Palestinian autonomy, will fail. The following could very well happen: Israel will insist on a limited autonomy, while Egypt will not be willing to accept autonomy without legislative council. The other three major problems and possible obstacles are Jerusalem, security, and the settlements. Egypt will then declare a freeze on the normalization plan, and recalls its ambassador to Cairo. Israel will then have to decide whether to break off the relations with Egypt, or to leave a small unit in the embassy to deal with trade relations etc. If the relations are completely broken off, will it still be possible to have some trade going on, as is the situation with some African countries? Will Egypt grant visiting visas to Israelis? Will there be any contact between the Israeli and the Egyptian armies in the Sinai, and will Israeli ships be allowed to go through the Suez Channel? And there is also the possibility that Egypt will decide to cancel the Camp-David Agreement. These are some of the questions that Israel has to consider before she takes part in the 26ᵗʰ-of-May meeting.

There are also the super powers and the United Nations to consider. It is very likely that the European countries will then support a resolution in the UN Security Council to establish a Palestinian state. Such a resolution might be introduced in the Security Council even if the 26ᵗʰ-of-May meeting will not break down, but its outcome might then be different. It is worth our while to consider also the following questions: How will the US vote in the Security Council, especially if Saudi Arabia will use the oil weapon? How will the vote affect Egypt, and how will Jordan react? Will such a decision by the Security Council induce the PLO to form a government in exile? Will the Palestinians in the territories (the West Bank and Gaza) declare independence? Will such a Palestinian state be recognized by the world, and will she be accepted as a member of the United Nations? These questions too will pose a difficult challenge to Israel, and should be considered before the Israeli-Egyptian meeting in May.

Israel will have to find answers to the above-mentioned possibilities, but what answers? The relations with the US might be affected before the presidential elections in the US in November, and the answers will depend on who will win the elections, Jimmy Carter or Ronald Reagan. Another interesting question is whether a crisis will strengthen the government of Israel, or it will force an election in Israel. In conclusion, an extreme disagreement in the 26th-of-May meeting between the Israeli and Egyptian delegations could result in the establishment of a Palestinian government in exile, which will be internationally recognized, with new pressure on Israel, which might even be expelled from the UN. If this happens, Israel will lose all the advantages she gained in the peace treaty with Egypt, and she might face a military confrontation from a politically inferior position. It is, therefore, strongly recommended that our government should do everything possible to prevent a breakdown of the meeting in May.

APPENDIX XI.
POLITICAL OBSERVATIONS

The following is a list of some political ideas that were raised in my discussions in Cairo in March and May 1980. No attempt is being made here to present a comprehensive, or even a balanced picture; rather the ideas are presented in order to indicate several personal points of view that are often overlooked. The ideas are clearly mine and do not represent the opinions of the Management of the Peace Project.

Attitudes. It is commonly accepted that Israel's expectations from peace and from the ensuing bilateral relations are high, while those of Egypt are low. The Israelis are considered enthusiastic about the future interactions with Egyptians; once the borders are opened and the green light is given, they are expected to flood Egypt with visits and offers of cooperation. In reality, though Israelis do show more interest in bilateral interactions, the anticipated enthusiasm has failed to materialize. To make matters worse, growing Israeli indifference and even disappointment with the peace is playing into the hands of the extremists, and creating a bad atmosphere in Israel for future negotiations and possible necessary concessions.

There is a widespread lack of appreciation in Israel for the Egyptian concessions and sacrifices to date. "We are giving them land, while they are giving us promises" is a popular statement often made by Israelis. Egypt's isolation from the Arab world, following the peace initiative, is overlooked, and there is still a large measure of mistrust. Israelis will often say, "The entire move can very well be a part of an all-Arab strategy to get the land back in order to launch a new war from better positions", or, "Sadat is O.K., but what will happen after Sadat?" The slowness of the political negotiations and the slow pace of normalization are causing mistrust in Israel and possibly in Egypt as well.

The Autonomy. Many observers wonder whether the new Egyptian-Israeli relations will enable Egypt to draw Israel out of its isolation in the region, or whether Israel will manage to drag Egypt down into isolation. The Palestinian problem, or that of the West Bank and Gaza, is the dominating factor in the Middle-East equation. While many Egyptians view the autonomy plan as an Israeli ploy to avoid solving the problem, and at the same time enabling a separate Israeli-Egyptian peace, many Israelis still believe that Egypt is interested only in paying lip service to the Palestinian problem. These points of view deepen the mutual mistrust.

Most Israelis now think that for Begin the peace treaty was a trade-off. He believed that he was giving (back) the Sinai ("too willingly", some Israelis might add) in order to keep the West Bank. It is, however, interesting to note that most Israelis now believe that the autonomy – any real autonomy – will eventually lead to a Palestinian state. They point out that Begin out-smarted himself. They add with a bitter smile, "Begin has found a way not to eat the cake and not to have it as well".

There is growing public opposition in Israel to the settlements in the occupied territories, and a growing uneasiness with the repressive measures taken there. Controlling the life of another people is repugnant to an increasing number of Israelis. It is no secret that for a variety of reasons, the present Begin government is not very popular in Israel today today.

Security. Israel did not appreciate the depth of Egypt's hurt after the 1967 war, and had to pay a high price in 1973 for this lack of awareness. On the other hand, anyone who misjudges the concern of Israelis for security, after the Holocaust in Europe and the 1973 war, is making a grave mistake.

In 1977, Sadat captured the trust of a significant fraction of the Israeli public, not only by his dramatic moves, but also by stating that Israel has a right for 100% security. Israelis became then more willing to "swallow" his demand for 100% withdrawal from Egyptian land. Sadat's formula of 100% security for 100% withdrawal was simple, and showed appreciation for Israel's concerns. Coupled with the statement of "no more war", it did marvels in changing Israeli public's attitude towards a complete withdrawal from the Sinai.

On the other hand, the Egyptian position on security in the West Bank, as presented at the last negotiations in Herzliya, was not welcomed in Israel. It is also unfortunate that it appeared to the Israeli public that the talks were deadlocked primarily on security issues. With regard to the West Bank, the Israeli public can be divided into three groups:

Group A, the hawks, want to keep the West Bank. Their reasons may vary, but the simple fact is that they want to keep it or control it forever. Security is one of their motivations, but they would want to keep the West Bank (and Gaza) even if it could somehow be guaranteed that no danger would ever come from it.

Group B, constitutes the majority of the population. The attitude of the people in this group towards the West Bank stems basically from one consideration – security. Until recently, and with the help of external circumstances, Group A has managed to convince Group B that the only way to protect the country from the east is to control the West Bank militarily, and in order to do so, Israel has to control it politically as well.

Group C, the doves, advocates self-determination for the Palestinians as well as withdrawal by Israel from the West Bank and Gaza, for moral as well as political reasons. People in this group also believe that Israel can never be secure unless the Palestinians obtain their rights for self-determination.

Several months ago, a group in Tel Aviv, consisting of academic and non-academic people from the political right to the political left, carried out a study of the development of the Egyptian-Israeli relations. Their first goal was to look critically at all accepted political axioms. It is interesting that following months of hard work, and a serious effort to re-examine the various questions with no bias, a large measure of agreement was reached on two points:
The Palestinian problem is indeed the key to many questions in the area, including Egyptian-Israeli relations.
If security can be guaranteed, there should be no objection to self-determination for the Palestinians in the entire West Bank and Gaza regions, and even to a Palestinian state there.
Israel and Egypt are now faced with a challenge of finding a solution based on two elements: Self-determination for the Palestinians in the West Bank and Gaza, and long-term security for Israel. The time is ripe for a new "Sadat formula" in the Israeli-Palestinian plane, similar to his 1977 formula in the Israeli-Egyptian plane.
The Coupled Equations. Until Sadat's visit to Jerusalem, the "Egyptian

equation of state" did not include any "Israeli variable", and the "Israeli equation of state" did not include any "Egyptian variable". The two equations were thus uncoupled; and each of them could be treated and even "solved", independently of what happened in the other state. The situation is now different. To a large extent, the two states find themselves in the same boat, so that each equation of state has a term (or terms), which depends on what happens in the other state. Thus, we now have a system of coupled equations, which can only be solved together.

Egypt often asks Israel to appreciate its internal problems and its difficulties in the Arab world. It is now in the interest of Israel to do so, since anything that happens in Egypt could affect the peace process, and therefore, Israel itself will be affected. Similarly, Egypt has to appreciate the anxiety in Israel as well as the internal political struggle in the country. It is in the interest of Egypt to appreciate the fear and mistrust in Israel, and to help overcome them.

Normalization of Relations. The normalization of relations, or rather its pace, is generally regarded as an Egyptian bargaining card. Few Israelis appreciate Egypt's genuine need to go slow to allow the Egyptian public as well as the observing Arab World to adjust themselves to the new situation. But is the pace of the normalization a good bargaining card? Clearly, Begin does not care much about the pace of the normalization, as long as he gets "his" West Bank and Gaza. Cynics say that Begin was willing to give up the Sinai for the "right" (in his opinion) to keep his hold on the West Bank, so why should he care about the pace of the normalization?

On the other hand, the slow pace of the normalization increases, for the Israeli public, the mistrust towards Egypt, as the normalization is taken as a test of Egyptian sincerity. Slowing down the pace plays into the hands of Group A. Many security-minded Israelis believe that the loss of strategic depth in the Sinai could be offset by common vested interests, which will make peace profitable for both countries, and will make war unthinkable. "But if we give up the Sinai", say people in Group B, "and we do not get peaceful and normal relations with Egypt, our country will be weakened by the peace. So let us remember this lesson when we deal with other Arab countries, or when the time comes to complete the withdrawal from the Sinai". With such an attitude, it will be hard to have a coalition between Group B and Group C (the doves).

The situation is, therefore, somewhat unfortunate. There may be compelling reasons for Egypt to insist on slow normalization, not necessarily as a whip, since it would then be aimed at the wrong opponent, but for genuine internal and external Egyptian interests. On the other hand, there are good reasons for Israel, and for constructive Israelis, to ask for a meaningful normalization. Since both countries are in the same boat, and since their equations are coupled, it is essential that both countries face the dilemma, and that they seek a solution *together*.

Some degree of normal relations already exists, and an increasing number of Israelis now interact with Egyptians. This is inevitable, once the peace treaty was signed. The question is no longer whether there will be an interaction; rather, the important questions now are: who will interact, where and when, as well as how fast the process will proceed? Therefore, the "interacting terms" already exist in our coupled equations, and the question now is that of whether the algebraic sign of these terms will be negative or positive. Will the wrong Israelis be the first to interact with their Egyptian counterparts, or should co-ordinated efforts be made to ensure that the pioneers would be those Israelis and Egyptians who will, most likely, contribute positively to the process of normalization, while minimizing any possible damage?

APPENDIX XII.
STARTING UP SCIENTIFIC COOPERATION

The goals and first steps of our Peace Project are described elsewhere[4] as well as in the document called The Tel-Aviv University Research Project on Peace[5]. The major challenge being faced by the Peace Project today is the proper startup of academic relations with Egyptian scholars. One of the major decisions that we had to make was whether we should immediately begin scientific cooperation, or wait for further political development and improvement of the atmosphere. The reasons for our decision to proceed now carefully with preparations for actual scientific cooperation were described in part in another manuscript, and will become clearer in the following pages. We will also present here the considerations for our selection of first candidates for scientific cooperation.

General Considerations. Like most academics in the world, Israeli professors and students are interested in scientific interaction and cooperation with colleagues the world over. The new opportunity to do so with scholars in a neighboring country, Egypt, is thus attractive for many Israeli academics. However, for personal as well as ideological reasons, an appreciable number of Israeli scholars display some measure of reluctance, and some even oppose cooperation. With few exceptions, the initial eagerness for cooperation, which followed President Sadat's visit to Jerusalem, has slowed down appreciably, and has given way to sober academic considerations.

Those of us who have visited Egypt have learned that Egyptian intellectuals and scientists have a more negative attitude towards cooperation than their Israeli counterparts. Many reasons are suggested for the negative attitude, and it is important for us to fully understand these reasons before any attempt is made to embark on a program of cooperation. The following is a list of some of these reasons as suggested to us by Egyptian and other colleagues:

4 An entrepreneur.
5 See APPENDIX IX.

1. *Emotion and psychology.* Hatred and misconceptions of thirty years of enmity and several wars cannot be expected to disappear in a year or two.

2. *Negative reactions from students and colleagues.* Before an Egyptian professor decides to be among the first to interact scientifically with Israelis (cooperate, visit Israeli universities, etc.), he has to weigh seriously the expected reaction of his colleagues and students.

3. *Appreciation of Egyptian interests.* A premature and publicized interaction may further alienate the Arab countries.

4. *Ideology.* Scholars in disciplines such as history, social sciences, law, Islamic and Arabic literature, still have reservations about the Camp David agreement and the whole peace process. In particular, these scholars are unhappy with the anticipated replacement of Arab scholars by Israeli and American ones.

5. *Profession.* Past, present, and future professional connections of professors in some academic disciplines are closer by nature to the Arab and Islamic worlds than to the West. These professors are afraid to lose these connections by interacting openly and voluntarily with Israelis.

6. *Material losses.* As salaries are about ten times higher in the Gulf countries than in Egypt, Egyptian scholars weigh seriously, and often unfavorably, any interaction with Israeli scholars, since such interactions, if publicized, may jeopardize their income from the Gulf.

On the other hand, I have discovered that most observers have failed to realize that the attitude towards scientific cooperation is not entirely negative. In fact, there are some encouraging signs of a growing measure of interest in scientific interaction with Israel. Based on many discussions with Egyptian natural scientists, I would suggest that an appreciable number of such scientists would welcome the opportunity to interact with Israeli counterparts. The following are two observations, which have led me to these conclusions:

Scientific isolation. Many Egyptian scientists feel isolated scientifically from the rest of the world, primarily because of lack of funds; this is tied to the fact that in most disciplines of the natural sciences, the international centers are in the West, and not in the Middle East or even in the Soviet Bloc. Furthermore, judging from a few examples, I have reached the conclusion that the host countries in the Soviet Bloc do not often make available their most advanced equipment to the visiting Egyptian trainees.

Front-line research. Scientists and students everywhere are eager to carry out research in the front line of their fields. Actually, for any research to be meaningful it has to be in the front line. Egyptian professors as well as academic administrators are aware of this widespread eagerness, and constantly look for ways to satisfy it. This situation can be improved by more interaction with the outside world, especially with the West. This interaction involves travel abroad, visits of foreign scientists, scientific cooperation, etc.

The obvious question now is: why Israel? It is clear that Israel is not the only, or even the major gate to modern (predominantly western) science, but it is *a neighboring* gate. Israeli scientists have good scientific connections with western scientists and institutions, which have sizable budgets for collaboration with foreign scientists. Nobody expects Israel to provide answers to all the healthy wishes of Egyptian scientists. However, my visits in several universities and research institutes in Cairo and my discussions with professors and students there lead me to believe that there is an appreciable interest in Egyptian academia in scientific cooperation with Israeli scientists. If my findings differ somewhat from those of most foreign observers, it is probably because most observers do not come from the natural sciences, nor have they had extensive discussions with professors and students in these scientific disciplines.

Criteria for Candidates for First Scientific Cooperation. The first consideration in the selection of first candidates is the likelihood of success. Looking at the list of negative reasons presented above, it appears that for reason of ideology, it is more likely to find good candidates in the natural sciences, or in medicine, engineering and business, than in the social sciences, or theology or law, on even in journalism. However, remoteness from ideology is not a sufficient criterion by itself to distinguish among the disciplines. Doctors, engineers, and business people are as far professionally from ideology as are mathematicians, physicists or pharmacologists, but are more reluctant at present to participate in joint endeavors. A second criterion, that of material gain and profession, should be applied simultaneously. While an Egyptian theologian or social scientist benefits professionally and financially by interacting mostly with the Islamic and Arab worlds, and would be reluctant to endanger these ties, an engineer, a doctor, or a businessman too stand to lose appreciably from publicized interactions with Israeli counterparts. On the other hand, an Egyptian mathematician, biologist, or physicist is not only removed from ideology by profession, but his professional interaction in the foreseeable future will be with the West, which also has many more high paying jobs at universities and research institutions than do the oil countries. Therefore, for reasons of ideology, profession, or even financial gains, candidates for first scientific cooperation should come from the natural sciences. It is not surprising that conferences in the last year have been unsuccessful in bringing Israeli and Egyptian scholars closer together, as none of these conferences has been in the natural sciences. On top of the discipline criteria, there is obviously a personal one, as some individuals may like or dislike cooperating for personal reasons.

Another principle has been used in the selection of the group of candidates; namely, the whole group of candidates should constitute a balanced program. For instance, if the Egyptian participants in one of the projects are stronger than the Israeli ones, this situation is reversed in another project of the proposed program.

The Proposed Program for First Scientific Cooperation. Out of many candidates, I have chosen to recommend that three be first for cooperation. They constitute together a balanced program according to the above-mentioned principles. Each of them can stand independently of the others, but together, and with proper preparation and continuous observation, they can present a meaningful controlled experiment in the social sciences. It is proposed that qualified non-Israeli and non-Egyptian social scientists overlook this three-project program. The three projects are the following:

1. Remote sensing. The Egyptian Academy of Scientific Research has an advanced center for remote sensing, in which pictures from satellites are analyzed. Cooperation in this analysis is expected to benefit both countries. Professor Mohamed Abdel Hady, the center's director, is interested in cooperation with our scientists, and even in training our young researchers. Professor Abdel Hady is also a professor in Oklahoma State University, and his American university has expressed interest in participating in the proposed Egyptian-Israeli collaboration. Professors from three faculties at Tel Aviv University (Exact Sciences, Life Sciences, and Engineering) have expressed similar interest.

2. Intermediate Energy Physics. Professor Mohamed El-Nadi from the Faculty of Science in Cairo University leads a large group of low-energy (nuclear) and high-energy (elementary particles) physicists. Their research equipment consists mainly of microscopes, which are used to analyze particle tracks in emulsions. Since 1967, I have assembled at Tel Aviv University a group of physicists who specialize in intermediate-energy (pion-nucleus) physics, a recently developed field that attempts to bridge the gap of knowledge between nuclear physics and elementary-particle physics. Our people work mainly in large-accelerator laboratories in Europe, the USA, and Canada. Professor J.P. Blaser, the Director of the Swiss national accelerator that is located near Zurich, has invited Professor El-Nadi's group to participate in an experiment, in which Professor Danny Ashery from Tel Aviv University is one of the principal investigators. The Egyptian scientists will perform the experiment in Switzerland, and bring back with them irradiated emulsions, which will then be analyzed in the microscopes at Cairo University.

3. The Productivity of the Black Goat. The desert goat is the main source of milk and meat for the Bedouins. Improvement of its productivity is therefore of great importance to both Israel and Egypt. Professor Tymour H. Kammal, the Head of the Radiology Department of the Egyptian Atomic Energy Authority and Professor Amiram Shkolnik of our Zoology Department have both worked extensively on this project, as well as on the study of camels. They have expressed great interest in collaborating in the research on goats and camels. Professor Johnson from the University of Missouri, who has already worked with both of them, is interested in a trilateral study of these topics.

Overlooking the Program. The responsibility in the individual projects will naturally be left solely to the scientists. However, the three projects constitute one program or experiment in scientific cooperation between scientists of two neighboring countries that have not had any tradition of scientific cooperation. It is therefore proposed that this pioneering and pilot program be observed by an experienced social scientist from a third country. Professor Steve Cohen of the City College of New York enjoys respect in both Egypt and Israel, and is therefore a good candidate for this task. Since he plans to be in the region for an extended period in the summer of 1980, it is proposed that he be asked to include the observation of the triple-project program in his activities. Tel Aviv University has decided to grant him partial financial support, and this decision has already been communicated to him.

A Visit to Tel Aviv University. We are pleased to learn that you, Dr. Boutros Ghali, have accepted the invitation of our president, Professor Haim Ben-Shahar, to visit our university. We welcome the idea of an informal and unpublicized meeting with a small group from our faculty. We would be happy if you could visit our university during, or soon after the next round of autonomy talks that will be held in Israel.

I sincerely hope that you will welcome the program, which was outlined in this manuscript, and I will be interested in any comment or suggestion that you might have. Speaking for myself, as well as for the groups of scientists that will be involved, I would like to express the hope that you and your government will find it possible to approve this pioneering program. I have been advised by representatives of the Ford Foundation that they will be ready to supply the program with some financial support, if they can be assured that the program be welcomed by the Egyptian government.

Finally, I wish to express my strong personal belief that the program outlined above is sound, with a reasonable chance for success. Many hours of preparation have been invested in it. The program is expected to benefit equally Egyptian and Israeli scientists, and could serve as a pilot for cooperative projects in the future. This program could increase our mutual trust, with little risk of damage to the involved parties.

APPENDIX XIII.
A MIDDLE-EAST UNIVERSITY SPONSORED BY UNESCO

The following report was prepared by Professor Avivi I. Yavin, a former dean of the Faculty of Exact Sciences at Tel Aviv University, at the request of Professor Maurizio Iaccarino, Assistant Director General for Science of UNESCO. The report includes the ideas discussed and the conclusions reached at a meeting in UNESCO Paris on January 16, 1997, which was attended by Professor Maurizio Iaccarino, Mr. Avi Shoket, Israel's ambassador to UNESCO, Dr. Vladimir Zharov, Mr. Alfredo Pinilla, Dr. Siegbert Raither, and Avivi I. Yavin.

The establishment in steps of a Middle East University was proposed in 1994 by a Palestinian physicist, Reyad Sawafta, and by an Israeli physicist, Avivi I. Yavin. The goal of this pioneering project was to enable cooperative teaching and research for all academic people in the region (professors and students alike), mainly in order to solve the problems of the regions and combat the brain drain. It was proposed to build the University in the Aqaba-Eilat-Taba region, i.e. on the border of Jordan, Israel, and Egypt (with the northern Dead Sea - the Jericho region - as an alternative, since this spot is a meeting place of Jordan, Israel, and the Palestinian Authority).

All the participants of the said meeting in UNESCO were warmly supportive of this idea and of the suggestion that UNESCO would play a major role in its execution, as it is in line with UNESCO's Culture for Peace Program and with UNESCO's Constitution, as had been stated by Professor Frederico Mayor, the Director General. The following are the points, which were stressed at that meeting:

1. The proposed Middle East University is an exciting major project that can only be initiated, prepared, and implemented by and through a major international organization such as UNESCO. It

should focus on science and technology teaching and research of relevance and importance to the Middle East. The University should be international and rely on the broad support of the international scientific community. Scientists from Mediterranean countries, and in particular Italy, are well placed to play a key role in developing and realizing the project.

2. Planning as well as preparatory activities could, by themselves, be useful, regardless of whether or not the University is finally established.

3. UNESCO will see to it that all UNESCO-supported Middle East science and technology activities and projects (such as the Bio-Technology Project, planned for Jericho, and the follow-up of the conferences in Dahab and Jerusalem) will reinforce and promote the University goal.

4. Although a limited amount of financial aid (seed money) will have to be provided by UNESCO for the very first steps, UNESCO is not able to provide adequate funds for planning and preparatory activities, and funds from external sources will have to be raised. The assistance and support of eminent scientists from around the world will be needed to assure success.

5. UNESCO will set up a Working Group for the planning and development of the University, which will report to the Assistant Director General for Science (ADG/SC). The group will be composed of presidents, deans, and institution heads (or former ones), as well as senior scientists, mainly from the Middle East, whom UNESCO will appoint as consulting experts (initially, only at nominal pay), so as to facilitate their meetings and movements within the Middle East region. A prominent scientist will lead the Group, preferably from Italy.

6. Avivi I. Yavin shall be a founding member of the Working Group, and will make a proposal to the ADG/SC on the group's membership and its initial plan of action. Siegbert Raither shall assist him and coordinate the project within UNESCO, under the overall supervision of the ADG/SC.

APPENDIX XIV.
A LIST OF NAMES APPEARING IN THE BOOK

The following is a list of names of people that either appear several times in the book, or that the author believes that their contribution to the book is significant. In most cases, only their position at the mentioned time is specified, although in some cases the author feels that it is important to point out what happened to them afterwards.

Abarbanel. Shalom...The Tel-Aviv University rector.
Abdel Hady, Mohamed...Director, the Remote-Sensing Center.
Abshire, David...Director, CSIS.
Aharonov, Yakir...Physics Professor at T.A.U.
Aharonson, Shlomo...Professor of political science at H.U.
Alberg, Ralph...travel agent in Paltours.
Alon, Yigal...Deputy prime minister and foreign minister.
Anabtawi...American professor of Palestinian origin, acting vice rector in University of Kuwait.
Arafat, Yasser...President of Palestine Liberation Organization.
Assousa, George... American physicist of Palestinian origin.
Avinery, Shlomo...Senior Professor of political science at H.U.
Azar, Edward...Political science professor in North Carolina, of Lebanese origin.
Badawi, Omar...Professor of physics at Cairo University.
Badr, Mahmoud...Professor of Urology at Cairo University.
Badran, Ibrahim...President of Cairo University.
Bahran, Mahmoud..Technical director, the Alsabah Group.
Bashir, Tahseen...Senior Egyptian diplomat.
Becker, Yehiel..Biology professor H.U. Conference organizer.
Begin, Menahem... Prime minister of Israel.
Beit-Or, Drora...Administrative director, the Peace Project.
Ben-Shahar, Haim...President, Tel-Aviv University.

Blaser, J.P. ...Director of S.I.N., the Swiss national laboratory.

Carmichael, William...Regional office head, Ford Foundation.

Chechanover, Joseph...Israeli manager general, foreign ministry.

Cohen, Steve...American professor of psychology.

Dayan, Moshe...Israel's foreign minister.

Dvoretzky, Aryeh...Mathematics professor, Head of Academy of Art and Science, Israel.

Dinstein, Yoram...Law professor T.A.U, later rector, president.

Eban Abba...Member of Knesset, formerly foreign minister.

El-Baz, Farouk...Astrophysicist, the Smithsonian Institute.

El-Bedewi, F.A...Head of Physics Dept. Ain Shams University.

El-Dorri, Mohamed...Eastman Travel Agency, Cairo.

El-Nadi, Adel...Physics professor, son of Mohamed El-Nadi.

El-Nadi, Mohamed...Physics Professor, Senior Egyptian nuclear physicist.

El-Saidi, Ali...Ph.D. nuclear engineering, later energy minister.

Faouzi, Hussein...Egyptian writer, honorary doctorate - T.A.U.

Ghali, Boutros...Egyptian minister of state for foreign affairs, later secretary general of the United Nations.

Ghobal, Ashraf...Egyptian Ambassador to the United States.

Gomah, Ahmed...Ph.D., first secretary Egyptian embassy.

Goralnik, Israel...General Manager ORT – Israel.

Harith, Mohamed Abdel...Ph.D., Egyptian nuclear physicist.

Havens, William...Professor, secretary general of A.P.S.

Helmi, Moustapha...Minister of state, science and education.

Henley, Earnst...Professor, formerly president of A.P.S.

Hirsch, Zeev...Professor, faculty of management, T.A.U.

Hirschfeld, Yair...History, Ph.D. from T.A.U. Started negotiations with P.L.O. leading to the Oslo agreement.

Hoffman, Stanley...Harvard professor of political science.

Horn, David...Physics professor, later director of Peace Project.

Iaccarino, Mauricio...Assistant director general-UNESCO.

Ibrahim, Saad Eddin...Professor of Sociology, American Univ.

Ismail, Hassan...Head of the Egyptian Academy of Science.

Israeli, Dov...Lawyer.

Jackson, Henry...US senator from Washington State.

Jacob, Maurice...Theoretical physicist at CERN.

Joseph, Joachim...Professor of Planetary science T.A.U.

Kammal, Tymour...Head of Radio-Biology, Egyptian A.E.A.

Kelman, Herbert...Harvard professor of psychology.

Keren, Moshe...Entrepreneur.

Lando, Edith...Vancouver philanthropist.

Lederman, Leon...Physics Professor, Head of Fermi Lab.

Lesch Ann...Ford Foundation director for the Middle East.

Lustig, Harry...Professor of physics, treasurer of APS.

Michaeli, Dan...Zahal' chief physician, later manager general of Ichilov Hospital.

Ne'eman Yuval...Professor of physics, formerly president T.A.U.

Noweir, Tabark...Ph.D., Egyptian A.E.A., formerly my student.

Osman, Ahmed...Professor of physics (nuclear theory), Cairo U.

Pail, Meir...M.K., historian (military history).

Patir, Dan...Secretary of Prime-Minister Menahem Begin.

Pearl, Richard...Assistant to Senator Jackson, later deputy defense secretary.

Peckman, Joseph...Economist, Brookings Institution.

Peres, Shimon...Foreign, defense and prime minister, today president of Israel.

Polack, Herman...Assistant secretary of state.

Rabinovitch, Itamar...Professor of history, later rector and president of T.A.U. and Israeli ambassador to the US.

Rafael, Gideon...Israeli retired diplomat.

Raither, Siegbert...Physics Ph.D., Harvard; UNESCO employee.

Richmond, Eddison...Councelor US Embassy in Cairo for science and technology.

Romahi, Saif...Jordanian college president

Rosen, Louis...Physics professor, formerly director of LAMPF.

Sackler, Raymond...Chairman of T.A.U. board of trustees.

Sadat, Anwar...President of Egypt, murdered in 1981.

Salmeron, Roberto...French physicist of Brazilian origin.

Sawafta, Reyad...American physicist of Palestinian origin.

Shamir, Shimon...Professor of M.E. history, later ambassador to Egypt and Jordan.

Shapira, Yonatan...Professor of sociology at T.A.U.

Shkolnik, Amiram...Biology professor.

Sokolovski, Mori...Biology professor, vice president of T.A.U.

Starr, Joyce...Coordinator of the task force, US state department.

Stone, Richard...Senator from Florida.

Vary, James...Physics professor, Iowa State University.

Violini, Galileo...Physics professor, director of C.I.F. in Bogota.

Vogt, Erich...Canadian physicist, formerly director of TRIUMF.

Weizmann, Ezer...Israeli defense minister.

Wilson, Robert...Professor of physics at Cornel University, formerly director of Fermi Lab.

Yaar, Ephraim...Professor of Sociology at T.A.U.

Yariv, Aharon...Retired major general, head of Center for Strategic Studies at T.A.U.

Acknowledgements

I am grateful to Professor Erich Vogt for his diligent review of the manuscript and for his advice and constructive criticism. Professors Haim Ben-Shahar, Professor Shimon Shamir, and the late Professors Judah Eisenberg and Eitan Berglas, all from Tel-Aviv University, supported and advised me throughout my efforts in establishing the Research Project on Peace at Tel Aviv University and in my attempts to form scientific collaborations with Egyptian scientists. Ms. Drora Beit-Or deserves special thanks for her administrative support. I am grateful to Professors Mohamed El-Nadi, Tymour Kammal, Mohamed Abdel Hady, Mahmoud Badr, and Dr. Tabark Noweir, all from various scientific institutions in Cairo, to Dr. Boutros Boutros Ghali, the Egyptian Minister of State for Foreign Affairs, and to Mr. Addison Richmond of the American Embassy in Egypt, for helping me in my endeavors. Professor Harry Lustig assisted me in my efforts to get the American Physical Society involved in the attempts to promote Arab-Israeli cooperation. Dr. Siegbert Raither from UNESCO and my late friend Israel Goralnik supported the initiative of Dr. Reyad Sawafta and me to build a Middle-East university. The willingness of my friend Zeev Bar-Gil to design the book is highly appreciated. I am especially grateful to Professor Parker Alford and to my daughter Talma, my son David, my daughter Mimi, and my son-in-law Gil for their contributions and advice. Last but not least, I am grateful to my wife Rivka for her love and active support and for her urging and encouraging me to write this book

CPSIA information can be obtained at www.ICGtesting.com
Printed in the USA
BVOW031015220413

318786BV00001B/175/P